THE SOCIAL HISTORY OF EDUCATION

GENERAL EDITOR: VICTOR E. NEUBURG

First Series — No. 7

SIXTY YEARS IN WAIFDOM

THE SOCIAL HISTORY OF EDUCATION

GENERAL EDITOR: VICTOR E. NEUBURG

First Series of Eight Titles

No. 1. Edward Baines

The Social, Educational, and Religious State of the Manufacturing Districts; with Statistical Returns of the Means of Education and Religious Instruction in the Manufacturing Districts of Yorkshire, Lancashire, and Cheshire; in Two Letters to the Right Hon. Lord Wharncliffe, on Sir Jas. Graham's Factory Education Bill; also the objectives to the Amended Bill   (2nd ed. 1843).

No. 2 Mary Carpenter

Reformatory Schools, for the Children of the Perishing and Dangerous classes, and for Juvenile Offenders   (1851).

No. 3. Central Society of Education

First, Second and Third Publications (1837, 1838, 1839). Three Volumes.

No. 4. James Hole

"Light, more Light!" On the present State of Education amongst the Working Classes of Leeds, and How it Can Best be improved   (1860).

No. 5. J. W. Hudson

The History of Adult Education, in which is comprised a full and complete history of the mechanics' and literary institutions, Anthenaeums, philosophical mental and christian improvement societies, literary unions, schools of design etc., of Great Britain, Ireland, America etc.   (1851).

No. 6. Sir James Kay Shuttleworth

Memorandum on Popular Education   (1868).

No. 7. C. J. Montague

Sixty Years in Waifdom or, The Ragged School Movement in English History with a Preface by the Most Noble the Marquis of Northampton   (1904).

No. 8. Thomas Pole

A History of the Origin and Progress of Adult Schools; with An Account of some of the beneficial Effects already Produced on the Moral Character of the Labouring Poor   (1814).

SIXTY YEARS IN WAIFDOM

OR,

THE RAGGED SCHOOL MOVEMENT
IN ENGLISH HISTORY

C. J. MONTAGUE

AUGUSTUS M. KELLEY PUBLISHERS
New York 1969

Published by
WOBURN BOOKS LIMITED
9 RUSSELL CHAMBERS, BURY PLACE, LONDON WC1

Published in the United States by
Augustus M. Kelley, Publishers
New York, New York 10010

First edition   1904
New impression   1969

Printed in Holland by
N.V. Grafische Industrie Haarlem

THE EARL OF SHAFTESBURY IN 1856.

SIXTY YEARS IN WAIFDOM

Or, The Ragged School Movement
in English History

By
C. J. MONTAGUE

WITH PREFACE BY
THE MOST NOBLE
THE MARQUIS OF NORTHAMPTON

LONDON
CHAS. MURRAY & CO.
11, LUDGATE SQUARE, E.C.
1904

PREFACE

By the

PRESIDENT OF THE RAGGED SCHOOL UNION

IN the following pages will be found the history of
the Ragged School Union, which for sixty years
has laboured incessantly for child-life in London.
The writer has painted vividly for us the wonderful
progress of a work of love, and on the canvas we find
the portraits of Christian men and women who, for
Christ's sake, have spent themselves to save His little
ones.

When ragged school teachers first began their
efforts to save the children in London, and subsequently in other great towns, loyalty, law and order
were all in danger. England had been sleeping on a
volcano, and wise men saw plainly what a sudden
eruption would entail. Poverty, ignorance and discontent were elements of danger, and the great chasm
between high and low, between rich and poor, seemed to
point to a serious outbreak of social trouble.

The part taken by ragged school workers at this
anxious moment this history relates, written by one
who knows his subject well. How much was done by
the Ragged School Union to remove causes of disorder
and to remedy a great evil, for no evil can be greater

than neglect of children, the readers of this volume will be able to determine.   But this fact seems to stand out plain and unassailable,that if a nation is to be prosperous and contented, the most careful supervision of child-life must be perpetually exercised, and that of all social subjects which should lie nearest to the heart of a patriot, the training of character in the young should take the front place.

It has been, and is still, the object of the Ragged School Union to help the children of the poorest class to become Christians, and therefore law-abiding useful citizens.   It has been a national work, for it has enabled hundreds of thousands to escape from the perils of degraded life and to rise to positions of comparative comfort and high respectability.   It has been an imperial work, for thousands of ragged school children have scattered throughout the empire, taking with them the good characters which they have gained in the ragged schools.   It is a Christian work, for the teaching of our Lord has been the foundation of all that has been done.

It is in a spirit of gratitude, and not of boasting, that this history has been written.   God has blessed, and is blessing, the Union for the work done in His name, and the author shows in his interesting narrative that the inspiration of this religious and philanthropic Society has come from the knowledge of Divine guidance and love.

Northampton

CONTENTS

CHAPTER VIII

CHAPTER IX

CHAPTER X

CHAPTER I

Introduction

" Has no one ever said that you were beside yourself, or
called you crazy, or a crank, or a pestilent fellow ?
  *   *   *   *   *
Mend your ways, or you can claim no kinship with the
saints and the heroes which were before you."

Plain Talk in Psalm and Parable.
ERNEST CROSBY.

SOME forty years after the Ragged School Union
was founded, Dean Bradley, upon Innocents'
Day, 1885, preached a sermon from the pulpit of Westminster Abbey on its behalf. As far as time allowed
he gave a sketch of the gloomy state of affairs existing
in 1844 in this dear England of ours, and in conclusion
said—" But good came out of evil, for as the result of
his (Lord Shaftesbury's) self-denying work came the
Ragged School Union, from which followed Schools,
Homes, Refuges, Industrial Schools, Institutes, &c."

It will be the aim of this book to show what share
this movement has had in national history. It will
strive also to indicate the high value of the principles,
upon which with changed forms of activity, it is working in the present day.

A too partial story should earn reproof from the
shades of departed men of large interests who were
ragged school teachers. Professor Leone Levi, reformer
of English Commercial Law, was one ; General Gordon,

1

empire-maker and sympathizer with the sorrowing in all nations, was another.

But if on the other hand there were any dwarfing of the claim, Lord Shaftesbury's statements about it would contain rebuke for the mis-handling of a great tradition.

The crying needs of London to-day also demand faithfulness in presenting the work as a solution of future social difficulties. Lord Shaftesbury himself was not a man of mean interests, or narrow life. The slave in America, the aborigines of all parts of the earth, the opium-smoker of China, and the oppressed Armenian and Jew had his sympathy and active help. Yet with a world-wide observation, to give him the proper sense of proportion and perspective, he said—" I firmly believe that the Ragged School movement is a most important episode in the history of mankind. I have never known or read of anything else like it. I know of nothing so remarkable ; I know of nothing so singular ; I know of nothing which has been so stamped by the finger of God as the Ragged School movement has been from the commencement."

It was not two months before the date of Dean Bradley's sermon that ragged school workers were called to be present and take a leading part in the national funeral of the great and good earl.

At that impressive service, and another so sadly similar that came sixteen years later, when the great and good Queen Victoria's funeral sermon was preached there, we felt that the story of the R.S.U. was one that every patriot should know.

On January 27, 1901, the ragged school teachers who gained admission into that "treasure-house of greatness" of our race, came not alone to mourn a

queen " rich in a plentiful exchequer of her people's
hearts " ; nor a rare, gifted and faithful woman only,
but also one who had been a friend to their work before
she or the work were popular in the country. Moreover, the Queen was Patron, and there was the bare
possibility that his present Majesty might not see fit

29th' April 1901.

My Lord,

I have the honour to inform you that I have
submitted to The King your letter of the 20th' Inst:
and in reply I am commanded to say that His Majesty is
pleased to accede to the request contained in it, to
grant His Patronage to The Ragged School Union.

I am Sir,

Your Lordship's obedient Servant,

Signature

General.
Keeper of H. M's Privy Purse

The President,
The Ragged School Union & Shaftesbury Society.

LETTER FROM KING EDWARD, ACCEPTING POST
OF PATRON.

to be her successor in that capacity. Since then that
cloud has been removed.

But there was another link yet, the occasion was the
anniversary of the death of General Gordon, who wrote
when abroad that he prayed twice daily for his fellow

teachers. The offertory was to be for the Gordon
Home for Destitute Boys. Canon Henson led the
thoughts of all to the coming King when he said :
" Once more an Edward sits on Edward's throne,"
reminding his hearers that of the six bearing that name
who have reigned since the Confessor, four rest within
the Abbey walls. There was, too, a strangely blended
tradition gathering around the familiar name. " The
ascetic purity of S. Edward, the masterful wisdom
of Edward I., the tragic fate of Edward II., the splen·
dour of Edward III., the popularity of Edward IV.,
the pitiful fortune of Edward V., the precocious piety
of Edward VI." But the most significant thing was
the honour assigned to the first of them.

" The most honoured tomb in Westminster Abbey is
that of one who was neither splendid, nor successful,
nor wise, only good." Around him, as in perpetual
homage, the proudest and most splendid of our feudal
monarchs, Edward I., Edward III., and Henry V. are
gathered. The esteem of his people was expressed in
the simple verse of the chronicle,—

> This year King Edward, of Angles Lord,
> Sent his truthful soul to Christ,
> Into God's protection. A holy spirit,
>   *   *   *   *   *
> A King in virtues good, chaste, and mild ;
> Edward the noble his country guarded,
> His land and people, until came suddenly
> The bitter death, and so dearly took
> The noble King from earth.

This is perhaps as fitting an opportunity as will occur
for an expression of gratitude to our patron for assuming a position that has great influence upon the
financial fortunes of the Society, as well as for a very
real practical interest that he and every member of the

Royal Family have shown. He has realized the hopes
of Englishmen, and his rule has already proved a blessing to the world.

But it was to the late Queen to whom we were paying our last homage on that occasion, and the preacher
in noble language expressed the thoughts of the nation
about her.

" The Queen's surest title to the enduring homage of
posterity, as to the reverence of the two generations
which have rejoiced to live under her mild and righteous
rule, will be her fidelity to duty. Englishmen can
understand the worth of this high claim to their
homage. They are a practical, unemotional, if you
will, a matter-of-fact people. A brilliant American
said of them truly that ' they are impious in their
scepticism of a theory, but kiss the dust before a fact ' ;
and here, in the Queen's life, they saw the fact of daily,
arduous duty faced and done with the pure enthusiasm
of girlhood, with the more disciplined ardour of middle
life, in the inevitable weakness of extreme old age—
they saw that fact under every variety of circumstance,
when in the sunlight of prosperity all things were easy
and full of gladness, in the grey days of adversity when
the landscape of life wore an aspect cold and repellent,
in the labour and sorrow of those last years when duty
proposed itself in its naked sternness, uneased by fortune,
no longer veiled by the illusions of youth—they saw in
their Sovereign, year after year, decade after decade,
the fact of a dutiful life, and they ' kissed the dust
before it,' they poured into their traditional loyalty
a deeper and holier sentiment, they revered the Queen
as the symbol of that which, in their lives also and in
themselves, was the one thing worthy of a man's
homage ; their own consciences and the conflicts of

LORD SHAFTESBURY'S MONUMENT,
WESTMINSTER ABBEY.

their own lives interpreted to them the intrinsic greatness of her life."

Sitting in the nave, one had but to look aside to see the marble statue to Lord Shaftesbury and link the two great workers for the English nation of sixty years ago. Others there were undoubtedly in all departments of activity in which the energies of a great people find expression, but none to equal them in the extent of service or amount achieved.

In 1844, when the Queen was twenty-five and Lord Shaftesbury forty-three, this country was beset with many of the difficulties that Russia has to-day, except that opinion was not so much repressed. It is very doubtful whether Her Majesty knew at the time the extreme danger of her position during the early years of her reign. It is a question if any one near the throne quite realized it.

The working classes and those lower, were in a state
of the greatest exasperation towards the official and
the property-holding classes. Their grievances were
intensely real and material ; they affected food, clothing and shelter. In addition to that, they had been
kept ignorant for generations, and many of them were
debased by influences that have now passed away. To
read of some of the things that were allowed in London
until quite recently will astound those to whom the
street-life of that time is unfamiliar. The evils, too,
were of so many kinds. They ranged from lack of
moral education to lack of drains and sanitation. They
embraced laws, municipal administration, prison
management, police, and all the transmitted sin that
centuries of neglect and oppression had fostered. It
really seemed as though all the social machinery had
been specially designed for the object of making the
masses of the people anti-social and dangerous.

To meet this democratic discontent with those in
authority, and hatred of the wealthy, there was no
uniting principle to combine the middle and upper
classes.

The aristocracy as a body were reserved towards the
Queen, partly from that dislike to a woman's control
that many men have, partly also because of the
liberality of her views, but mainly because she was
the most resolute and thorough reformer of Court
morals the English throne had known. This could
not be welcome among a nobility accustomed to the
moral atmosphere of the Court of George IV.

" A corrupt Court is a centre of corruption," said
Canon Henson in his sermon ; " An evil monarch is a
national calamity. Who can measure the influence
for good which the pure life and ordered Court of

Queen Victoria have had on English society during her long reign! Every clergyman, philanthropist and social reformer has had, these sixty-three years past, an ally and sympathizer on the throne of his country. Look through history and see how few are the periods, and how brief, in which this could be said. When we consider all these things, our sorrow, great as it is beyond words, passes into another and more religious sentiment. We thank Almighty God for the gift of that gracious and serviceable life, we add to our national treasures the priceless jewel of a pure and lofty tradition bound about the ancient and famous English Crown, and henceforth we connect *our civic duty* with a dear and honoured name."

Queen Victoria added that new jewel to the Crown at great cost to herself, and it may even be said at great risk of life and throne. Not that she was ever in any danger from the nobility; she always had friends, and those who were not her friends were not disloyal. The danger lay in the want of unity between Crown, aristocracy, and the well-to-do if they were to save themselves and each other when the apparently inevitable conflict came.

A German thinker who came to this country in 1844 wrote—"The war of the poor against the rich will be the bloodiest ever waged. The Revolution *must* come; it is already *too late* to bring about a peaceful solution." [1]

The Times in that year, in one of its leaders during the month of June, had this passage—"War to *Palaces*, peace unto cabins—that is a battle-cry of terror that may come to resound throughout our country. Let the wealthy beware."

[1] Engel's *Condition of the Labouring Classes in* 1844.

The backwardness of public men in supporting the Queen is a very marked feature of the early years of her reign. The government of England was no sinecure, and loyalty to the throne was scarcely as much as tepid.

The Duke of Wellington excused himself from service on account of his age and deafness, Sir Robert Peel in a burst of confidence told the House of Commons that he found it " no easy task to ensure the harmonious and united action of an ancient monarchy, a proud aristocracy and a Reformed House of Commons."

Lord John Russell's *gaucherie* caused the Queen many a heartache. Till Prince Albert came, Lord Melbourne alone gave her a real support. His assumption of coolness, the air of' the bored exquisite that masked his seriousness, doubtless gave the Queen nerve for her task. Good men in the early years of the last reign saw in him only a cynical fop, who received deputations lolling on a couch, a man who blew feathers in the air when grievances were talked of, and balanced chairs or dangled cushions when Government action was asked for. In reality we know him as working hard with his secretaries for Queen and nation in his bedroom, to escape bores for whom he could do nothing.

If the monarch was isolated from the aristocracy because the latter were largely a reactionary body, out of sympathy with modern progress and less in touch with life's verities than they should have been, there was an unbridgeable chasm between the aristocracy and the manufacturing capitalists.

The latter had already dealt the first blow at the ancient privileges of the landed interest by the Reform Bill. By repeal of the Corn Laws, for which at this time they were agitating, they would gain an ascendency over all other capitalists in the country, whose interests were bound up with land, bankers, stock-jobbers, fund-holders, &c. A little later on, the aristocracy would be recruited from the ranks of these aggressive men, but in 1844 there was a very cordial hatred between them.

A letter from Mr. Joseph Hume to Professor Leone Levi brings this out very clearly. In it he asserts that the merchants are as limited and as selfish as the landed interests, and he believes that if merchants had had as much power as the landed interests, the commerce of the nation would not have been so free from fetters as it now is.

The attitude of the wage-earners was that of suppressed revolt. The street folk and the criminal classes only waited for the artisans and mechanics to give the word to rise. The rural labourers had such hardships that they were ready to join in any movement that promised to better them. The miners were being treated with cruel injustice.

Between this mass of labourers and the manufacturers, were the middle classes, and these, at this time and for the following three years, lent a moral support to the fermenting revolution.

In the next chapter we shall go a little more into detail, but what we desire here to show is—on the one hand a lonely queen, criticised and barely supported by a nobility that could not protect itself from the class below it, while yielding to, yet hating, the new aristocracy of wealth. The latter returning the hatred and not scrupling to condone insurrection if it served their plans. Arrayed against these three on the other hand, was the whole mass of the population possessed by a burning sense of wrong, with respectability to support it, for a time at least. Well might Sir Walter Besant write, in the year of the Queen's Jubilee—

" How this country got through .without a revolution, how it escaped the dangers of that mob, are questions more difficult to answer than the one which continually occupies historians—how Great Britain, single-handed, fought against the conqueror of the world."

That the country would be saved no man was sanguine in 1844. " The country *may* be saved " was the feeling of the most advanced reformers. To be in time to avert calamity they were men and women of many hobbies.

How it was that the Queen was not popular with the masses will be best dealt with in the next chapter, in which we shall hope to show what hell-broth was brewing in England out of sight.

What the Queen was like in appearance at this time is so well known that nothing on that point need be written here, excepting that Professor Leone Levi, coming from Italy, his native land, in October of that year, congratulates himself upon being in time to see the Queen " in all the glory of her youth and beauty " at the opening of the Royal Exchange.

Lord Shaftesbury's appearance is not so well known. He was then Lord Ashley, and is thus described— " Lord Ashley possesses perhaps the palest, purest, stateliest exterior of any man you will see in a month's perambulation of Westminster." The description, after stating that he looks ten years younger than his age (forty-three), compares him to a classic statue in a fashionable suit. " The fine head has also much of the marble about it." " His fine brow and features

are distinctly cut, the nose perhaps a trifle too prominent to be handsome. He has light-blue eyes,
deeply set and near each other, with projecting white
eyelids ; his mouth is small, retiring and compressed."

" The whole countenance has the coldness as well
as the grace of a chiselled one, and expresses precision,
prudence and determination in no common degree.
To judge from the set form of the lips, you would say
not only that he never acts from impulse, but that he
seldom, if ever, felt an impulse in his life."

When we come to the position occupied by the Queen
and her subject in the public mind in 1844, Lord
Shaftesbury has the advantage.

Her late Majesty's seven years' record was known only
in the main to the people who did not like it. To the
outside world she was the wearer of an inherited crown
upon which her immediate predecessors had cast no
glory. The throne was little thought of when men's
minds were occupied with coming revolution. Yet
Victoria had purified the Court, kept free from cliques,
had declined to associate herself with an anti-national
section of the Church, and had laid the foundations
deep and broad for her glorious reign. We cannot
claim her as our patron at this date, but she was
certainly Lord Shaftesbury's ally, and when the R.S.U.
was four years old sent £100 to the funds.

Lord Shaftesbury had already done enough in public
life to make his name live in English history. The
principles he represented are thus described—

" The path he (Lord Ashley) has marked out for
himself in public life is one altogether independent of
party consideration and party conflicts.

" Lord Ashley is well known as the author and persevering advocate of those legislative measures which
are intended to interpose between master and workmen,

so that the power of the former shall not become too oppressive to be borne by the latter.

"To rescue whole masses of men from this ever probable evil, the 'Factory Bill' and 'Mines and Collieries Bill' are framed.

TABLET AT HARROW, WHERE LORD SHAFTESBURY
AS A BOY DEDICATED HIS LIFE TO THE POOR.

"The principle of both is this—that capital, all powerful as it is, should have some limit placed to its power of purchasing ; and great as are the necessities of labour, it should be restricted in its eagerness to sell what capital would buy up, even to the last stage of human exhaustion." [1]

[1] *Illustrated London News*, July 23, 1842.

What this cost him is shown by an extract from his diary in 1847.

" I quail when I think of the concentrated hatred against me. The League (Anti-Corn-Law-League) hate me as an aristocrat : the landowners as a Radical : the wealthy of all opinions as a man of inconvenient principles . . . Every class is against me, and a host of partisans of every grade. The working people, catching the infection ,will go next, and then ' farewell, king,' farewell any hopes of future usefulness."

The price of reform to the Queen and her husband we shall never fully know. The present King has some notion of his parents' sufferings, and could doubtless give his subjects facts that would surprise them. It was a very genuine martyrdom endured till nearly the close of the married life of the royal pair. A harassing pettiness pursued them in nearly all they did for the good of the nation. Strenuous and unselfish workers, both of them, they were pained at being excluded from sympathy in the higher circles of English society. The Queen could bear much for herself, but injustice to her beloved husband made her angry and ill. The culmination was reached when crowds collected around the Tower in the confident expectation of seeing her and Prince Albert committed to it as prisoners. We know from a letter the Prince Consort wrote to Baron Stockmar that this very seriously affected the health of both of them.

So Queen Victoria, like Lord Shaftesbury, did not give to the English people that which cost her nothing. Our progress was an evolution bought by tears, instead of a revolution brought in with an expiation of blood. The latter, however, as we have already said, seemed inevitable in 1844, for reasons that will now be given,

CHAPTER II

Social Problems in 1844

" Alas, what a business this will be : —which must be taken ou
of the hands of absurd, windy persons, and put into the hands of
laborious, modest and valiant men to begin with it straightway,
to proceed with it and succeed in it more and more, if Europe, at
any rate if England is to be habitable much longer.

" God knows, the task will be hard ; but no noble task was ever
easy. This task will wear away your lives and the lives of your
sons and grandsons ; but for what purpose if not for tasks like
this were lives given to men ? "

CARLYLE, *Past and Present* (1843).

QUEEN VICTORIA as an unpopular personage
with the masses is so inconceivable to the
modern Englishman that the grounds for the statement must be given. They did not like her because
knowing nothing of her and hearing only libels they
formed their opinions accordingly. Such bias as they
already had was *against* the House of Hanover. A
London mob broke the windows of . George III's
carriage and sent him hurrying into St. James's
Palace, where he told those he met that he was the
last king of England. Another exploit of these
denizens of the capital's underworld was to turn back
the hearse containing the coffin of George IV's much-
wronged queen. This they did in spite of the military.

But discounting all this and giving fullest value
to the sentiment that a young queen would excite,
it is clear that it would not stand too much strain.
If they were told, as they were told, that she was a

selfish girl, given to frivolous pleasures while her subjects were starving, the hatred of the dynasty would come back like a flood. But had they not the daily papers ? it may be asked. Yes, they could have them if they liked to buy them at 3*d.* or 6*d.* each.

LORD SHAFTESBURY PLEADING FOR THE CHILDREN AT THE BAR OF THE HOUSE OF COMMONS, 1843.

They never did. The few who could read and wished to read a paper read it in shop or public-house. An entry in Lord Shaftesbury's diary after his successful speech upon the condition of the nation's children (February 28, 1843), is to this effect : " Shops and public-houses crowded by people wanting to read the speech." The papers themselves were not all of them fostering loyalty. When Queen Victoria, acting upon a view that is not old-fashioned yet, viz. that rank and wealth should promote the spending of money for the general benefit, organized festive gatherings, it told against her. She commanded for Court dress home-manufactured articles such as Paisley shawls for the ladies. Her intention was to stimulate trade. The papers however, printed parallel columns. In one would be a description of dresses and jewels. Beside it would be tales of starvation, and then a contrast would be made and commented on. But this was in the green tree of middle-class and upper artisan life. What was done in the dry tree of poor-life, ready to flare up at any chance spark, was far more serious.

The expensiveness of the taxed newspapers left an opening for something cheaper. The want was supplied by Mr. Catnach of the Seven Dials. When anything of a sensational character occurred, whether a political event, a great fire, a murder, scandal in high life, or anything that promised to be of sufficient general interest to ensure the sale of some quires of broadsheets, a simple but huge organization was at once set in motion. A poet of the Dials would write the verses at once and receive a shilling for his pains. Afterwards he might receive a few pence extra if the copies sold well. The copies when printed were taken by patterers and chaunters to all parts of the kingdom. Patterers were plausible street orators and chaunters were very much the same; the names denote different occupations, but in practice a chaunter could patter and a patterer could sing ballads. There were stock tunes to fit these rhymes, so it did not take long to transmit ideas to the mob and the working classes. There was not always distortion of facts, but it was unusual for a fair statement to appear from this source. The broadsheets were hawked by the same class that disposed of last dying speeches and confessions, and they had palates that could only be tickled by highly spiced wares. A tame news-sheet would not go off in any quantity. Literary blackmail was the only thing that paid. There was no malice against Queen Victoria, far from it; the Catnach press could at times be generous. Here is a verse from a rhymed Queen's speech—

> My lords and my gentlemen all,
> The bishops and great house of commons,
> On you for protection I call,
> For you know I am only a woman ;
> I am really quite happy indeed—
> To meet you like birds of a feather,
> So I hope you will all struggle with me,
> And pull away boys altogether.
> My name is Victoria the Queen.

The schoolmaster was not abroad in the slums so the patterer taught history. In a raucous voice he would personate Her Most Gracious Majesty as expressing herself thus—

> I heard my old grandfather say
>   His greatgrandmother easily could reckon
> When they made a fool run away,
>   Whose name was King Jemmy the Second.
> Billy gave him a ticket for soup,
>   Though Bill married old Jemmy's daughter,
> He knocked him from old Palace yard
>   To Ireland, across the Boyne water,
>   Long life to Victoria the Queen.

This was sung at the time of the " No Popery "

agitation, and we may suppose the concluding line was put in to satisfy passing policemen.

The Queen was not marked out specially. Her doings came in for treatment that would yield "tidy browns" just the same as any one else who made good copy. Louis Philippe or "Lewis Fillup" as they called him was, so one of the professionals declared, "good, many ways. When he used to be shot at—if the news weren't too early in the day—and when he got to England, and when he was said to have got back, or to have been taken. I have nothing to say against him. I wish he was alive and could do it all over again." The patterers were impartial in their favours. At one time the mother of the public hangman became chargeable on the guardians of her parish. Directly this was known there were patterers down the quiet street in Hoxton where Mr. Calcraft lived, declaiming in awful and mysterious terms against the unfilial executioner. The neighbours bought copies and Calcraft himself sent out for two. The remainder of the edition was sold in his native village. Nothing worse than extravagance was attributed to the Queen by the street minstrels, but it was just the one thing that hungry and unemployed men would hear with least patience. At the time of her marriage there were as many as twenty-three songs about it, all of which sold well, but the favourite was one which went to the tune of "The Dusty Miller" in which the patterer personated Prince Albert and appeared in tatters to be "in character."

The news that reached the poor were such items as the reduction of the vote to the Prince Consort by the Duke of Wellington and the Opposition, and the Duke's inquiry as to whether the Prince was a Pro-

testant. They would never hear of Sir Robert
Peel's well-earned tribute to Her Majesty's scrupulous
economy, and for the simple reason that under no
kind of treatment would that fact yield money to
the poor man's newsagency.

Before Prince Albert came, Lord Melbourne was
the scapegoat. His whole attitude and bearing
reminds one of a famous picture in which a French
dandy of the time of the Revolution, being summoned
to execution, walks to the tumbril with an air of indifference that infuriates and temporarily paralyzes
the ruffian sent to fetch him.

But after the courageous resolve of the royal pair
to visit Ireland in the time of her trouble the scales
fell from the eyes of the democracy, and the people
of Great Britain saw the royal pair for what they
were.

But according to Mr. Justin McCarthy it was not
till 1848-9 that the Court emerged into practical
acceptance as "actual head of the British people."
In 1844 the misunderstanding was not removed.

As between the capitalist and his labourers there
was a far more definite feeling of dislike. The Rt.
Hon. W. E. Forster upon Lord Shaftesbury's eightieth
birthday said—" I remember when I first went to
Yorkshire I was struck by the feeling of distrust—I
might almost say hatred—on the part of workpeople
towards the employers," and in conclusion said,
" These things are, however, entirely changed, and
Yorkshire is in consequence vastly improved. Now,
what has caused this change ? Other men were connected with the matter, but no man was so prominently
connected with it as Lord Shaftesbury."

What was the position in 1844 ? On the surface there was calm, but it was the peace of a slumbering volcano.

The riots of 1842 had been suppressed and the leaders had been sentenced to heavy terms of imprisonment or banishment, but 1844 cannot be understood without a glance at those riots. At this time the manufacturers were working for repeal of the Corn Laws, partly from patriotic and partly from self-interested motives. It was a very prevalent thought among employers that if starving factory hands were to go into the rural districts and plunder the produce, landowners would be more favourable to Corn Law repeal. John Bright in the House said that when they did go, it would not be " as paupers begging for bread, but as an army quartered on the enemy." To help things forward a little, a general lock-out was decided upon at Manchester, just about harvest time, and following an improvement in trade. Upon second thoughts most of the employers gave up the idea, but one firm, Bailey Brothers, told their people " to go and play a bit." If the reader cares to turn to the August numbers of the *Illustrated London News* [1] he will see the result. The first item is " Departure of troops from London for the manufacturing districts." In fashionable Regent Street, a groaning and booing crowd follow the soldiers. Many call out to them to " Remember they are brothers ! " Then an ugly movement is made in the middle of the street. The crowd closes in upon the troops, and the command is given to the band to stop playing and to the soldiers to fix bayonets. At Euston the mob nearly forces its way into the yard.

In the next scene we have " Attack on Messrs.

1 August 5, 1842.

Wilson's Mills, Salford. Mob fired on." Following
it there is a colliers' strike in Warwickshire. Riot at
Preston—rioters shot. At Heywood 3,000 rioters
enter the town and at once thirty-three cotton mills
stand idle. At Lees and Saddleworth 10,000 persons
are out, and deputations from Rochdale are on the
way to Colne, Padiham and Burnley to get them to
rise, and a private letter from Wakefield says that
there is a general strike of colliers. Standing on the
edge of a crowd a reporter hears the following from
one of the leaders—" The Anti-Corn-Law League have
caused us to make this movement, but it is our
own fault if we do not get more than they think."
Then we go on again and find a mob of 5,000 at
Rochdale, cotton and woollen mills stopped and business of all kinds at a standstill. From Bury and the
out-townships there is at Macclesfield another crowd
of 14,000. The operatives of Bolton have struck work,
and 20,000 rioters hold the streets of Stockport. The
workhouse has been broken open and 672 seven-pound
loaves given away. At Burslem a bishop's palace
has been burnt, but the dragoons have restored
quiet. Other towns affected are Coventry, Whitwick,
Warrington, Halifax, Leeds, Blackburn, Huddersfield,
Derby, Clitheroe, Wigan and Glasgow, besides all
Yorkshire.

This conflagration was soon stamped out. Business
was good, and harvesting was in progress, the wrong
time of year for getting the help of farm-hands, who
at any other time doubtless would have joined. If
there was any bond at all between bourgeois and
proletarian before this occurred, there was none in
1844 when many a good man had received a life or a
twenty-one years' sentence.

The working-man, the agricultural labourer, and the miner were all at war with Society. How the workman was disposed towards it may be judged by some of the happenings late in '43 and throughout '44. Before they are given let it be remembered that the poor-rate was twice as high as in 1839.

Applicants for relief were trebled in number, and many came from a higher class than had been customary. The working classes commanded two-thirds less of the means of subsistence than from 1834 to 1836.

The consumption of meat in some places had been 20 per cent. less than usual, in others as much as 60 per cent. less. Skilled labourers and craftsmen were out of work.

The right of working-men to combine for trade purposes had been conceded in 1824. Joseph Hume, the man who shed tears during Lord Shaftesbury's plea for the children in the Commons in '43, had been instrumental in sweeping away the last vestiges of the tyrannous labour laws. But the application of this principle of free combination was a struggle extending over many years. The power to combine, it should be frankly admitted, was unwisely used by working-men, at first—not by the miners, because they had good leaders, but by some of the others. But then, as Dr. Thorold Rogers very properly says—" The blame of so ill a use lies much more at the door of those who have for their own ends refused the liberty of spontaneous action, than it does at the door of those who abuse what they have recovered." [1]

Here are some of the disastrous follies of '43 and '44 in the factories of the manufacturing towns.

[1] Vol. ii. p. 314.   Thorold Rogers : *Economic Interpretation of History.*

September 29, 1843. Attempt to blow up the saw-mills of Messrs. Padgin, Howard Street, Sheffield, by means of a closed iron tube filled with powder. Damage considerable.

September 31. A similar attempt on Ibbetson's knife and file works, Shales Moor, near Sheffield. Damage considerable.

October 6. Attempt to set on fire the works of Messrs. Ainsworth and Crompton, Bolton.

January 4, 1844. A machine of cast-iron containing four pounds of powder found in the works of Messrs. Kutchen, Earl Street, Sheffield.

January 20, 1844. An explosion caused by a package of powder—Sawmill—Messrs. Bentley and White, Bury, Lancashire.

February 1. Soho wheel works, Sheffield, set on fire and burnt down.

The rural population was no more contented than that of the towns. Agricultural distress was very acute.   Rick-burning was becoming appallingly common all over the country. The causes of discontent were three, the working of the new Poor Law, the severe laws against poaching, and the displacement of labour by machinery.

The first was felt most keenly, although it was a beneficent change. To give State doles to supplement wages is a practice no nation can indulge in for long and live. Yet the full wickedness for the assessment of wages by the country justices of the seventeenth century under the old labour laws was only seen, when the out-door relief that masked it, had been stopped. The wage payment of men who by law and circumstance could not very well leave the parishes where they were born, were

brought down to the very lowest subsistence level,
and that for constant employment.   For all accidents,
slackness, and other contingencies, parish relief
was the remedy.   Bad management of this relief
had placed a premium upon pauperism, and a change
had to be made when the nation was on the brink of
bankruptcy.   But reform which left out of account
the antecedent injustice, not a dead transaction but one
still operative, chafed and goaded a population
corrupted by the combination of robbery veneered
by a disguising almsgiving.

A law placed on the statute-book in slow-moving
times takes a few years to be fully felt, and at this date
there had been a decade of new Poor Law.   Its effect
at this time was that instead of " three or four millions
of half-paupers " there were " a million of total paupers,
the rest still half-paupers but going without relief." [1]

And what kind of preparation had these three
millions had for the change ?   The old system had
been, according to the Loor Law Commissioners,
" A check upon industry, a reward for improvident
marriage, a stimulus to increased population, and a
means of counterbalancing the effect of an increased
population upon wages ; a national provision for
discouraging the honest and industrious and protecting
the lazy, vicious and improvident ; calculated to
destroy the bonds of family life, hinder systematically
the employment of capital, scatter that which is
already accumulated, and ruin the taxpayers.   Moreover, in the provision of aliment, it sets a premium
upon illegitimate children."

This could scarcely be a preparation for endurance
or energy and initiative.

[1] Engel's *Condition of the Working Classes in* 1844.

If they became indoor paupers they were doomed to a fate not unlike that of Russian prisoners before the present Czar's reign.[1]

The Game Laws pressed heavily on starving people, for under them a man convicted twice of stealing game, even though for food, could be transported for seven years. The hatred of machinery must be taken with the bed-rock conditions to which the rural population had been reduced.

In June *The Times* sent a correspondent into the rural districts. He found 6s. a week to be common wages for full time.

The *Morning Chronicle* also sent a commissioner. This gentleman, who signed himself " One who has whistled at the plough," wrote—" I boldly assert that the condition of these people, their poverty, their hatred of the Church, their external submission and inward bitterness, is the rule among the country parishes of England, and its opposite the exception."

Our boldest peasantry were the poachers of the country, and the smugglers on the coast. It made things uglier that agricultural labourers had just formed a union.

As for the mining population, they were engaged in a terrible struggle, not only for their own rights but for the rights of labour generally. The conflict was protracted throughout the year, and all England followed it through the journalism of Fleet Street or St. Giles'. The nation became exasperated to the last degree by the cruelty and injustice of the mine-owners.

Though Lord Shaftesbury had succeeded in placing on the statute-book a law for the protection of women

[1] Engel's *Condition of the Working Classes in* 1844.

and children in the mines, it was as yet a dead letter
in most districts because no inspectors had been
appointed.   In 1844 the Miners' Union sent an official
notice to the Home Secretary that in the Duke of
Hamilton's Scotch mines sixty women were employed.
The struggle between the miners and the mine-owners
to secure for the former some very reasonable conces-
sions, was fought by the latter, with the view of crushing any attempt to make use of the power of combination the law had given.

It was a manful, heroic fight, conducted with great
restraint by the men and with great harshness and
provocation by the mine-owners.   On March 31 40,000
miners laid down their picks.   They held out till the
end of September.   In July they were all evicted from
their homes with their families.   The sick, the feeble
old men and little children, even women in child-birth,
were mercilessly turned from their beds and cast into
roadside ditches.

Soldiers and police were there, and the troops had
orders to fire at the first sign of resistance.   Justices,
interested men, were present to give the word, but not
one act of revenge on their part spoiled the miners'
war.   For eight weeks of the fag-end of a wet summer
they were under the open sky with their wives and
little ones.

Lord Londonderry and the other mine-owners who
were with him won in the end by importing Irish
labour, but at the cost of inflaming the passions of
every man in this country worthy of the name.

Of the remaining section of English poor, the street
folk of London and the large towns, it need only be
said that, whether following legitimate trade or otherwise, they were all against the authorities.   Moreover,

they were appallingly numerous and tolerably well
organized. When Henry VIII. indulged in wholesale
massacre of beggars, the sturdy rogues took counsel
with the gipsies who had just arrived in this country.
By these ancient vagrants they were taught arts
whereby vagabondage could be made a relatively safe
occupation. They gave them a secret language known
as thieves' cant, sometimes called pedlars' French or St.
Giles' Greek. The street folk had had 300 years in
which to organize for mutual protection, and in various
ways they had done so. We have seen that they had
a literature of their own, a journalism that was smarter
in publishing news than the regular press. These
dangerous masses were behind the exasperated working people, and England's ruin seemed inevitable.
What really happened will be shown in a later chapter.
The awful prediction of Carlyle in '43 might have come
true in '48, but in that day of wrath England, through
the labours of many men and women in varying fields,
could already say, Emmanuel: " God with us."

CHAPTER III

The Early Schools

" We are not able to say when exactly the first beginning
was made, nor to apportion the merit of the earliest efforts."
LORD SHAFTESBURY, 1846.

THAT the direct and indirect influence of the
ragged schools of London and the great towns
did a great deal towards turning aside the threatened
trouble there can be little doubt.

Lord Shaftesbury never tired of saying so. Cabinet
ministers and judges of his generation allowed that
it was true. What the schools were like will perhaps
possess more interest if what they did be first told.

In a later chapter the doings of a "great" day will
be described, a day when the citizens of London did
honour to their fellow-citizen Lord Shaftesbury on
his eightieth birthday in the ancient Guildhall. The
occasion called together perhaps a more representative
body of people concerned in the making of the Victorian
era than any within living memory up to the time of
Queen Victoria's Jubilee. The Earl's speech will
be given now because, in a form that cannot be improved
and with an authority least likely to be called in question, it states the claim of ragged schools. The Earl
said—" What is the main object of our gathering
here ? It is the honour of the Ragged School Union.
Now, let me tell you—it is a thing worth mentioning

specially to you citizens of London ; that you may
know what manner of people you have long had
among you, and have still to-day ; that, hitherto, you
have not known the fortitude, faithfulness, zeal, vigour,
and ability of those men and women who have achieved
such great and mighty results in the removal of the
causes of suffering among the lowest classes of humanity. This Ragged School Union began, as you have
heard, about forty years ago—began with a very
few children indeed (there are men on this platform who
can remember the time when one school only was
to be found with five or six children). It gradually
took root, then rapidly grew, and assumed the immense
proportions of its palmy days, when these five or six
children had become fully 30,000 in daily attendance,
receiving a sound religious and industrial education,
and every one of whom had been picked up in the
streets of London, and who, but for the intervention
of the ragged school teachers, would have swelled the
category of the dangerous classes. In this way we
have taken off the streets of London 300,000 such
children, and have placed them in the paths of honest
industry. Well, in 1870 the School Board was
founded, and although that School Board seriously
limited at first our operations, I do not speak with
disrespect of it, as I believe its institution was a real
necessity. The various members of the Board carry
on their arduous work with great zeal and ability, and
I am able to say we understand each other better
now. We have different spheres. If we cannot
ascend to their height, they cannot descend to
our depth, and be assured that there are terrible
depths yet to be fathomed of ignorance and misery
None was better aware of this fact than Sir Charles

Reed, whose death I look upon as a public calamity ;
and I do not believe that England has for a long
time had amongst her sons a man of wiser head
and nobler heart. Now about the Ragged School
Union. That you may understand the character of
its operations, I may tell you that the movement was
commenced by persons of comparatively humble
station in society, who were oppressed by alarm, pain,
fear, and shame at the state of things they saw around
them, and by the scenes which they witnessed amongst
the neglected and impoverished classes. It is almost
impossible to describe, perhaps to imagine, the then
existing state of things. The first comers to the
schools seemed to have no notion of anything which
obtained in respectable, decent life ; no notion of
order, obedience, discipline, cleansing, or washing of
any kind ; no notion of propriety, or of the first elements
of education, of parental care or filial duty, or right
or duty of any kind. In fact, the ragged schools had
to set to work at the mighty task of redressing these
evils by endeavouring to supply by all the means in
their power at the very outset the want of domestic
training, of parental care, and family teaching. They
followed these neglected children to their homes, got
them into the ragged school, inculcated the first
principles of morality and religion, and in the end
they trained thousands of such children, imparting
such an education and such habits of diligence and
order as to put them in the way of getting an honest
and decent living, and so become useful and loyal
members of the nation. All this time these people
were working from pure love to the perishing ; these
worthy people were not seeking fame, they were not
guided by personal ambition, they made no claim to

recognition or gratitude. Small and humble they may have been, many of them, yet they had, and they have, a claim upon our honour and respect. I assert for them, that they were working while the mighty men of the Government and the mighty men of the Empire were deliberating; they were educating the people while astute politicians and learned heads were considering how the thing was to be done. They were, in fact, reversing the policy of the devil, for they were sowing the good seed while the nation slumbered and slept. This they did, and they claim very little for it. I on their behalf claim gratitude and recognition. I claim for them that they have made government more easy. I claim that through them we present a spectacle such as no nation or civilized community had ever presented to it before. We see vast numbers of men and women of all sorts and conditions of life; it is very various. I have now an address signed by 3,000 ragged school teachers, representing 1,700 different callings of society, even to a crossing sweeper among them; who, although not highly educated, taught his class, I believe, very well. We have, then, these large numbers of men and women living by their labour, giving up their spare hours for evening work, and occasionally a few hours in the morning; giving all this time without fee or reward; giving their time, their talents, and their hearts to the cause, diving down into the recesses of human misery, caring for nothing but the welfare of the lost children and to spend and be spent in the service of their Lord and Master. Well now, that is the state of things and the character of fellow-citizens who are doing this work. I speak with the deepest reverence and affection for all such, and I trust you will throw into it equal heart and soul, and energy and life. Now I do not name these London workers to the exclusion of others who have toiled, and successfully, in this great city; I do not speak to the exclusion of those who in all the great towns and cities of England, Scotland, and Ireland took up their example, and of whose success great things are recorded; nor do I speak to the exclusion of agencies of a kindred character which have also been instrumental in accomplishing much good. But I do claim for the action of all such that, as my honourable friend said, you are making government easy, you are making government tolerable, you are superseding the necessity for extraneous acts of legislation, you are making it possible to keep the vast population of the largest city on the earth in order with the fewest police and the smallest armed force to be found proportionately in any other large community in the world. Of course there are other agencies acting simultaneously with the Ragged School Union, but it happens to be the Ragged School Union that I have to bring before you to-day."

It occurs no doubt to the reader that before there be a Ragged School Union there must be schools to band together. That being so, there is a natural wish to learn how the schools sprang up. Lord Shaftesbury in 1846 in the *Quarterly Review*, wrote— " We are not able to say when exactly the first beginning was made, nor to apportion the merit of the earliest efforts."

It is such a very natural and obvious thing to get poor children together and instil the first principles of duty into their minds, if their parents have not done it, that a Sunday ragged school is more the product of instinct responding to necessity than of ingenuity

seeking to solve social problems. The Rev. William
Hurlin, of Antrim, U.S.A., wrote to the headquarters
in October, 1902, that he was a London City missionary
in 1840 and founded a ragged school in Kingsland in
1842. He claimed that London ragged schools were
founded by London City missionaries, and gave in
his letter the following extracts from early L.C.M.
reports in support of his statement—

"The first published reference to ragged schools
is in 'The Fifth Annual Report of the London City
Mission,' which was presented at the annual meeting
held at Exeter Hall, on Monday, May 18, 1840. I
copy from page 16 of that report—

"'To the pages of the *London City Mission Magazine*
your committee would refer you for many interesting
reports of the labours and successes of the missionaries. During the past year several schools have
arisen out of their labours, and *five have been formed
exclusively for children raggedly clothed ;* one in the
West, a second in Lambeth, a third in Rosemary Lane,
a fourth in Bethnal Green, and a fifth in Shoreditch,
at which 570 children are attending.'

"In the *City Mission Magazine* for June, 1840, in
some remarks preceding an account of the annual
meeting just referred to, it is stated on page 82—
'Besides sending many children to schools, no less
than five new schools have originated out of the
labours of the missionaries, into which children raggedly
clothed are admitted. There are now 570 children
attending these schools.'

"In the Tenth Annual Report of the London City
Mission, presented in May, 1845, it is stated at page
27—'It may here be stated that there are now about
forty ragged schools in existence in different parts

of the Metropolis, all, or very nearly all, of which had their origin in the efforts of the missionaries, and to many of which the missionaries still devote considerable time.'"

It is beyond all question that the number of ragged schools in London was very largely increased by the agents of the London City Mission, but ragged schools existed long before 1835, when the L.C M. was started, as part of the Sunday school movement, and probably it would be found that even mediaeval England knew the ragged school as an ancient institution.

The late W. H. Watson in his *First Fifty Years of the Sunday School* wrote in reference to the Sunday Schools founded by Thomas Cranfield, the Rev. Rowland Hill and others—" These schools may be considered as the precursors of what have since been called ' ragged schools,' in the formation and carrying on of which John Pounds, of St. Mary Street, Portsmouth (who while earning an honest subsistence by mending shoes was also schoolmaster gratuitously to some hundreds of children of his poor neighbours) ; the Rev. Dr. Guthrie, of Edinburgh ; Sheriff Watson, of Aberdeen ; the ' Poor Tinker' of Westminster ; and the Poor Chimney Sweep of Windsor, have been so useful ". (p. 50).

The connexion of the London City Mission agents with ragged schools was given by the Rev. John Branch at the R.S.U. annual meeting 1850—

" The simple matter of fact was this, the City missionary found not only adults living in ignorance and sin, in filth and mental degradation, but he found a mass of children growing up around him, the boys making expert thieves, and the poor girls driven to a life of infamy at fourteen or fifteen years of age. He found, moreover, this unfortunate class in rags and filth. He could not find admission for them into any decent school, and hence the necessity and origin of ragged schools."

That they were not the only ragged schools existing in 1844, is shown by an extract from our first report. It is there stated that—

"Many of these schools (there were twenty then) have been started by private individuals, several of whom are agents of the London City Mission." Five years later when the number of schools had increased to eighty-two, institutions which had developed agencies unthought of at the outset, there is a paragraph to this effect—

"The Committee, ere concluding, desire to express their thanks for continued and valuable assistance rendered by the agents of the London City Mission, in the formation of new schools and in the visitation of parents and children. They regard the aid thus received as one of the collateral benefits conferred upon the poor of this vast metropolis by this excellent society, whose labours first paved the way for ragged schools, and showed the necessity for their existence."

As a matter of fact, the fully developed ragged school was a much more elaborate thing than the school of the first efforts. When the workers sought for the nearest corresponding agency, in the history of the past, to that which they were forming, they found the type in the work of John Pounds, of Portsmouth. John Pounds in practical ways cared for the bodies, minds and souls of his scholars. Moreover, he gave large numbers of them a start in industrial life. The distinctness of his philanthropy from his means of gaining a livelihood, taken with the foregoing features of his efforts for poor children marked him out as the founder of the ragged school movement by his example.

It is quite likely, as Mr. Hurlin says in his letter, from which an extract has been given, that what John Pounds did was little known among the conductors of ragged schools in the late thirties and early forties, and had no part in calling them into existence. But these were merely Sunday Schools for excluded, dirty and unruly children. The ragged schools of the late forties and early fifties derived a great deal of suggestive help from Portsmouth. It came to London via Edinburgh through the " apostle of ragged schools," Dr. Guthrie, the awakening of whose interest in them he himself describes—

" My first interest in the cause of ragged schools was awakened by a picture which I saw in Anstruther, on the shores of the Firth of Forth. It represented a cobbler's room ; he was there himself, spectacles on nose, an old shoe between his knees ; that massive forehead and firm mouth indicating great determination of character ; and from between his bushy eyebrows benevolence gleamed out on a group of poor children, some sitting, some standing, but all busy at their lessons around him. Interested by this scene, we turned from the picture to the inscription below ; and with growing wonder, read how this man, by name John Pounds, by trade a cobbler in Portsmouth, had taken pity on the ragged children. whom ministers and magistrates, ladies and gentlemen, were leaving to run wild, and go to ruin on their streets. How, like a good shepherd, he had gone forth to gather in these outcasts, how he had trained them up in virtue and knowledge, and how, looking for no fame, no recom-

pense from man, he, single-handed, while earning his
daily bread by the sweat of his face, had, ere he died,
rescued from ruin and saved to society no fewer than
five hundred children.

"I confess that I felt humbled. I felt ashamed of
myself. I well remember saying to my companion,

JOHN POUNDS AND HIS SCHOLARS.

in the enthusiasm of the moment, and in my calmer
and cooler hours I have seen no reason for unsaying
it—'That man is an honour to humanity. He has
deserved the tallest monument ever raised on British
shores.' Nor was John Pounds only a benevolent
man. He was a genius in his way—at any rate, he

was ingenious; and, if he could not catch a poor boy in any other way, like Paul he would win him with guile. He was sometimes seen hunting down a ragged urchin on the quay of Portsmouth, and compelling him to come to school, not by the power of a policeman but a potato. He knew the love of an Irishman for a potato, and might be seen running alongside an unwilling boy with one held under his nose, with a temper as hot and a coat as ragged as his own."

Dr. Guthrie's books were much read in England and when he began his ragged school work in 1847 his methods, based upon those of Sheriff Watson, of Aberdeen, were followed in sympathy by the workers of London. To them his "pleas for ragged schools" as they came out were very welcome. Lord Shaftesbury and Dr.

JOHN POUNDS' HOUSE AT PORTSMOUTH.

Guthrie may be said to have popularized what John Pounds and Sheriff Watson had done, and while doing so they insisted upon its public importance. Under such stimulus many of the old ragged Sunday schools quickly added social operations. In a very short time there was an entire transmutation of the movement. It was largely due to the persistence with which John Pounds' memory was upon all occasions brought under notice.   Another eloquent passage upon the old cobbler may here be given—

" Were we to make a pilgrimage, as soon as to the lonely heath where martyrs repose, we would direct our steps to the busy streets of Portsmouth, and would turn from the proud array of Old England's floating bulwarks to seek out the humble shop where John Pounds achieved works of mercy and earned an imperishable fame.   Honour to the memory of him, beneath whose leathern apron there beat the kindest heart—there glowed a bosom fired with the noblest ambition.   Without fee or reward from man, while he toiled for his hard-earned bread with the sweat of his brow, this poor cobbler educated not less than five hundred outcasts before they had laid him in his lonely grave !   Honour, we say again, to the memory of this illustrious patriot.   Princes and peers, judges and divines, might have stood uncovered in his presence ; and marble monuments might be removed from the venerable walls of Westminster to make room for his."

Lord Shaftesbury's article in the *Quarterly Review* for December, 1846, upon the second annual report preceded Dr. Guthrie's advocacy, but was similar in the two respects that it placed the claim of the work for support upon the broadest grounds of social service and it emphasized the philanthropic phase.   Lord Shaftesbury's article, Dr. Guthrie's pleas and the pressure of the work itself upon the honorary workers combined to cause a type of institution similar to John Pounds' school to become recognized as being what was meant by a ragged school.

Nearly everything in the operations of the R.S.U. existed in germ in that wonderful little shop, six feet by sixteen.   Even the fresh air movement had its counterpart, for the scholars took turns at sitting on the step and the form outside. The clothing department was represented by the garments Pounds loaned to the children to enable them to attend Sunday school. The cripple department was foreshadowed by that curious contrivance of leather he made for his crippled nephew in the imitation of an orthopaedic instrument he had seen, and which we are told effectually cured the distortion.

When there was a competition for places in his little academy he always gave the preference to the little " blackguards," thus forestalling in practice Lord Shaftesbury's advice, " Stick to the gutter." When he went out upon the Portsmouth quays at night he put baked potatoes in his pockets for the " drifts." Not only so but he taught his girl scholars to cook simple food, so that the ragged school cookery class had its origin in the shoemaker's shanty. To the lads he taught his own trade, and this would represent industrialism, while the reading, writing and arithmetic in which they were thoroughly grounded, stood for education. Being doctor and nurse to his young charges he may be said to have had a medical department as well. As a maker of bats, shuttlecocks and crossbows for the youngest he exhibited an interest in recreation.

That he succeeded in emigrating any of them does not appear, though he sent many a boy away to sea. The last of his talking starlings was given to the wife of the port-admiral to mark his sense of indebtedness for help in this direction.

Even the Robin Dinner was anticipated by the good old man in the plum-pudding feast for the children he held every Christmas Day He was not an ascetic,

but he lived simply. The uncooked sprats found in
the gallipot on the mantelshelf on January 1, 1839, the
day he died, showed what he considered good enough
for his dinner on New Year's Day. In his death, too,
he was representative. A week before, when the
children were picking out the plums from their slices
of pudding, he told the woman who boiled it for him
that he had no earthly want unsatisfied and he hoped
when he died he might go off suddenly just as one of
his own parrots, jays or starlings might "drop from
his perch." His wish was gratified, for he expired in
the very act of asking a favour for a poor child. He
therefore was the first of the noble company of those
in the cause who have died standing up and with their
armour on, fighting sin and selfishness for the children's
sake.

This brief sketch is sufficient to make clear towards
what ideal the schools would tend after Lord Shaftesbury had assumed the leadership, and when there was
a combining agency in existence to make the best
information common property. The R.S.U. did more
than that, however. A school of industry and refuge
was started at Westminster in 1847, under the auspices
of the Society, on the lines of the Aberdeen effort.
It is quite plain what these early schools were. The
largest did not accommodate 250 scholars and the
smallest had 25. The large schools were at the outset
either barns, cowsheds, stables, covered-in railway
arches or disused storerooms; the small ones, rooms
of ordinary dwelling-houses. In either case the rent
was not a serious matter, the voluntary teachers and
their friends being able to defray it in most instances.
Lights were provided, usually candles, and little more
was needed except a few bibles. The seats were

frequently planks placed upon bricks. For a long time after such a school was opened there would be constant disturbances.

The superintendent of one of these schools came to Lord Shaftesbury in great trouble once and said —" The neighbours are alarmed, the landlord will close the doors, the teachers will flee." " Well," said the Earl, " you cannot have a ragged school without the preliminaries."

The work at first

DRAWING BY JOHN MACGREGOR, M.A.

was to teach reading, with a view to subsequent Bible study. Most of the schools were open on Sunday nights, many of them in the afternoons, and some few on the Sunday morning as well. Week-night operations were as extended, though not as varied, nor on such a scale, as now, in some of them. Four or five nights a week was not an uncommon programme in the larger schools in 1846.

Schools that had begun in a small room at a rental of two or three shillings began to launch out, and as financial responsibilities increased the control passed to the volunteer workers who raised the money. Their work must have been exceedingly trying, a seemingly hopeless attempt to incise characters in a sand-drift. Few in numbers and without any professional training for securing discipline, they must have continually gone over the old ground in the teaching of the alphabet and made little headway. Then some of them, greatly daring, thought that if a paid teacher could be secured to give his services several nights in the week for a modest sum, they could be released for the work they had in view, the influencing of character. The R.S.U. then came forward and helped with a grant, and at once the enterprise took a more businesslike shape. The plan succeeded and became pretty general, and so the day-schools began. In 1846 there were four schools open every day and evening (Saturdays excepted), and the Union had reason to be proud of them, though the feeling was chastened perhaps by anxiety about the expenses, simple though they were. The schools in Westminster, Clerkenwell, Marylebone and St. Giles' were the forerunners of the free board schools of our time. Cruikshank's etching gives a very good idea of the difficulties of the work, but a nearer view of life in a ragged school will require ampler treatment.

The RAGGED SCHOOL
In West Street (late Chick Lane) Smithfield.

CHAPTER IV

The Scholars—(the Thieves)

" It is a great wrong to leave a child uneducated. It is a still greater wrong to punish it for crimes which are not its guilt, but ours—the infallible consequence of our criminal neglect."—DR. GUTHRIE.

THE Union, starting as it did, with the object of giving added value to local efforts already put forth for the benefit of the poorest children of London, had to define its position with the greatest care.

Only a few of the many primitive institutions existing in 1844 joined at first. Men and women enjoying a living touch with poor life have an instinctive dread of officialism. They discount in advance the most sanguine dreams of the benefits that concerted action will bring. It is with a great price that the comfortably circumstanced and better endowed in. faculty purchase the trust of the poor. When they get it, the price paid for a simple unimpaired human intercourse so far exceeds their first estimate, that they examine narrowly the terms upon which any partnership in their possession of the flickering faith of crushed, bleeding, charred, or broken hearts are offered.

The inviolable sanctity of human nature to the advances of anything but the most reverent touch of an uncalculating sympathy comes as a great revelation to many. Afterwards they give no man credit for arriving at their position intuitively. The memory of what it cost, in abandoned prejudices and ruined self-appreciation makes them as doubtful of new-comers as the centurion was of Paul when he claimed the Roman citizenship as a free-born man.

The founders of the R.S.U. had to consider, when framing the constitution, the schools that were already affiliated, the schools that might become so, and new ones that would be subsequently formed. They felt that the basis must be broad and deep but the aim must be specific. Accordingly, they drew up very early a list of the children who should be the special subjects of ragged school labour. They were—

1. Children of convicts who have been transported.

2. Children of convicts in our prisons at home.

3. Children of thieves not in custody.

4. Children of the lowest mendicants and tramps.

5. Children of worthless drunken parents.

6. Children of stepfathers or stepmothers ; often driven by neglect or cruelty to shift for themselves.

7. Children of those suitable for the workhouse but living a vagrant semi-criminal life.

8. Children of honest parents too poor to pay for schooling or to clothe the children so as to enable them to attend an ordinary school.

9. Orphans, deserted children, and runaways, who live by begging and stealing.

10. Workhouse lads who have left it and become vagrants.

11. Lads of the street-trading classes, ostlers' boys, and labourers' assistants, who otherwise would get no schooling.

12. Girl-hawkers working for cruel and worthless parents.

13. The children of poor Roman Catholics who do not object to their children reading the Bible.

It needs a little reflection to realize how very large these groups were sixty years ago. One main fact thoroughly grasped may explain much. It is that the great metropolis was, as regards its administration, in a state of chaos for more than ten years after 1844, and was the subject of bungling experiment for long after. The police force was not many years old. The means of conveyance within the London area were very much the same as any race of civilized men had had since the dawn of history. Telegraphy was in the experimental stage. There was a surprising number of circumstances to favour the thief and the nomad.

To take one fact alone, there were but 30,000 street lamps and 40,000 private consumers of gas for all London in 1846. We are apt to forget how large London was. At Queen Victoria's accession it was twice the size of Paris in her Jubilee year. Yet this great city, which must have been larger still in 1844 and the following years, was governed partly by a commission appointed by that enlightened authority upon modern cities, King Henry VIII, and partly by 112 independent and mutually jealous parochial bodies. The City proper was, as now, under the control of the Corporation. Vagabondage had its recognized entrenched strongholds, where it had strengthened itself during centuries, and could almost defy, and very frequently succeeded, in baffling authority. London under so many masters was a fairly safe place for robbery of a simple kind. The fashions made the pursuit a profitable one. A pig-skin purse in a hip pocket under the coat is the despair of a modern pickpocket, but a long silk purse in an outside pocket was convenient and tempting in those days. When there was no purse there was often a silk handkerchief worth several shillings to repay trouble.

The thieves, from whose families three sections of the early scholars were drawn, constituted an hereditary but not exclusive caste. Recruits were numerous and welcome. The reason the profession was inherited was because there was no other opening in life for the children. Lads and girls from decent families drifted into it also because there was so little employment even for them in other directions. There was an indirect compulsion in their cases as well.

Re-absorption, after a lapse, into the ranks of honesty is a slow and painful process for the young offender in the present day, but at that time it was out of the question.

The ranks of the criminal classes were always being augmented, and although the convict ship and the hangman's rope were in constant use, they did not thin the class as quickly as it was being made. The laws, too, were wicked in their severity, especially to the young.

A case that was cited from the Exeter Hall platform at our annual meeting in 1853 may be given as an illustration. A little fellow eight years of age was tried in August, 1845, at the Clerkenwell Sessions, for stealing boxes, and sentenced to one month and a whipping. In January, 1846, he was again tried for robbing a till; after that he was twice summarily convicted, and then tried at the Central Criminal Court, in 1846. As a consequence of this record against him he was sentenced to seven years' transportation when only

nine years of age. The sentence was commuted to
three months' imprisonment, but there was no mercy
or common-sense in this or the previous treatment the
poor child had received. Conviction followed conviction, so that in 1852, when he was only twelve years of
age, and four feet two inches high, he was a hardened
jail-bird with whom the law was powerless to deal.

In the Rev. J. W. Horsley's *Jottings from Jail* an
autobiography of a thief is given. It is in thieves'
cant. This we shall not reproduce, but give a compressed paraphrase of the story. It is very instructive
as showing the kind of work done by him as a juvenile
and as an adult.

He tells us that the thief's parents lived at Stamford
Hill. He and some companions robbed an orchard at
Stoke Newington when he was quite a little fellow. His
father thrashed him severely and tied him to the bedpost.
He escaped, let himself out of the bedroom window
by the bedclothes, found his companions, and then all
three went off to sleep under a haystack. After that
they were too frightened to go home. The robbery
of a food-safe followed.

Then his mother found him and he went home for
a time, but he soon fell into the old ways. Stealing
linen from gardens, and bread from bakers' barrows,
were the next exploits, after which he left home a
second time. He next made the acquaintance of
some experienced thieves, and they took him to help
them in parlour-robbing. He, being still a young boy,
used to be put through open windows. An acquaintance with silver plate came next. He soon learned
how to break it into small pieces, and dispose of it
to watchmakers and dealers in stolen goods down
Petticoat Lane. With the proceeds he would go to the

" Brit." in Hoxton, or the " Gaff " in Shoreditch. Sometimes he slept in his companions' houses, at other times
in a shed where there was a fire kept burning night and
day. At last he was caught, and got twenty-one
days for robbing a baker's cart. In prison he made
friends with a Shoreditch lad, and when they came out
they worked together. At St. John's Wood, when after
silver plate, he frightened a cat. Puss knocked down
a pile of crockery, so the young thief was taken again
and tried at Marylebone. This time he was sent to
Feltham Industrial School (1868).

He was not yet sixteen. After attempting to run
away, and being brought back and punished, he culti-
vated the acquaintance of lads who knew more of
thieving than himself.

When he came out, he took to costermongering.
He persevered at this till times were bad, then most
unfortunately he was treated roughly and with injustice
by a policeman. Not content with bullying the youth,
the officer dragged up the boy's past to the crowd
that gathered round.

Sore at heart and sore in body, for the constable's
blows upon his head made him ill for days, he found
his resources at last reduced to 5s.

Then he threw himself into the old life again.
With the little remaining money he had, he took a
ticket to Sutton and came back with five pairs of
boots stolen from a gentleman's house, for which he
received 30s. from a Jew. Next day he went to
Forest Hill, succeeded in stealing some plate and
clothing, and the seduction of easier circumstances
completed his backsliding. Knowing more than
formerly, he now obtained as much as 4s. an ounce for
his stolen silver, and was in comparative affluence.

Flash dress and access to concert-rooms, the predecessors of the West-End music-halls, though far
more questionable in character, were now possible
for him, and he had money to spend and for gambling.
A pugilist taught him to box, and then he entered the
charmed circle of some of "the widest people in London."

They were a pretty set of watch-stealers, confidence-
trick men, sham loan office men, card-sharpers, box-
stealers, burglars, utterers of false coin, passers of
false jewellery, turf swindlers, and skittle - sharps.
For nearly a year he had great success in robbery
for large amounts, and then for the first time he got
drunk. Drinking became more or less habitual with
him, and a woman he met at a Whitechapel concert-
room did not help him to regain lost ground. At
Blackheath, when attempting burglary in a semi-
intoxicated state, he was caught. Tried at Greenwich,
and being unknown, he was sentenced to two months
at Maidstone jail. When he came out he found that
the woman had been inconstant and the home was
gone. His fellow-thieves raised £6 for him, and he
lived on the money for a month.

Then he began again. Nineteen pounds was the
sum his first venture brought him, the proceeds of a
plate robbery at Slough, and then, to use his own words,
he "carried on a nice game." Habitual drunkenness
and the commission of deeds "he would have been
ashamed to do before he took to the accursed drink"
were now quite customary. Next he acquired facility
with skeleton keys. Two months more at Maidstone for being found at the back of a house was
followed by a year of prosperous business, and then
he was sentenced to two months for assaulting policemen. This time Coldbath Fields was the prison.

Here the autobiography digresses to give an incident that shows how a receiver of stolen goods overreached himself. This man had taken advantage of the author of the strange life story now before us, at a time when the latter was intoxicated. He had given him far less than he·should, according to accepted standards, for a gold watch and chain. When sober, the thief went back to him and remonstrated. The receiver gave him half a sovereign, and a piece of advice. This was contained in the words—" Do anybody, but mind they don't do you."

Some time after, the thief and a companion had a burglary planned for a certain evening, and were on the way to it when they saw this receiver and his family going to the Surrey Theatre. Abandoning their first scheme they went to this man's house, took £32 in cash and a gold watch and chain. Shortly after the receiver was sentenced to eighteen months for some illegal transaction. The thief was also sent for a short term to the same prison. When they met in the prison yard the receiver threatened with his fist, but the thief laughed. When at last they met outside the walls the thief returned the other's advice—" Do anybody, but mind they don't do you."

After several other robberies and committals to jail he was out with a companion one Boxing Day when the latter, who like himself, was intoxicated, stabbed him. The tragedy sobered both, the aggressor asked permission to see his wife and child before being given in charge. The other man, however, would not give him in charge. For some time after this occurrence he had serious thoughts, but they passed away in time.

There are hairbreadth escapes in the story which

need not be given, but one little circumstance showing the man's better side is very suggestive. He had been out upon an unsuccessful quest one day in the neighbourhood of Acton. From there he went to Shepherd's Bush, but so many dogs had been poisoned in that locality that the police were on the alert. While waiting for the train at Uxbridge Road for Brondesbury, where he had hopes to find things quieter, a tract was given him headed with the text—"What shall it profit a man if he gain the whole world and lose his own soul ? " He thought, " What good has the money done me what I have had ? " So instead of getting out at Brondesbury he went on to Broad Street, went home, and did not go out for a week.

On the Sunday following he walked to Clapton, where his childhood was spent. Walking down Mount Pleasant Lane, he leaned over the railings to the left to admire the fine view of Epping Forest, though feeling very miserable. From this spot there was, between the sixties and the eighties, a very impressive view—it is not quite spoiled yet. The freshness of the morning, the bright weather, the Sabbath calm, his old memories and the moving scene were means of grace to the man, and then the bells of St. Matthew's played a hymn he had learned at Feltham Industrial School. " This was the first time in my life that I thought what a wretch I was." But his companions were looking out for him. A moody penitent thief is a source of anxiety to his fellows. If he should open his heart to any one he may compromise them. These friends soon had him in the public house, where he drank hard to drown his thoughts, and on Monday he was " ready for the old game again." On Monday he secured some silver plate and a purse with £5 in it at

Maidenhead. Soon after he took £50 at the Alexandra Park Races.

Next he went to Redhill and broke into a house, but finding it to be a clergyman's came away, leaving things as he found them. He says—"I could have robbed several in my time, but I would not." So he went to Croydon, obtained some silver plate, and went home.

Henley-on-Thames came next, and then Portsmouth, on the occasion of the return of the Prince of Wales from India. He and a confederate found after they "knocked off" that they had between £60 and £70 to share. After that, an uninhabited house yielded £43 in goods. From another house at Erith he took some plate and clothing, though he wasted a little of his valuable professional time at the outset in throwing drugged liver to a stuffed mastiff in the hall. At the Harpenden Races he and a confederate took a diamond pin and nearly £100 in money. Then followed a period of loose living, when he very nearly went mad. After that came a number of exploits very similar to those already described. Ultimately, so far as the incomplete story of this sordid life is concerned, he ventured too far in robbing a house at Willesden, and was convicted and sentenced to eighteen months' imprisonment.

There is reason to believe that this man's life was entirely changed at a later period, through the exertions of his heroic young wife, married subsequently, and the prison chaplain.

Our interest in the story is the insight it gives into the conditions that must have obtained in the families of thieves. The anxiety, tension, alternating lavish waste and acute privation, give a home atmosphere of the most poisonous kind for young life.

The story, long as it is, has been inserted advisedly,
although space is valuable. The thief-constituency
of the early schools was a large fraction, yet this
seemingly hopeless group provided most excellent
colonizing material, and the reason needs seeking.
The career of the clever and educated swindler not
unseldom displays a ruthless cruelty towards the
victims of his crimes, as well as a reckless indifference
to the consequences of actions that have as their
object the gratifying of self in a region well outside
the pressure of urgent necessity. A callousness un-
mitigated by the faintest streak of altruism is too often
present in these cases.

With the poor thieves it is not always so. These
men who take chances often have imagination, and
they hide the ugliness of their means of livelihood
from themselves by regarding it as a species of fair
sport. Society has everything in its favour, and the
odds are against them. They are the hares, the
police the hounds. Doubling of all sorts is in the
game. They are not without scruples, but these
relate not to the rules that Society has framed, but
some of their own making in which, in a rough and
ready way they seek to preserve, pathetically enough,
a nodding acquaintance with abstract equity.

We have seen that our young thief would not rob
a parson or give away a confederate who had stabbed
him. In the same way a young pickpocket who had
robbed his teacher in the street, not recognizing him
in the dark, restored the silk handkerchief and expressed
regrets. This restoration and apology required a very
large amount of moral courage. But there is no lack
of real fibre in the class. They possess too what the
settled-dwelling, regular-living man often lacks, initia-

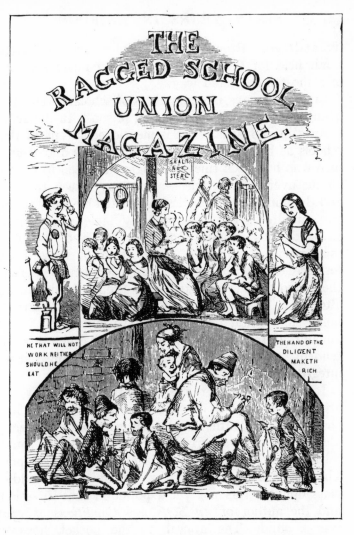

FRONTISPIECE OF THE MAGAZINE, DESIGNED BY JOHN LEACH.

tive and " go." Brought under discipline early, and given
a fair field for their energies, they often rise socially
in a most unexpected way.

In the old days, large numbers of scholars were frequently absent " doing time " in prison. In the 1849
report an industrial class is mentioned in one of the
schools as being composed entirely of lads and young
men who had been thieves. Eight had been in prison
on the average five times—in custody fifteen times—
and the number of robberies committed by each, about
two hundred. For the property stolen they only
received about one-fifth of its value, and yet they
each made about £3 a week. One of these lads,
formerly the worst among them, had, since entering
the school, been entrusted with property amounting
altogether to about £1,500. This he had carried
home safely, and returned with various sums, in all
amounting to £50, for work done, to the superintendent, and in every instance had maintained strict
integrity.

It occurs, no doubt, to the reader that a very powerful
argument in favour of such work as that which had
changed these youths could be drawn from expediency
alone. It may surprise him that outside a small
religious circle it was the main argument relied upon.
Charles Dickens, the great re-humanizer of middle-
class opinion, was not yet a power in that direction,
and the author of *All Sorts and Conditions of Men*
was a child. The appeal to the pocket, however
was practical, and Dr. Guthrie was the first to make
a striking use of it. In *Seed Time and Harvest*
he gave a list of fifteen thieves' incomes, which
would, of course, represent a dead loss to the community.

1. Richard Clarke, during a career of 6 years, £2,820
2. John Clarke, ,,   5 ,,   500
3. Edward Clarke, ,,   3 ,,   1,650
4. Ellen Clarke (O'Neill) ,,   2½ ,,   1,550
5. John O'Neill, ,,   9 ,,   1,450
6. Thomas O'Gar, ,,   6 ,,   300
7. James O'Brien, ,,   3½ ,,   1,400
8. Thomas M'Giverin, ,,   7 ,,   1,900
9. Thomas Kelty, ,,   20 ,,   8,000
10. John Flanagan, ,,   14 ,,   5,800
11. John Thompson, ,,   5 ,,   1,800
12. John Bohanna, ,,   6 ,,   1,500
13. J. Shawe, ,,   3 ,,   600
14. W. Buckley, ,,   7 ,,   2,100
15. Sarah Dickenson, ,,   3 ,,   630

          £32,000

The figures were striking, but he proceeds—" Let us fix our attention on one individual of this group ; let it be Flanagan, of Liverpool. He was seventeen times in prison, and caught fifteen times besides, but discharged for want of evidence. He was at length transported. Here are his transactions during three years ; and the tables, be it observed, do not include any sums under £10, although he stated that these considerably exceeded those above that sum—

1838 and 1839.

Value.	Where robbery committed.	From whom.
£20	Concert, Liverpool . .	A gentleman.
15	Theatre, Liverpool . .	A gentleman.
11	Zoological Gardens . .	A lady.
30	Coach-office, Liverpool .	Proprietors.
46	Auction, Broughton Road	A lady.
30	Auction, Cheetham Hill .	A lady.
15	Auction, Pendleton . .	A lady.
21	Manchester	A till from a liquor-vault.
50	Manchester	A till from a public-house.
11	Leek, Stafford . . .	A shopkeeper.
85	Hanley Races	A gentleman.
49	Northallerton Fair . .	A drunken farmer.
12	Liverpool Packet . . .	A passenger.

Value.	Where robbery committed.	From whom.
£18	Liverpool Packet . . .	A passenger.
30	Liverpool Packet . . .	A passenger.
45	Horncastle Fair . . .	A lady.
47	Leeds Fair	A butcher.

1840 and 1841.

10	Lincoln Fair	A gentleman.
14	Lincoln Fair	Captain of a boat.
10	Spalding Fair	A farmer.
11	Horncastle Fair . . .	A maltster.
10	Liverpool Races . . .	A gentleman.
16	Liverpool Races . . .	A farmer.
17	Chester Races . . .	A lady.
11	Manchester Races . .	A lady.

1841 and 1842.

10	Manchester Theatre . .	A lady.
70	Bury Fair	A cattle-dealer.
250	Manchester (in the Street)	An officer.
15	Knutsford Races . . .	A jockey.
30	Doncaster Races . . .	A publican.
18	Nottingham Races . .	A butcher.
14	Derby Races	Unknown.
13	Crowle, Lincoln . . .	A publican's wife.
12	Caister, Lincoln . . .	A farmer.
11	Market Rasen . . .	A gentleman's servant.
60	Brigg Fair	A farmer's wife.
21	South Lincolnshire . .	A coachman.
	&c. &c. &c.	

£1,168

These facts, reduced to black and white, were full of meaning, but the actual money loss caused by the pursuit of thieving was not all, there was the cost of the entire judicial, police and prison establishment to be added.

A magistrate stated at a public meeting in 1849 that 18,000 prisoners in the prisons of Middlesex alone cost at an average, first and last, £120 to £150 each. Also that 550 juveniles, under 17 convicted in the year at the Clerkenwell Sessions had cost £1,200 to prosecute, the stolen property being valued at £160.

The lessening of juvenile commitments after the establishment of ragged schools was very appreciable. Dr. Guthrie was able to give figures of the results in Edinburgh. The school there was opened in the summer of 1847.

Percentage of children under 14 in Prison.

1847	5·6
1848	3·7
1849	2·9
1850	1·3
1851	·9

" Formerly all these children found their way to the jail. No man cared for their souls, or commiserated their condition. Banishing what it did not hang, the country shipped off thousands to rot and fester in our colonies, till these, rising as one man, declared that they would have no more of our refuse and waste ; that, if we would grow criminals, we should keep them. Many seemed born for the gallows, and coolly calculated on being hanged, as sailors do on being drowned, or soldiers, in time of war, on being shot. I happened once to find them at their rehearsals. They had a ragged urchin suspended by a rope thrown over the door-lintel of an old house. The noose was dexterously placed under his arm-pits; but the way he hung his head and mimicked the dying spasms, drew up his legs, and kicked, was perfect. So thought his companions. The young savages danced round him in wildest glee, and greeted each kick with roars of laughter. They were familiar with hanging ; nor much wonder, since Newgate, for instance, used to show ten or a dozen old ruffians with boys, strung up like vermin, and slowly turning round in the morning air, with their white caps—waiting to be cut down. Horrible sight ! "

[1] Dr. Guthrie, *Pleas for Ragged Schools.*

The obvious inference to be drawn from the costliness and ineffectiveness of the punishment of crime compared with the success and economy of ragged schools was thus emphasized by this author—

" Nowhere else can labour and money count with such certainty on meeting with an ample reward.

" It seems like lowering a noble cause to introduce the consideration of money to plead for it on the score of economy. It is a great stoop to come down from the lofty heights of Religion, Pity, Humanity, Justice, and Mercy, to pounds, shillings, and pence. Yet I can demonstrate that ours, the kindest and holiest, is also the cheapest policy. It has been calculated, as I have already stated, that every child left to grow up into a criminal costs the country, on an average, not less than three hundred pounds. Let us suppose then that but one half of the five hundred, whom this single school has saved, had run a career of crime ; they would have involved the State in an outlay of £75,000. Now, during the twelve years of its existence, our school has cost some £24,000 ; the amount, therefore, saved to the country is just the difference between that sum and £75,000 —that is, £51,000. But make the much more probable supposition that at least two-thirds of these children would, but for our school, have developed into full-blown criminals, then, besides rescuing them from a life of crime and misery, we have saved the State in actual money a sum, in round figures, equal to the difference between £24,000 and £96,000. With that fact before them, a saving in twelve years of £72,000 effected by this one benevolent institution, were our Governments and Parliaments wise, and not, to use a common proverb, penny wise and pound foolish—

ragged schools would be regarded as having the fore-
most claim on the public funds. They would be made
to cover, as a net-work, all the wretched districts of
the large cities of our land."

A speaker at one of our annual meetings (1849)
gave testimony in the same vein. " The more the
public mind is imbued with the truth, that it is cheaper
(to put it upon the lowest grounds) to raise the population in religion, virtue, and intelligence, than to allow
them to grow up in vice and crime, the more will
ragged schools be promoted, and the less will be the
necessity for enlarging our prisons. When I state that
in the prisons of Clerkenwell and Westminster there
were last year 1716 inmates below the age of 16, you
must see the need for your exertions, and form some
idea of the expense entailed upon the country in the
support of so many criminals. I find that 8,000
children may be educated for about £3,000 a year,
while in the prisons 500 children are not kept at less
than £10,000 a year. If, therefore, you wish to be
benevolent, to be useful and economical, increase
your ragged schools."

It was indeed pressingly necessary when the educating of children in the arts of robbery was carried
on as a system. A little fellow whose father and
mother were dead, who was alone and uncared for,
told his teacher one Sunday that he and twenty more
boys were kept by a man and a woman in Wentworth
Street, Whitechapel, and taught to pick pockets.
The training took six months. . Daily the woman
dressed herself, put a bell in her pocket, also a purse
containing 6d.; any of the pupils who could take
the purse from her pocket without causing the bell
to tinkle got the 6d. as a reward for his dexterity.

When proficient the boys were sent out to plunder for
the pair. The confession of another thief's tutor was
as follows—

" He had been twenty years living a criminal life,
and had been twenty times in prison. He resided in
a low lodging-house, where he carried on his craft of
training young lads to steal. The best hands among
them were sent into the streets, and they brought
home the plunder, on which the criminal.school lived.
He was too well known to the police to dare to go out
himself. ' But,' said he, ' I never can keep the young
'uns long, for as soon as I have made them clever at
their profession, if they are not taken by the police,
they leave me and start for themselves ; so that I am
obliged to look out for new hands.' Being asked how
many lads he supposed he had trained to be thieves
during the twenty years, he replied that he had kept
no account, and he could not exactly tell, but of this
he was sure, that it was not less than *five hundred*.

Apart from the work of ragged schools in connexion
with the prevention of crime and the restoration of
the lapsed, the great service rendered to the cause of
reform in the treatment of criminals by Dr. Leone Levi
ought not to be forgotten. To be exact it was not a
reform at all, though it was the means of producing
many.

Dr. Levi brought before the Law Amendment
Society the need for judicial statistics. Without figures
to guide them the authorities could not tell whether
the nation was advancing or falling behind. He told
the story of his mortification when attending an
international congress of statisticians at Brussels at
being compelled to confess that this country could
supply no figures. He pictured the astonishment of the

continental savants at their colleague's admission.
Lord Brougham was present and wanted to know
what judicial statistics might happen to be. As soon
as he understood he was heartily with the Professor.
He gave notice in Parliament that same evening
that he would put certain questions and bring in a
bill. The great lawyer drove the matter somewhat
for time, and Dr. Levi gives a graphic sketch of
Brougham in his room in the House of Lords with a
glass of brandy by his side, taking down figures, of
which the former feared he would be able to make
nothing when he rose to speak, writing at such a speed
that his pendulous nose shook with the energy of his
movements.

But when the time came he gave a most lucid
explanation of the whole subject. Next morning
Dr. Levi had a letter from him which practically
asked him to draft the bill. Since then our public men
have been able as it were to watch the moral health
of the country, and the opportunity to do so has been
productive of many reforms.

It must have been a very difficult position in which
the teachers of early days were placed in dealing with
the poor little jail-birds in their classes, but it must
have been a great comfort to the children to have
disinterested friends whom they could love. After
twenty-one days in Bridewell what a happiness to have
the hand grasped, to be addressed kindly, and to look
up into a loving countenance, knowing that there, at
least, was no contempt nor harshness of thought. We
have read of the missionary and the negro orphan.
Resting in the shadow of his wagon one day the white
man was startled by a touch. Before him stood a
little emaciated piccaninny, naked but for a wild-cat

skin about his loins. By his side was a starving
springbok, a pet, and the creature licked his hand.
The child's friends were dead, but he managed with
his swollen tongue to say—" Stranger, I am alone," and
the next he knew was that the missionary was caressing
him and ministering to him while hot tears fell upon
his bare skin. Then the man told the boy that God
loved him also, and the child believed him and grew
up to be a help to his helper and to many another.
It was much the same with the child-thief.

CHAPTER V

THE SCHOLARS—(*continued*)

Paupers—Vagrants and Waits

" Death ! The life of crime before them, should they survive the cold and hunger and neglect, under which they sink
by thousands into an early grave, is such that I have been
thankful to see them dead ; lying in their rude coffins ; safe
in God's arms."—DR. GUTHRIE.

WE shall have to refer again perhaps to the interesting thief-class, but for the moment we
are free to consider another contingent of ragged school
scholars, the parish-bred element, the families of tramps
and the ownerless children.

Reference has been already made to the corrupting
influence of out-door relief upon the normal family life
of rural England. It remains to call attention to the
thoughtlessness shown in dealing with pauper children
towards whom the guardians of the poor had assumed
direct responsibilities. There was not a little cruelty,
too prevalent to be quite disregarded, but still nothing
to be compared with what had existed at the beginning
of the century. The official mind was saturated with
the teaching of Malthus, that " the poor man had come
to the feast of Nature and found no cover laid for him
and Nature had bidden him begone." Good men had
steeled themselves to the suppression of pauperism,
and pauperism was discouraged to the point of harsh-

ness.   It is never fair to take the exceptional and treat it as typical, and it is not in that way that the following scrap of news of 1844 is given.   Though barbarous enough to rouse indignation at the time, it was but an expression in extreme form of a general attitude.   In the Greenwich Workhouse there happened to be a disobedient child of five.   This truculent and unmanageable little rascal was sent as a punishment to sleep all night on the lid of a coffin in the dead-house.   If there were any point in it, the reader might be sickened with much more of the same, but our practical interest lies elsewhere.   The 50,000 workhouse children of that year hardly at this point concern us—we have to think of a certain proportion of the adult London population bringing up families, and who had received their start in life from the provincial or London unions.   Those who did not drift back to the workhouse would, in very large numbers, settle in London, and in the vast majority of cases they would be social failures to the end of their days.   The apprenticeship system lingered long after the abuses of the old Poor Law had gone. What is about to be sketched is not a panorama of horrors of the pre-Victorian period, it has nothing to do with physical pain or hardship at all.   But it is a story of moral damage reacting upon the resources and life of the nation nevertheless.   Moreover, it is not an account of an influence, remote in time from our period.   It is founded upon the matter found in eleven closely-printed pages of a Blue-book of the year 1843. That which was still an unabandoned practice in dealing with pauper children in that year must have been tolerably general ten or fifteen years earlier when the adults of 1843 were receiving their life-equipment and bias as children.

At that time British pauperism was at high-water mark. Large numbers of agricultural labourers who did not themselves come upon the guardians of their parishes to be provided with work, confidently looked to them to support their children at an early age.

This is what happened in the case of a boy. His name was put on the guardians' list for parish apprenticeship. At nine he was ready, and having said goodbye to father and mother till he should be twenty-one, he made his way with other boys and girls to the parish offices. Here he would find a number of grumbling farmers, talking aloud among themselves against the system. They would

SCHOLARS OF SIXTY YEARS AGO.

complain that they were not able to employ the well-trained healthy children of their own best labourers at wages because they were compelled to take the children of the careless or vicious folks of the village into their houses. These nice lads that they would have been glad to have would, upon leaving school, have nothing to do, and if they got into idle bad ways whose fault would it be ? Then, if they took to poaching, the squire would get them transported. Perhaps at this point one farmer would say that he personally would not mind so much if he had some choice of the individual who was to stay in his house for twelve years whether he wished it or not. There were girls on the list whom he did not want mixing with his children. His own daughters were very young and well in hand, but his boys were quite free enough in their ways, and he couldn't always have his eye on them.

Our apprentice-elect would begin by this, to see that whoever had him, his welcome would not be a warm one, and he would study the angry faces in hope and fear, desiring that the one that he minded least might be that of his future master. Then the parish clerk, trying to laugh off all ill-humour from himself, might be seen writing the names of the children on separate pieces of paper which he put into a hat in the hurried manner of one who had a disagreeable task to perform that he wanted to get through quickly. The farmers dipped their hands into the hat, each withdrew a slip and led away a child. The silence of the homeward journey made our little friend uncomfortable, and the sharp tongue of the farmer's wife upon arrival at the farm finished him. Tears began to flow. What hurt him most was the aloofness and scorn of the farmer's

children. The bitterness of his degradation crushed
his childish soul. However, being a healthy, cheerful,
obtuse boy he soon recovered, and having a fund of
high spirits and good nature to draw upon, soon
managed to turn the keen cutting edge of persecution.
The farmer's household liked him in a way. He, on his
part, found he was better clad as to warmth, wore better
boots than before, and had good regular meals. Still
he was a pariah, an outcast. The slightest childish
freedom might bring upon him a cruel snubbing from
young people his own age. Schooling was at an end
for him. Sunday school was dropped partly because
the farmer did not care to provide him with a second
suit and partly because he did not care for him to appear
in his everyday clothing.

So all his friends were gone, mother, teacher and companions. All the people he did meet, made him feel
his inferiority. The loss of intercourse with the village
he felt less than he otherwise would, as by keeping
away, he had thereby escaped the taunts of boys a
little older than himself. These boys would regard
his class as enemies and interlopers, injuring the prospects of decent families. Much of the pain of the position would wear off in time, if the lad were moderately
active so as to be worth his keep to the farmer. But
there would be more to bear later. As the youth neared
manhood, possessed of a strong well-knit frame and a
head that would think, the injustice of the arrangement would make him brood. Can we not fancy him
at nineteen, denied education, denied religion, denied
the simplest of rights. No time could he call his own.
For ten years he had not handled a coin of the realm.
His self-respect had been ruined, he had no ambitions,
no social ideals. The sustaining prospect for that

strong, healthy, passionate, animalized man is that in two years' time he will be able to indulge in harmful, forbidden things. Passing a group of youths and girls off to a country fair, the girls looking slightingly as he went by, fancy how he would feel it. When they had passed he might hear one of the young men make a joke at his expense, and might hear the remark received with boisterous unrestrained laughter. The sound

A CHRISTMAS TREAT—LAMB AND FLAG RAGGED SCHOOL.

would madden him and he would turn as if to thrash the yokel, but the local magistrates would have had him whipped if he had, and then there would be more laughing. That thought would restrain him. One can easily imagine a type of lad of finer clay who would be more effectually ruined. Smarting under the treatment caused by his employer's irritation, he might so act that even fairly reasonable relations could never be established through the entire twelve years. When once the hatred was there, the boy's spite would perhaps take the shape of supineness. With twelve years of dependence before him he might doggedly set himself to do only the least that he could not escape doing. The master, exasperated beyond endurance, might be tempted to violence and other degrading treatment. Human beings under such rearing when their natures are forming, lack initiative or stability, usually both, and when a system like this is a national one the results are appalling. It is to the great cities that the victims gravitate, These workhouse lads neither made good workmen, expert thieves, ingenious beggars nor brisk street hawkers. In *Oliver Twist* the country-bred pauper-boy, Noah Claypole, is put to do the most sneaking kinds of robbery by Fagin the Jew, but his ultimate calling, it will be remembered, was that of informer. There were many Noah Claypoles with families in the early days of ragged schools, living in the low lodging-houses of London. There were means of living that did not tax bodily strength, the mental faculties or the courage unduly. The disposal of counterfeit coin was one.

To beg by means of a letter written by a screever was another. A screever was a lodging-house character of brains and education. There have been instances where screevers were university men. The screever would write a letter to which the appearance of his customer would give an air of reasonableness.

These were his prices :—

		s.	d.
Friendly letter	. . . .	o	6
Long ditto	. . . .	o	9

	s.	d.
Petition	1	0
Ditto with signatures	1	6
Ditto with forged names	2	6
Ditto " Very heavy " (dangerous)	3	0
Manuscript for a broken-down author	10	0
Part of a play for ditto	7	6

When " Lawyer Joe " or some other screever had written the letter, he would fold it in official style after appending the signatures of the clergyman and church-wardens, each written with a different shade of ink, crease it as if it was long written and often examined, and dipping his finger in the ashes under the grate smear it till the newness had quite gone. The money would then pass and Noah Claypole became a " lurker." Upon reading the document he would find that he was supposed to have lost his all in a fire, or he was a crockery merchant whose horse had been suddenly afflicted with the " mad staggers." His little stock had been shivered, and he was now seeking money for the purchase of a " new animal."

But if this were too risky to suit him, he might become "a turnpike sailor " under a mariner. He took the risks, represented the shipwrecked crew in all con-versations with the unbelieving, took charge of the subscription list and the takings, and gave the crew who had never seen the sea, a shilling a day each for walking about with him. Or he might, on the same terms, be a miner who had lost a limb in a colliery explosion, being led, in company with other maimed ones, by a man who really had been underground and could answer all questions. This was a very safe venture because the leader had a convincing parchment document with him, headed by a blood-curdling drawing of flying limbs and heads. It cost him £2,

but as he had been known to draw £60 in one week
from its use it was a good investment.

There were many other little branches of the business
that a lazy unventuresome man could engage in.
" Finding " was a fairly safe calling. The " finder "
with a bag on his back might be seen at any of the
meat or provision markets. He was usually occupied
when folks' eyes were upon him in looking for pieces
of string and other useful things on the ground. If

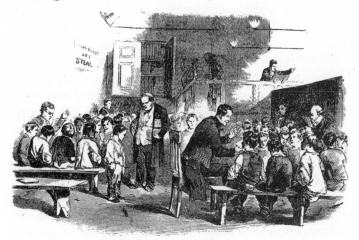

LAMBETH RAGGED SCHOOLS.

caught in the act of finding a piece of meat that had
not been mislaid, a cuff and a kick were the extent of
the penalty.

Last of all there were his children as a source of
revenue. There was a scale of hire for them.

	s.	d.
Loan of one child without grub	0	9
Two Ditto	1	0
Ditto, with grub and Godfrey's Cordial . .	0	9
If out after twelve at night, for each child extra	0	2
For half a dozen children	2	6

The children when not earning for their parents, would come with others from the lodging-houses in large numbers to the ragged schools. So would the children of the patterers and the singers of thoroughfare ballads, and the retailers of street pennyworths, grease-removing compounds, plating powders, china cement, blacking, tooth-powder, pills, herbs and all the other wonders of the London kerb. Such people for the most part would be without settled homes where family life was possible. A London lodging-house would be their winter quarters. There were of course higher grades of all these classes and exceptional individuals. Some of them had rooms of their own, sent their children to day and Sunday school, caused them to say grace before and after meals, to attend public worship and always speak the truth,[1] but they were rare. There were also individuals in the lodging-houses themselves who deserved and received respect and esteem.

" Hopping Ned and his wife," both Catholics, were people of this stamp. The woman is described as strictly virtuous, a most devoted wife and tender mother, and very charitable to any in want of a meal. She was a woman of " great personal attractions, a splendid figure, and teeth without a parallel." Another unnamed man had a wife called Maria. Her beauty was the theme of applause, and whenever she opened her mouth there was silence in the lodging-house kitchen. Her common conversation was " music and mathematics combined, her reading had been masculine and extensive, and the whisper of calumny had never attacked her own demeanour or her husband's."

[1] *London Labour and London Poor*, Vol. i. p. 219. Henry Mayhew.

This is the bright side of vagrant life. The dark side is represented by groups of men waiting in the early morning to meet young workhouse-bred girls as they came from the casual wards without prospects of work or the day's meals.

In addition to the cadgers already described, there would be the well-trained vagabonds, the successors of an historic caste. Vagabondage was a science and an art that required considerable ability. There used to be an expensive initiation for the novice in old days. The course of study embraced all kinds of roguery practised by the allied groups of thieves on the one hand and patterers on the other, and there were special features of the craft itself. A knowledge of roads and towns was one of them, a knowledge of lodging-houses and casual wards was another. Directories, too, were made with human-nature paragraphs beside the names, as for example—

"Countess of Essex (only good to sickness or distressed authorship).

" Marquis of Bredalbane (good on anything religious).

"Mrs. Taggart, Bayswater (her husband is a Unitarian minister, not as good as she, but he'll stand a ' bob ' if you look straight at him and keep to one story).

"Lady Cottenham, used to be good, but spoilt now unless you have a letter from any one she knows, and then she won't stand above five shillings."

Foresight, insight and powers of combination were required also for some branches of the profession. A plausible beggar, for instance, would call upon a wealthy man and tell a touching story. Not altogether unmoved the gentleman would yet plead the frequency of imposture and express a wish for a reference to confirm the tale. Thinking quickly of a town where some friend of his would be putting up in a day or two, he would give the fictitious name and address of a non-existent gentleman, whom he would invest with the titles of Hon. and Rev. He would then be told to call in a week's time. Judging by the impression made that the gentleman was worth further trouble, he would write to the postmaster of that town as the Hon. and Rev. So-and-So, who would be obliged if any letters coming for him could be forwarded to his present (the beggar's) address. If the man wrote, the beggar got

BROOK STREET, RAGGED SCHOOL.

the letter. It was an easy matter then to write the reply, send it under cover to the friend in that town at the lodging-house, with directions to post it, when a dole worth calling for was usually the result. If the beggar was not a complete letter-writer, a screever would write both letters for a shilling and was equal to all emergencies.

Still greater resource was needed for the task that an Irishman cheerfully undertook. He suggested to a certain Member of Parliament deeply interested in the emancipation of the Jews that he should be employed to visit the provinces, hold meetings and get up petitions. He drew £10 on account and the money for a suit of clothes. He never left London and did not intend to from the first, yet he pleased his employer and was paid a good round sum. Sending to Ireland, he obtained boxloads of petitions for repeal. The front pages were stripped off, new and suitable prefaces were written, the reams of signatures that followed of course seemed in order, and when they reached the legislator from Bath and Bristol he was delighted. The money draft sent to one of these towns was, of course, forwarded to London, and the money spent one jolly night at " Tom Spring's," in Holborn. During the whole affair the Irishman had not moved a quarter of a mile from Drury Lane.

A still more daring, disgraceful and even impious exploitation of enthusiasm was that perpetrated by three worthies rejoicing in the nicknames of Chelsea George, Jew Jim and Russia Bob. They had all been in prison and came out about the same time.

Chelsea George was bronzed and weather-beaten and had grown a long and patriarchal beard. He might pass for a distinguished foreigner with people prepared to expect to see one. He had picked up some French, Italian, Dutch, German and Spanish when upon the Continent.

Jew Jim had been in the South Sea Islands, on the coast of Africa, all over Hindostan and a good many other places besides.

Russia Bob was an Irishman who had been in Russia.

These three were passing a rag-shop one day when they saw a large black doll on sale for fourpence. It suggested an idea. They bought it and dressed it in Oriental style. Then they went down into Staffordshire to see what they could make out of the Methodist miners and their wives

The parts they were each to play were as follows—

Jew Jim, a converted Israelite, who had become a missionary. He had rev. before his name and half the letters of the alphabet after it.

Russia Bob, a self-denying colleague.

Chelsea George, the first-fruits of their ministry.

The doll, an idol from Mural in Hindostan, that had been rescued from the moles and bats of India to serve a more useful purpose in Staffordshire.

The bronzed and bearded convert was tested before a crowd of upwards of a thousand pious people with the idol, but in well-acted pantomime and mixed Spanish, German and Italian gave the miners to understand that he abhorred the idols he once worshipped. When presented to him for his worship and embraces, he became profoundly agitated, pushed it from him, spat in its face, and cut capers like a dancing bear. Then all three appeared to converse in low-toned gibberish.

The missionary came forward and said his convert, who knew only a few words of English, would now make his profession of faith, after which the collection would be made.

The tanned old sinner then went through his part of the performance amid the fervent " amens " of the audience. An offering was taken up amounting to £16, a verse of a hymn was sung and the crowd dispersed. Had it not been that Jew Jim was wanted for robbery from the person with violence, committed just before, perhaps no one would have discovered the fraud.

Such performances could not be matched by all in the vagabond fraternity, but most of them could do crooked things cleverly and free from any amateurishness of touch.   One of the ancient arts, which often saved a rogue's neck and procured for him a licence to beg unpunished, was that of producing the surface appearance of wounds and sores such as might be expected to maim the sufferer if they were real.   It was called the " scaldrum dodge."

A woman in the sixties succeeded in deceiving the public, and even physicians, by the expedient of pricking her skin with a pin and then treating the punctures with acid.   Her husband used also to show what appeared to be terrible excoriations, but were really only skin stains produced by various acids and gunpowder.

Henry Mayhew estimated the number of vagrants in England and Wales nearly two decades after our date as 22,000, so it will be seen that there must have been a large body of children from mendicant families to be dealt with.   The unsupervised, unregulated lodging-houses, in spite of all their physical abominations, had their attractions for this class.

For orphans and ownerless children there were many means of living, and large numbers roamed at large.   Night shelter would be their chief expense, and that could be obtained at as low a rate as a penny a night.   Of food they would get scraps from thieves and mendicants, from street traders and even shopkeepers.   Pence they could get, for small services in the markets or by trading with oranges, flowers, onions, blacking, lucifers and the like. Clothes and boots were never a source of worry.   The river-sides swarmed with irresponsible urchins.   From London Bridge to Westminster, where the Embankment is now, there were coal wharves and wood-yards. A scanty living for these gamins could be obtained from the loose coal to be picked up on the foreshore, and not unfrequently things better worth finding were left by the tide. Anything over from dossing-money went in drink and larks. Not unfrequently the urchins preferred to sleep in doorways and under arches, though it was cold and draughty. It was sweeter for one thing, they could spend the money at the Gaff for another. They were also able to keep out of the clutches of their elders. Still it was an awful life, even regarded from the physical point of view alone, though the exposure made those who survived as hard as nails. When, however, they were taken in hand, they proved to be well worth all the trouble taken on their behalf.

There still remain the children of the great street-trading class to describe. The home-life of these people was, regarding it broadly, distinctly higher than that of the classes hitherto considered. Father, mother and children did seem to belong to each other in a special way. The need of having storage room for unsold stock made a rudimentary home a certainty. Parental example, perhaps, would not satisfy a high standard, but life with all its blemishes was direct, open and above-board, and the coarseness was not nearly so harmful as the double-living and nervous tension of the thief's home atmosphere. With the nomads who had no special home it is impossible to compare them.

CHAPTER VI

THE SCHOLARS—*(continued)*

The Street-traders

" Father too has told me about our Saviour what was nailed to a cross to suffer for such poor people as we is.   Father has told us too about His giving a great many poor people a penny loaf and a bit of fish each, which proves him to have been a very kind gentleman."—*A Coster Girl to the late Henry Mayhew.*

THE aim of this and the two preceding chapters is to give a general view of the constituency from which the scholars were drawn.   Unless a full treatment were given there could be no conception of the extent and variety of occupations it represented.   Moreover, the conditions that remained, unaltered, except for some unimportant changes during nearly two-thirds of the period we are dealing with, and which, with modifications considered later, are with us to-day, require more than a slighting touch.   An intelligent sympathy on the part of the reader with the R.S.U. being the object of this book, he must now be introduced to the very large class of street-folk from whose families the largest proportion of scholars was drawn.   A few were not traders and not beggars.   The street entertainers, odd-job men and street labourers, for example, and these would comprise showmen and performers, acrobats, jugglers, stilt-walkers, cocoa-nut and rifle-gallery men, as well as the street musicians, pavement artists and silhouette cutters.

The odd-job men would be made up of wall and pavement stencillers, bill-stickers, bill - deliverers, boardmen, street-porters, horseholders, night - watchmen, and supers at the theatres. The street labouring class would take in some that belong to a higher social grade, turncocks, sweeps, and the watering-cart men, for instance, but the crossing-sweepers, scavengers, flushermen and dustmen would be of it.

The street traders, however, were the main body. Many of the open-air restaurants have vanished, and all that we now have are the whelk-stall, the baked potato can and the trotter stall. The cheap coffee-shop and eating-house have elbowed out the street caterer of former days. Sam Weller's interesting pieman has gone, so have the street purveyors of fried fish, ham-sandwiches, pea-soup, hot green peas, plum " duff," meat-puddings, spice cakes and Chelsea buns. Yet at one time they were a very large class.

The muffin and crumpet man and the cat's-meat woman are still with us, but many of the retailers of hot and cold drinks have gone. One of Charles Lamb's chimney-sweeps resurrected would search London in vain for a saloop stall. At a time when there was nothing between the tavern and the chop-house except the street stall for any one wishing for refreshment but not wanting a solid meal, the caterers flourished. Another group were the dealers in printed matter. A great deal of street literature was disposed

of under false pretences, the vendors trading upon
human nature. They exploited a curiosity they
knew how to raise to the point at which it is past bearing, and understood well, man's hankering for the forbidden. The individual expecting to read in the
broadsheet he had purchased an exposure of some
one "not a hundred miles away," whom he hoped
might be a neighbour, was disgusted to find, upon
arriving home, that the whole thing was "a sell,"

AN EARLY R.S.U. EXCURSION AT MUSWELL HILL.

and the lad who had bought a straw, and been presented with a mysterious something which he had
been given to understand would endanger the
stationer's liberty if it had been a purchase, instead
of a gift, was deceived also. It might be a tract or
some anti-Corn-Law particulars. The trade in prurient

suggestive matter had not by any means gone ; it was curtailed, but was scarcely a street trade.

A street stationer giving good value for money was the " pinner-up." He sold three yards of songs in a slip for a penny. The dealers in back numbers and old books were of the fraternity.

The sellers of second-hand goods cannot be classified. Farringdon Road, the Cattle Market or High Street, Aldgate, in the present day show how apparently infinite in variety are the objects to be found on stalls given up to that trade, and from the large number of men, women, lads and girls in charge of them we may guess that it was a much larger group sixty years ago. Such thoroughfares as have been mentioned, and many others throughout London, are lined with sellers of home-made articles on certain days at certain hours, and in many instances every day. The home industries would not vary much, though some no doubt have been crowded out by machinery. All we see now would have been seen then and some that have gone.

The cheap roasting-jacks of worsted and wire, upon specimens of which compo. ribs of beef and shoulders of mutton were wont to revolve are seldom seen, now that penny-in-the-slot gas-stoves are so common, and knitted nightcaps and cabbage and onion nets do not seem to be so much used. The glassblower still does a brisk trade in penny micro-scopes, glass bulbs filled with water, of which the sale is helped by a pink shrimp. The toy-makers are a shrunken group, though many still get a living out of home-made playthings. The hawkers of pennyworths that are not home-made have probably largely increased, but in the old days the toys were " young lambs,"

" buy-a-brooms," paper houses, cardboard carriages, clowns, and donkey men on sticks, feathered cocks, and black velvet cats. Cloth penwipers, iron and kettle holders, tea and egg coseys would also be on sale, though these have now become bazaar articles.

Many things that are now bought at shops would be purchasable of the makers at a stall, the tinware of the jobbing whitesmith, rolling-pins, clothes-horses, and other white wood articles of the worker in wood, and the clothes props and clothes pegs made by the less skilled. The wire-worker also sold his toasting-forks, grid-irons, fire-guards and bird cages. Such primitive craftsmen, with slender stock-money, dependent upon the weather for their sales were, as now, often very poor. It is impossible to enumerate them and the class of small retailers. The sellers of patent compositions for polishing leather, or metal, for sharpening tools, cleaning grease from clothes, reviving faded black then, as now, gathered little circles of admiring students to watch the demonstrations, and the lecturer's manner was always professorial.

So did the black man with tooth-cleaning powder gain patronage when operating upon one of the crowd, laughing all the time, that the sight of his own teeth might stimulate the sales. The gold-paint man had not arrived, but the wood-stainer had, and he did things in the public eye you could not have imitated in your own home, with his material. The seller of liquid and other cements tugged convincingly at the plate whose shattered fragments had been just re-united, the razor-paste proprietor hacked a wood-stump, and then with a few stropping strokes got that marvellous edge upon his blade that no others could get with their enchantments. Then as now he swiftly

put it to the test. With an aptitude for seizing opportunity which characterizes his tribe, he would snatch
what hairs he wanted from the nearest boy's head and
slice them deliberately as an artist enjoying his work.
Itinerant herbalists, too, were there discoursing profoundly upon the healing or medicinal properties of
" the root."

In addition to all these were the mending pedlars,
who used no magic, tinkers and umbrella menders,
chair-caners, knife-grinders, and glaziers.

The street dealers in live stock, birds, dogs, gold-
fish, etc., would be a branch, as would sellers of green-
stuff, turf, cut-flowers, watercress, and " chickweed
and grunsell."

Then there would be the buyers of old clothes,
rags and bones, bottles, and hares' and rabbits'-skins.

Lowest on the list came the bone-grubbers, collectors of cigar-ends, and the dredgermen, or coal hunters
of the Thames shore at low tide.

This catalogue reminds the reader of many things
already known, but it serves to show what an extensive
underworld there has been, and still is, in London,
whose connexion with ordinary machine-made produc-
tions, or association with customary trade, is but
slight.

The coster, at the head of the tribe, calls for special
notice. Undoubtedly he is in the direct line of succession, from the primitive retailers and distributors of
ancient England.

The mercer, and other traders, whose stalls stood
beside those of his ancestors at fairs and in open
markets perhaps in those early times, were not above
passing the time of day and inquiring after the families
of their humbler brethren. The improvidence or

misfortune of the poorer salesmen kept their stock-money so low that they kept to perishables. The pushful and saving men invested in goods that brought a better return. At the same time theirs was stock that suffered more from weather, and packing and unpacking and the larcenies of crimps were a serious loss.

R.S.U. ANNUAL SUMMER FÊTE.

To take a house on the " chepe "-side the groundfloor of which could be made an open booth in the daytime was a course that common-sense, business enterprise, and economy would suggest. The provision of an apprentice (with a premium) to look after things by day, take down the shutters, put them up at night, and sleep under the counter with a cudgel beside him, would complete the arrangement. The extra rent would be set-off by the saving of brocades and other stuffs from ruin, while losses from thieves would be smaller. He saved and had enhanced comfort from being home to meals, and customers knowing he was " always there " would have greater confidence, which would mean increased business. From that point the coster-monger and the tradesman drifted apart.

The go-ahead man under the pressure of heavy rent, rates and taxes, the social ideals of his wife and daughters, his self-imposed burdens connected with the equipment of his children for life, and the trans-mission of advantages to them, would soon see a beam in the eye of his brother of the stall. The open-air stallkeeper might fancy that there was more than a mote in the eye of his critic, and for his part if he could have framed a theory of the effects of settled dwelling, or even have understood one when it was framed, it would be very much in substance that of Robert Louis Stevenson—

" The dull man is made, not by the nature, but by the degree of his immersion in a single business. And all the more if that be sedentary, uneventful, and ingloriously safe. More than one half of him will then remain unexercised, undeveloped ; the rest will be distended and deformed by over-nutrition, over-cerebration, and the heat of rooms."

Like the novelist, he may "have often marvelled at the impudence of gentlemen who describe and pass judgment on the life of man, in almost perfect ignor-ance of all its necessary elements and natural careers.

" Their own life is an excrescence of the moment, doomed, in the vicissitude of history, to pass and disappear. The eternal life of man, spent under sun and rain, and in rude physical effort, lies upon one side, scarce changed from the beginning."

What an early "costardmonger" would have said to this we know not. Any one who had the hardihood to read it to a modern one and escaped unhurt would be told "to stow the barrikin," as a costermonger hates to be mystified.

A matter into which no surmise enters is the fact that this historic class has kept a position of independence as regards the prosperous classes above them, and although at one time able to earn good money, it is only fair to say that there has been no general hankering among them to enter the ranks of the middle classes. Among fruiterers, and fishmongers, salesmen in the meat, fish, vegetable and fruit markets, among licensed victuallers, horse dealers, milk purveyors, etc., are numbers of former costers, but though they have all taken to the wearing of collars, and are able to hold intercourse with other people of property with the frank bold dignity of those who know they have succeeded, yet they are never ashamed of their origin, and it is rare to find their children so. "To live and let live," and "to stick to a pal," were part of the coster's creed, even when ignorant of the rudiments of education and religion. Often there was a third article—"give a helping hand where you can."

Centuries of self-reliance, freedom from the need to bend to the wills of others, out-of-door life and active pursuits have left their mark upon the tribe. Even their fashions were their own. They have also been, at least within recent times, a fighting race, and it is to this fact that Henry Mayhew attributes it that property estimated in the aggregate to amount to about £10,000 could be left almost unprotected at times. Robbing costers was not attractive enough to thieves. " They know we would take it out of them," was a coster's explanation. " It is Lynch law with us, we never give them in charge."

The absence of banking among them kept them back as a class. Their want of enterprise was due to it, and their addiction to drink, gambling, and other things, when doing well, was in part owing to possessing more money in their pockets than they needed for stock at any given time. Accordingly, as merchants, they repeated themselves, remaining dealers in perishables. In Henry V's reign they sold hot-trotters, pepper and saffron and other things, so they had ceased to be apple-sellers (the meaning of the name) at a very early stage. No doubt the process we have witnessed in our own day, of capable and thrifty members of the class adopting more profitable pursuits has been a continuous movement.

Their close association in the Alsatias of the City and its purlieus with the thieves and the vagabonds, though they avoided their practices, may have been due to a poverty which compelled all three to live side by side. Or it may have arisen from a fellow feeling between aggrieved and oppressed people. There has been a very close touch between the gipsies and the English nation. Were it not so the former could never have given us the endearing word " daddy." That closeness of touch must have occurred in the reign of Henry VIII, when there was much justifiable discontent, and men had sympathy with outlaws. It was then that thieves' cant was coined from Romany and used by the dispossessed, who took to the road. Probably at the same time the gipsy

words in the coster's back-slang crept in. At
any rate we find the costers, as a class, solid in
their resistance to authority, at the time our R.S.U.
history begins, not as the result of abstract views, or
recent trouble, but as though from traditional habit.[1]
They hated the police, whom they called "the crushers,"
most intensely. The latter they considered were in the
pay of the shopkeepers, whom they regarded as their
natural enemies. All shopkeepers are not averse to
stalls, as they know that shops both sides of a road

AN EXCURSION IN EARLY DAYS : WESTMINSTER
CHILDREN AT CLAYTON PARK.

and stalls in the gutters make a market, draw crowds,
and every one benefits. But it must be allowed they
prefer to own the stalls as well as the shops.

When some stalls in the New Cut, Lambeth,
were removed, the tradesmen's receipts dropped, in
some cases one-eighth, in others one-fourth. Old custom and public convenience has created unauthorized
markets everywhere. The costers considered themselves

[1] The ancient enactments of Common Council were very
stringent, especially in the reign of Elizabeth.

to be an unfairly treated class, and we are not surprised that a journalist of the fifties asking for information of a coster for the Press, should meet with a rebuff. "Press! I won't have anything to say to it. We are oppressed enough already."

The coster's social and religious views were very hazy. Any one who seemed to be living without work as he understood it, was in his belief being kept by the Government out of the taxes. "Sermons and tracts gave him the 'orrors." He had heard that God made the heavens and the earth, but as to the sea he didn't know. It would be as well to inquire of the salesmen at Billingsgate. One costermonger said he "had never heard of Christianity, but if he was to let a cove off once he'd do it again, so he never gave him the chance. He would see a henemy of his shot afore he'd forgive him—where's the use?"

The duty of neighbourliness was pressed upon him. "He could understand that all as lives in a court was neighbours; but as for policemen they were nothing to him, and he should like to pay 'em all off well. In coorse God Almighty made the world, and the poor bricklayers' labourers built the houses arterwards. He had heer'd a little about our Saviour. They seemed to say He were a goodish kind of a man; but if He says as how a cove's to forgive a feller as hits you, he should say He know'd nothing about it. Prayers, yes, before father died he said them, but after that mother was too busy getting a living to mind about his praying. Yes, he knew in the Lord's prayer they says, 'Forgive us our trespasses, as we forgive them as trespasses agin' us.' It's a very good thing, in coorse, but no costers can't do it."

The dislike of policemen was so great that many of

them suffered from the violence of coster lads more than they did if the youths had not been restrained by vanity. In prison they would lose their figure six curls or their " Newgate knocker " tufts over the ears, and appearance was a good deal to them. Most lads who did not start for themselves at thirteen or fourteen usually quarrelled with their parents and went to work for other men. If they went to lodging-houses to sleep, they were robbed or corrupted for the sake of their money. If they lodged with their employers, the men's wives petted them and fed their vanity, making them utterly selfish. A coster lad's landlady had one haunting fear. It was that if the boy quarrelled with her husband he would take some of his custom. The lad knew the round, the customers, the markets, and he could borrow stock-money upon as good terms as his master. Accordingly, he had the best of everything, was encouraged to squander his money on dress instead of save it, and flattered to the limit of his desire. His clothes cost a great deal of money. A coster jacket had a good deal of work in it. There were pockets on each hip, at each side, and several rows of them. They were arranged in groups one over another with lappels outside, large ones overlapping smaller inside ones. There might be perhaps thirty-two pockets in one jacket each pocket covered by a velvet flap. These pocket-flaps have been known to be handsomely embroidered in coloured silks, with devices such as the rose, shamrock, and thistle. Buttons, each costing several pence, were sometimes used to the extent of hundreds upon a suit. Occasionally there would be stripes of velvet down each leg of the trousers. In one instance to our knowledge, there were three colours, red in the centre,

and blue and green on either side of it.   One youth had
a band of dark blue cloth worked into the grey of the
garment, graduating in breadth from the tight knees
to the broad bell-bottoms.   Upon this ground
diamonds of light-blue cloth were sewn.

An influence that spoiled the coster girl as well as
the coster lad was that of the penny gaff, or penny
theatre.   Unlet shops were rented by travelling
showmen in populous districts, and in these a form of
entertainment objectionable in itself was presented
under conditions of over-crowding and bad lighting
that were still more so.   The direct and indirect
moral corruption of these places resulting to the young
people who frequented them it is impossible to exaggerate.   It is not surprising that the age at which the
sexes entered upon the full responsibilities of adult
life was very often for the lads fourteen years, and the
girls sixteen.   It is sad to think that the latter did
not have for their support in these arrangements
either the sanctities of religion or the practical
guarantee of law.   In too many cases the loyalty
they considered a sufficient substitute did not stand
the wear and tear of a hard life.

In not a few instances these young couples would
start life by underselling their own parents, with whom
they had quarrelled, and so in some cases taking the
bread from the mouths of brothers and sisters.

Under all the circumstances it is surprising that the
costers as a class did so well.   Improvidence among
them made moneylending common.   Banking they
considered was mixed up with Government and the
taxes, and there would, they were certain, be " cheatery
at the bottom of it."

Accustomed to pay heavily for any temporary

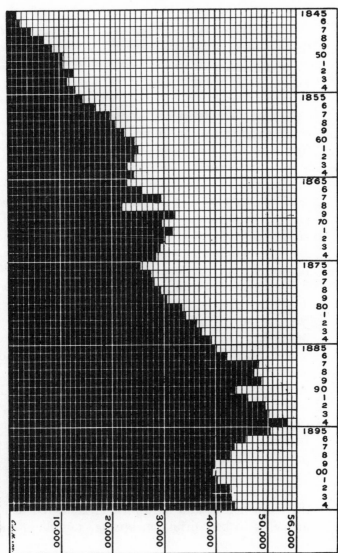

DIAGRAM REPRESENTING THE NUMBER OF SUNDAY SCHOLARS UNDER REGULAR TEACHING IN THE
AFFILIATED SCHOOLS OF THE LONDON R.S.U. FOR THE PAST SIXTY YEARS. EACH COMPLETE
BLACK OBLONG REPRESENTS A THOUSAND SCHOLARS.

pecuniary convenience or assistance, they would consider themselves defrauded in receiving 7½d. for the use of £1 for a whole year.

Twopence a day was the usual interest for a loan of 2s. 6d.; 3d. a day for 5s.; 6d. a day for 10s.; and 1s. a day for £1.

A money-lender with a floating capital of £150 could easily make an annual income of £350 upon it. One man who borrowed a pound paid 2s. a week for a year, and when he had paid £5 4s. he was still liable for the pound. These money transactions were considerable, but no I O U's or memoranda of any sort passed, no law-suits arose out of them, and it was an extremely rare thing for a lender to lose money. And this was in a money market where £1,040 per cent. per annum was the ordinary rate.

The coster paid heavily, too, for his barrow and anything else he hired. A man who let out 120 barrows, drew 160 per cent. profit on the year's business.

Yet in 1850, when they numbered some 30,000, costermongers bought one-tenth of the cheaper fruit at Covent Garden, one-eighth of the warren rabbits, poultry and game that came into Leadenhall, one-third of the vegetables at Spitalfields, one-sixth at the Borough Market, while of fish at Billingsgate they purchased half. This was a ready-money trade with the salesmen.

Though associating with thieves, the costers were in the main honest and hardworking, addicted in leisure moments to beer-drinking, boxing, gambling, and the twopenny hop.

Still, taking the most generous possible view of their good qualities, they were sadly depraved, and,

as the late Henry Mayhew, to whom we are indebted
for much of this information, very truly says—

" The fate of children brought up amid the influence
of such scenes—with parents starving one week and
drunk all the next—turned into the streets as soon as
they are old enough to run alone—sent out to sell in
public-houses almost before they know how to put
two halfpence together — their tastes trained to
libidinism long before puberty, at the penny concert,
and their passions inflamed with the unrestrained
intercourse of the twopenny hops—the fate of the young,
I say, abandoned to the blight of such associations
as these, cannot well be otherwise than it is."

This lengthy sketch of the classes whose children
were the flotsam and jetsam of the tide of humanity
which surged in the lanes and the alleys of the London
streets may prepare us for the difficulties of the
teachers. We leave the consideration of this " law-
less horde," unkempt, habituated to crime, and to the
punishments' of crime, half-naked, wholly ignorant,
many of them orphans, homeless, hopeless, and
deserted, to notice the kind of men and women to
whom the forlornness of the children appealed.

CHAPTER VII

The Teachers

" I should like much to hear of half a dozen heroes from the Horse Guards generously doing honour to the heroism of the ragged school teachers, either by a visit to their battle-fields or by a contribution to the cause in which they are so nobly struggling."—Old Humphrey.

THE most interesting fact connected with the ragged school movement is the spontaneous character of the beginnings of the schools. It is very remarkable that a large number of independent institutions in germ should be in existence in 1844, not the product of any concerted effort, but simply responses by individuals to an unadvertised need. To realize the full meaning of the pregnant years between 1844 and 1851, it is necessary to regard these little schools as representing in action a very general sentiment in the churches. The diffused idea that something ought to be done for the very poorest children became here a resolution that something should be done.

Christians all over London had embarked in small, personal, inexpensive ventures, having for their object the moral benefit of as many neglected little ones as they could manage.

The people who made the beginnings would rarely be men and women of very exalted social position.

The tragedy of a slum-child's life would press heaviest upon such pious and benevolent individuals as were brought constantly in situations where they witnessed it.

These persons were often working men, occasionally they were of the middle class, but in very few instances was anything of a public nature expected or intended to arise from their efforts.   All schools were not alike. There were a few brought into being as the result of resolutions passed by religious bodies, but these were exceptional.

So that the first teachers were individuals of some force of character who had in view the teaching of a small bible class, the expenses of which they would themselves defray.   None of them realized, however, what the work would involve, and to how much pressure of various kinds they would be subjected by the needs of the children, and their own limitations, in strength, faculty, and means, to compel them to take partners into the work.

The first difficulty was, the number of children who crowded into those little rooms of a half-crown, three shillings or four shillings weekly rental.

The pioneers would be compelled to have neighbourly assistance if only to secure order, to gain a hearing.

Then would arise the difficulty that a bible lesson could only be given in the form of an address if the children could not read.   Indeed so much individual care and personal attention was required by these neglected ones that the first workers could not be satisfied with general exhortations to hordes of un-recognized children.   They would feel that individual interest was so essential, that they must impress their friends into service, and teach the children to read, so

as to make class teaching possible. But the presence
of additional friends would alter the first plans. The
smallness of the room would be felt at the same time,
that the willingness of the new recruits to contribute
to the expenses of the school became apparent. Or
the necessity for change might be brought home in
another way, the landlord would perhaps give the
teachers notice to quit. A primitive ragged school
held on the ground-floor of a dwelling-house was enough
to scare the most easy-going landlord imaginable.

The next move might be to a stable down a mews, a
cow-house, a loft, a railway arch, or any other structure
that was roomy and cheap. So far the teaching staff
would be the friendly circle of the founder to which
would be added a few earnest local people. The school
could hardly at this time be called a public institution.
But notwithstanding the fact that such a mission
was sustained by private support, and the managers
were only responsible to themselves and each other as
sole subscribers, yet in most cases so orderly a system
of procedure would prevail, that no radical change of
constitution would be necessary, when increasing expenses made it necessary to seek outside financial help.

The new school would soon glide from the proprietary
to the public status.

The work of teaching to spell and read on the Sunday
would be regarded by the teachers after a time as
displacing worship, and it would then occur to them
to have classes of a distinctly educational character
during the week evenings. But there might be an
amount of uncertainty as to regular attendance on the
part of the teachers on the week evenings, and then a
friend, apt to teach, would be paid to conduct the
school, the volunteers would assist him, but it would

be incumbent upon him to be at the night school, under all circumstances.

This would be the first serious expense, and the appointment of some trustworthy woman living near the school to mind the key and keep the place clean would be another. Ultimately when other operations besides the night school were started, some requiring utensils and furniture of various kinds, it might be a gain to have a resident caretaker. Thus would the expenditure advance by leaps and bounds. It was fortunate in one respect that the teachers of a school were brought face to face with these responsibilities in a somewhat sudden fashion. The need almost invariably led to a request for a church collection. Emerging from their seclusion a deputation from a growing cause would wait upon a clergyman or minister in the locality where the school was situated, describe the work and ask for his help. In most cases not only was the help readily given, but the pulpit advocacy of the new found friend would bring other workers. In selecting the preacher to be approached the teachers would be likely to choose one with a large and wealthy and influential church. In consequence the congregation would include a large number of capable and zealous members to whom this new work would commend itself as a field for the useful employment of their leisure and energy.

Thus it came about that the only avenue through which enlarged resources might be expected to come, quickly enough, and in sufficient measure, to keep pace with the needs of a mission that had passed out of the private ownership stage, was often to be the channel also of a still larger blessing.

The calls for money would be recurrent, and the

practice would arise among the clerical friends of these struggling schools to invite the officers to annually plead their own cause before the congregations who had given assistance. The pulpit orators, however eloquent, could only deal with generalities, and their sagacity would unite with their convenience to cause them to bring these missioners and their flocks into close contact.

It is a very fortunate circumstance that the general public appeal by means of a lithographed circular, bearing a honoured name, was not yet the means of money-raising.

It was providential also that the appointment of honorary collectors was not an adequate provision.

That earnest pioneers in the slums should be forced to take their work and show it, as far as they were able, to the laity of Christian communities was the very best thing that could happen.

Not only was financial relief forthcoming, but, better still, men and women offered for service. The new teachers were also in a different social position in most cases to those who had begun the work, and had had greater advantages in general and commercial education. By these friends, links would be formed with supporting churches, resulting in a measure of stability in finances and a more or less continuous supply of workers.

At this point the strong personal influence of the great leaders like Lord Shaftesbury, Dr. Guthrie, John Macgregor and others came in to fan into a flame the growing enthusiasm. In a very few years by their tongues and their pens, aided by a sympathetic press, they made all London aware of the possibilities there were in the work, and raised the entire conception of

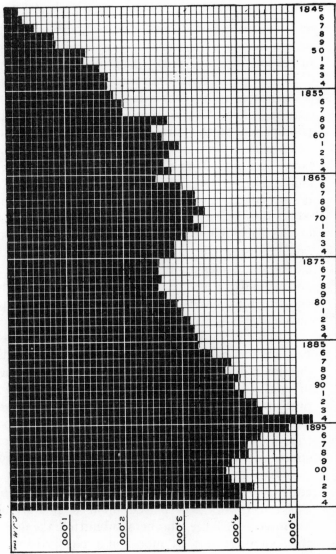

DIAGRAM REPRESENTING THE NUMBER OF VOLUNTARY TEACHERS IN THE AFFILIATED SCHOOLS OF THE LONDON R.S.U. FOR THE PAST SIXTY YEARS. EACH COMPLETE BLACK OBLONG REPRESENTS 100 TEACHERS.

105

it that was prevalent.   Other clergymen and ministers
and laymen initiated new work, or assisted established
causes, merely as the result of reading press accounts
of schools, or the reports of speeches.

Hence it was that some struggling city missionary,
who had begun to teach a few children in a back room
and had enlisted the help of one or two sympathizing
poor people at the time, might find himself in a few
years with an important work under his charge and a
large and mixed staff under his control.   The self-
elimination of some of these first founders of schools
is worthy of a more extended imitation where growing
work absorbs men and women of capacity.   In some
of the early schools might have been seen cobblers
and tailors teaching side by side with merchants and
bankers and men of private means, liberal education
and abundant leisure.   The management ultimately
fell into their hands, with the result that educational
day-schools, industrial classes, etc., were started.

Although the influence of caste was stronger in
English society sixty years ago than it is to-day, it
did not in the least interfere with the welding together
of workers in widely differing social positions.   The
problems to be solved in the ragged schools were so
difficult, and the evils to be removed, so appalling,
that all else was forgotten.   A mutual appreciation
sprang up between the workers, and a comradeship
that had no connexion with abstract views on social
equality.   It should not be forgotten that when once
this novel work was placed upon a public footing,
volunteers in large numbers submitted themselves to
the exacting tests of moral and physical endurance
that the work involved.

By a process of natural elimination, the best

alone remained, uniting as the staunchest of friends.

Ordinary social work lacks the cohesive and annealing force that the prayer meeting among religious
workers supplies. Any one who has served upon a
modern committee must feel this. The very fact of
bringing the difficulties of class-teaching, and the
difficulties of school administration, to the mercy-seat
in company by the members of a band of teachers, with
the glimpses of aspiration and earnest purpose that
the petitions afford, must have an effect upon every
individual. At every fervent out-pouring of spirit,
the observer who could listen unmoved must either
lack faith in the Deity, or doubt the sincerity of the
suppliants. In either case the stay in the work will
be brief. But if on the other hand there were the smallest
value attached to such a gathering by those present,
a sacred communism was its product. The thought,
" *Our* communion is with the Father and with His
Son," was inevitable, and caste in its meaner aspects
died.

Lord Shaftesbury and his Socialist correspondent
afford an illustration. In 1841 the Earl (then Lord
Ashley) had lost few of his inherited prejudices. He
was opposed to the repeal of the Corn-laws, and had in
many other respects not yet ripened.

A man that had been represented to him as a dangerous revolutionist, wrote to him requesting an interview in order that he might place at his disposal certain
information and experience that he had. He concluded his letter thus :—

" That your Lordship may long be spared to advocate the rights of the poor, the oppressed, and him
that hath none to help him, and that you may continually enjoy that greatest of all rewards, the blessing.

of an approving conscience, is the sincere prayer of your Lordship's admirer and humble fellow-worker in the cause of the white slave."

The letter reached the conscience and touched the heart of the nobleman, and the reply he sent shows how far superior is the touch of grace to the touch of nature in making the whole world kin.

" You have been represented to me as a Socialist and an advocate of principles that I regard with terror and abhorrence ; and you will therefore readily believe the pleasure with which I observed the spirit and language of your letter. I could not but apply to you the words of that Book whose expressions you have borrowed, and say, as was said to Ananias of Saul, ' Behold, he prayeth ! ' I deeply rejoice in this, because I respect your talents. I admire your zeal, and I hope to find in you a true and faithful ally in these great and final efforts for the moral, social, and religious welfare of the working people."

The spirit of caste in so far as such a spirit is harmful to individual development and efficiency of public service was exorcised in these new communities, as it has been in all ages, by religious fervour; yet an aristocracy of real worth lost nothing by it, but received always its rightful homage.

The removal of causes of friction between the classes, as England's prosperity increased, had nothing to do with it, neither had the writings of socialistic novelists.

When the landed gentry in pre-Reform days were holding the fortress against the possessors of the new wealth of trade, the knowledge that several of the great families had sprung from City trade made no difference to their rigid exclusiveness. Yet they knew that the first English Protestant queen, Anne

Boleyn, was the descendant of Sir Godfrey Boleine, Lord Mayor of London in 1457. The Earls of Denbigh owed their origin to a Lord Mayor of London who occupied Whittington's chair five years earlier. Some ninety years after, a Duke of Buckingham and a Lord Braybrooke were descendants of a Lord Mayor. The peerages of Salisbury and Fitzwilliam sprang from a similar source, as do also those of Warwick and Brooke.

With the Marquises of Bath it was just the same. Like Lord Palmerston, the President of the R.S.U., Lord Northampton, has a City ancestry. When, after fraternizing with the Lord Mayor and aldermen at the dispatch of cripples' New Year hampers from the Guildhall, he has gone home to lunch with the Lord Mayor at the Mansion House, he may have mentioned that his ancestor Sir Wolston Dixie of the Skinners' Company occupied the civic chair in 1585.

Yet what commonsense was powerless to effect in the aristocracy as a whole, the influence of religion did bring about with many of the best. The late Duke of Westminster, who came in touch with a ragged school at Chester in very early days, Earl Cairns, connected with the general cause for over thirty years, Sir Harry Verney, schoolfellow of Lord Shaftesbury, who took an interest in one of the earliest Westminster ragged schools, Lord Mount-Temple and many others obtained, through the ragged school movement, a just view of their reasonable claims. The classes and masses below them, who gained knowledge of them, gave them the respect they deserved, the result being that although the power of England has been transferred to the democracy, the aristocracy have lost none of their privileges and honours.

It would, however, be an error to represent that the

modern interest of the aristocracy in social, philanthropic and humanitarian enterprises is due solely to
Lord Shaftesbury and those of the nobility with whom
he associated. Quite as earnest and high-motived,
and perhaps farther-reaching, were the influences emanating direct from the throne. The Prince Consort,
Queen Victoria, the Royal Family and their household have exercised a very great power for good, and
a power independent in origin.

Chambers' Journal for 1847 records the fact that
the Hon. Miss Murray, one of the ladies in direct attendance upon the queen, had taken a deep interest in the
subject of industrial schools, and had dedicated a small
book upon the subject to Her Majesty and Prince
Albert.

Its object was not so much mental education as
moral training. At the same time that Captain
Edward Brenton established his school at Hackney
Wick for boy offenders, she had one at Chiswick for
girls. Lord Cottenham at her instance and suggestion
drew up an Act for the purpose of dealing with juvenile
offenders. It had passed the Commons at the end of
Lord Melbourne's administration ; but the dissolution
prevented its ever reaching the Lords.

There were probably other powerful influences at
work among the upper classes producing the modern
spirit prevalent among them. Into all kinds of social
service they have penetrated, and in no pedantic or
amateur fashion. Evangelism, it is to be deplored, is
the cause that has of recent years attracted fewest
recruits, although of all social movements it has
given the best results.

Those who have come into contact with members
of the aristocracy who seriously engage in social work

know the unfairness of describing such efforts as " a fashionable craze." Some of the most modest, genuine and solid work in this country is being done at this day by them. The " Home Arts and Crafts Association," and many another enterprise of a quiet unobtrusive character, where the titled enjoy free movement, afford channels for their labour among village and town children throughout the land. Even the ephemeral, unexacting patronage of all humane work that general Society engages in, is not insincere however much human nature may occasionally mingle with it. Royal leading has less to do with it than is sometimes asserted, and fear of the masses has long ceased to be a consideration. Now that the countryside has been so largely deserted for the towns, the girls of our noble families cannot exercise the old feudal kindliness as their grandmothers were able, upon their estates. Yet the inherited habit is with them, and our hospitals and workhouses and other charities derive benefit.

Underneath all that kind of charity, which it may be conceded, is on no higher moral level than the general, unheroic easy-going effort of all classes in the present day, there is something very much deeper and better in many.

It is probably as much due to woman's struggle for justice in the matter of education as to the religious life of the country, stimulated by the churches. The same Miss Murray who directed Royal attention to the children of our prisons collected the nucleus fund for the foundation of the first woman's college in England—Queen's, in 1846. The hopes of the ragged school cause are bound up with the service of woman.   Woman's struggle for a fair equipment in life nearly covers our period. Following "Queen's" came Bedford College in 1849, and the pioneer public school that Miss Buss founded in 1850. Then in 1860 Madame Bodichon at Glasgow stirred the members of the Social Science Congress by bringing before them in an effective way, the scandalous lack of provision there was for the education of girls. The year 1865 saw a scheme of lectures and classes at Oxford arranged by Miss Smith and the opening of the Cambridge Local Examinations to girls through the efforts of Miss Emily Davies. In the same year the Yorkshire Ladies' Council of Education was founded, followed by the Ladies' Educational Society of Liverpool in 1866. The opening of Girton took place in 1869. In 1871 Newnham was founded, and in the same year Princess Louise became President of a National Union for improving the Education of Women of all classes. The Oxford Association for the Education of Women came into being, with four colleges, in 1878. The high-water mark of achievement was reached when a Royal Commission on Secondary Education sitting in 1894–5 had upon a committee of seventeen three lady members. Out of fourteen Assistant Commissioners five were also women.

Other appointments followed in the following year in connexion with the Science and Art Department and Education office, but our legislators and administrators have, upon the whole, cut a sorry figure in their treatment of this question that ought not to be a question. Everything that could be done has been done to delay progress, and the practical result amounts to little short of criminal conspiracy against the interests of English girlhood.

The effect of all this want of fair play has been to drive many of the most active women of capacity, education, and culture, into work where the triumphs of intellectualism, will tell in favour of the average middle-class girl. But it has given to their efforts all the intensity of religious devotion, even where the paramount claims of religion in all social work may be unacknowledged, though not denied, and all emotion may be as firmly repressed, as a woman can succeed with such a violation of her nature.

The Evangelicals succeeded mainly because of woman's help, and they will again advance with a fresh accession of feminine strength. That in work similar to that in which their grandmothers engaged in London the ladies of the present will ultimately find freedom and satisfaction, can scarcely be doubted, as the following passage from a paper by Mrs. Healey of Oxford upon work among women in laundries very clearly shows. She says : " I have stood in a laundry, knowing the women who were at work, looking at some of their faces, and have felt that *almost super-natural power* was needed to master the difficulties." Through such an experience more than one intellectual woman has passed in the early ragged school work. They came to the same conclusion as Mrs. Healey, and ultimately went a step further, deciding that nothing but a supernatural power with which their own powers must be allied, could master the difficulties. Workers amongst the lowest invariably come to this, or, abandon a hopeless struggle. Mrs. Healey is a member of the National Union of Women Workers. Another member, a Miss England, writing about the same class of women—laundry hands—says—

" We need a reverence for their dignity as human

beings, and a deep sympathy, which shall take away all danger of patronage, and keep us ever remembering that our aim is not to make humble, characterless disciples, but so to help each to help herself, that she may live out her own life to its full perfection, and follow the Divine leading for herself, becoming in her turn a centre of light and sweetness to her own special circle."

How much the ladies learned, who met to teach the first girls' classes in the ragged schools would be most instructive information. The chances are, that every preconceived notion had to be abandoned. They found themselves among girls who were the offspring of sin, and already in their early teens the victims of sin. Their lost virtue was not a matter of a single lapse. Daily bread was earned by infamy. Not unfrequently they drank to excess as well. The brains of the cleverest woman in the world would not have been much use under such circumstances. Intellect alone could not bring regenerative power into these girls' lives. "Filthy, ragged, crime-worn, with countenances scowling hope out of countenance," they would sit around the novice whose first impulse might well be to put her face into her hands and have a good cry. But such teachers as persevered were rewarded. They gained the affections of the girls, and a vast accession of knowledge of human life and their own hearts as well. Personal power was also developed. Every side of the teacher's nature was tested. There are plenty of disagreeables to offend the senses in teaching a ragged school class at the end of sixty years' work, but these we may suppose are as nothing compared with the inflictions of years ago. With a bad and incomplete water supply for all London and a tax on soap there were excuses to be made, but the concentrated effect of it all on a warm and steamy Sunday night must have been sickening in the extreme. One thinks of the herb-women strewing fragrant herbs in front of a procession during a royal progress, the similar provision made at Bow Street and the Old Bailey, the note-books and clothing of Howard, the prison reformer, airing for days before a fire to get rid of the smell, and admiration for the women who passed through this first test, rises high. But there were other trials. The general habits of the girls could not but be abhorrent to delicately nurtured ladies, or indeed to any women in any station, living normal lives. In those first small schoolrooms it must have been a terrible torture to know that the ribald remarks shouted across a class must be heard by the gentlemen in the room.

The next test was that of physical endurance. The schools were woefully ill-equipped. A testament that costs a penny now cost tenpence then, hymn-books were correspondingly expensive. Any one who has witnessed a Salvation Army lieutenant or captain conducting a meeting in a small poor corps, where the members cannot afford to buy the *War Cry* with hymns on the last page, can realize what it must have been like. In such a meeting the woman's power is used for all it is worth. The testimonies are few, likewise the prayers, the Scripture reading, the choruses, the address, and the backbone of the service generally have to be hers alone. Whatever her personal magnetism may be, at the end she is pretty well played out, whether she come from Lancashire, Yorkshire, or Scotland, and have the inherited strength of generations of agricultural ancestors as a reserve to fall back upon.

Superadded to the physical strain there must have been heavy and disheartening disappointments. But when success came, how terrible it must have been for a woman to have her life threatened by the reckless and abandoned mothers of her girls because she was able to persuade them to live better lives, whereby the hope of profligate gains was gone.

Yet in spite of every drawback those who plunged deeply into the work soon acquired a passion for it that nothing could alter, and no other interest displace.

Such an one was the late Miss C. A. Howell, of Vincent Square, Westminster. Among her intimate friends were Lord Henry Cholmondley, Lord Congleton, Captain Trotter, and the clergy of the churches in Eaton Square and Queen Square, Westminster, all of whom she used for the work. In fact, so well did she use them and others that twelve schools in Westminster and Pimlico were kept going. An old day school teacher of New Pye Street gives this sketch. " Her influence over roughs was remarkable. She had a soft musical voice and winning easy manners, which, being so unlike those they were accustomed to, seemed to awe them, and her Bible talks charmed them into attention and interest at once."

The ladies who taught boys had, generally speaking, an easier time : sex told in their favour.

" One of such teachers of youths has written to say that having been with her husband to Palestine for their honeymoon, she was able to make her Bible lessons interesting with illustrations. The thought occurs that she may have been the lady to whom

Lord Shaftesbury refers as one respecting whose safety he had grave fears.

" I saw there," said the Earl, " thirty or forty men, none of them with shoes or stockings on, and some without shirts—the wildest and most awful looking men you can imagine. They all sat in a ring, and the only other human being in the room was a young woman of twenty-six or twenty-seven years of age, and, allow me to add, one of the prettiest women I ever saw. She was teaching all these wild, rough, uncouth creatures, who never bowed the head to any constable or any form of civil authority, yet they looked on her with a degree of reverence and affection that amounted almost to adoration."

The nobleman sought out the superintendent and remonstrated with him, saying that he was much alarmed. The superintendent said he had his fears also. But his fears were that some stranger might wander in and perhaps offer her some disrespect, " and if he did so, he would never leave the room alive ; he would be torn limb from limb."

Another teacher of the same type was a friend of Mrs. Sewell, author of *Mother's Last Words*. At the time that touching poem was written she was conducting a class at a school in Seven Dials. Mrs. Sewell was doubtful whether it was worth publishing, so she lent it to her friend in manuscript to read to her ragamuffins. The effect upon them induced the author to print it.

What the experiences of some of the men teachers were may be guessed by the following extract from a document written in 1851, about events occurring in 1843—

" About six or seven of us met in the little room in

B—— Street on the Sunday afternoon, little expecting
what we should have to contend with." The boys
rose in rebellion after the opening of school. "We
soon got several of the bigger boys on our side, and
such a scene followed as I shall never forget : some
swearing, some dancing, some whistling, and the
teachers looking, some of them, as pale as death, and
some quite ·exhausted. . . . Some of the teachers I
have never seen since ; most of the boys were reformed."

A short time after this there was a raid on the
furniture, candlesticks, books, etc., and had it not
been that the teachers were able to get four big lads,
whose number was brought up to sixteen, before the
skirmish was over, the place would have been sacked.

All the unsectarian societies in London have a
common ancestor, " the Society for Promoting Religious Knowledge among the Poor," founded in 1750.
Porteous, Bishop of London, Romaine, John Newton
Thornton, Wilberforce, and Rowland Hill belonged
to it. One rule was, " That the members be selected
from Christians of various denominations." The
last of the numerous family of societies that sprang
from it was the ragged school movement. At the
school where the fight, that has just been referred to,
took place, we are told that " By a kind of tacit agreement, Wesleyans, Baptists, Independents, etc., joined
with members of the Established Church, both high
and low. The children saw that Christianity was
indeed an all-embracing system, since those who parted
in their places of worship met in their charities."

John Macgregor, a teacher and a Churchman, wrote
in 1855 : " Nor shall I hesitate to declare among you
that the Church itself to which you and I belong is

most certainly preserved and edified by that hearty unsuspicious union of all denominations which is confessedly a result of our movement."

In cases where churches and chapels started ragged schools of their own, which they afterwards sustained with money and supplied with workers, the same broad teaching as in other schools was given. They also received teachers from outside, who were not of their communion.

The position of the York Ragged School was a little peculiar. It was started by Wesleyans as Wesleyan work. After a while they thought it desirable to make the school unsectarian, and throw the enterprise upon the sympathies of the town. To effect this and make a distinct change apparent, the office-holders resigned and invited Churchmen to take their places. Ever afterward the practice obtained of appointing Wesleyans to office, only when Churchmen were not available, yet the teachers were Wesleyans and the property as well.

It is worthy of comment that the Establishment of late years has shown a diminishing amount of readiness to co-operate with outsiders in work not distinctly its own. This is the more curious because the Victorian age has seen her claim and secure more latitude and liberty for herself in doctrine than at any other period in history, as a brief survey will show.

The Tractarian movement began five years before Queen Victoria ascended the throne with Keble's Assize Sermon. It grew in strength, and its influence began to be seen by 1846. Convocation, which the *Times* declared was only " a clerical debating society with a long name," revived by 1850, and by its action extracted the sting from " the Thunderer's " gibe.

In 1847 the appointment of Dr. Hampden, a theologian of neological views, to a bishopric, may be regarded as the charter of the broad church. The decision upon Baptismal Regeneration, arising out of the Gorham dispute in 1850, defined the Evangelical status, and the Frome case in 1871 was a victory for High Church views upon the Eucharist. When Dr. Temple was made Primate a tribute was paid to a variety of ecclesiasticism to be described " not as the broad, or high, but as the hard Church." [1]

It has been a loss to the Church, to the Ragged School Union, and to the poor that the balance of Established Church and Free Churches has been shifted in the London ragged schools, though churchmen are still well represented. The decay of theological liberalism is not easily accounted for, and High Churchism alone is not the explanation. It seems to have set in most inexplicably at the very time that a great Baptist, C. H. Spurgeon, and a great Congregationalist, Dr. R. W. Dale, of Birmingham, had carried their influence into Anglican pulpits. The Congregationalist and the Baptist communities have been strong supporters of ragged schools all along, and their rapid growth was due in no small measure to sharing in the prosperity of these churches. During the late Queen's reign the Congregationalists increased from 170,000 to 400,000, and the Baptists from 125,000 to 340,000.

It may be asked, How did it happen that in a London that was so strictly Sabbath-keeping that the very tobacconist used to put up one shutter as a distant mark of respect for it, that London ragged

[1] See *Social Transformations of the Victorian Age* (Escott), pp. 406–7.

schools could be supplied with teachers ? Of course
they would not ride. Probably they could not. A
glance at an early Victorian map of London shows,
instead of a huge conglomerate of bricks and mortar
covering two hundred square miles or more, an arrangement of dwellings that looks like an enlargement from
a micro-photograph of the shell of an insect with many
long legs and enlarged joints, or a potato-root taken
up and laid flat with its rootlets spreading upon a
sheet of paper. In the centre is a large mass corresponding with the insects' body or with a large potato
in the centre of the root, branching out from this are
roads in all directions, to which the limb sections of
the insect's legs, or the rootlets of the potato, correspond. All along these roads are swollen patches
smaller than the central one, like the joints of the
micro specimen or the new potatoes on the suckers.

The great central patch is London within and without the walls. The detached patches are numerous
suburbs like Hackney or Dulwich. These suburbs,
now merged into the London area, were then compact
and distinct, and such as needed a ragged school had
plenty of people to draw upon for workers and subscribers living on the spot. It is only then the central
portion for which an arrangement was needed. A
large provision existed in the prosperous number of
people who till the late sixties lived there as in John
Gilpin's days. They were able to go north, south,
east, and west, and not only deal with the ragged
schools of the City proper, but also with those in
Holborn and Southwark. Outside the City and con-
veniently away from it to become new centres of radiating
energy were the middle-class districts, Bloomsbury,
Islington, and Clapham. East London had its Stepney

squares and Bow population for dealing with the north, and the inhabitants of the Commercial Road squares for the schools on the north bank of the river. Every poverty patch was thus within easy walking distance of middle-class homes, which was an enormous advantage. We have now, in such work, to deal with entirely different conditions.

This chapter, which has covered a great deal of ground, may now be summarized. Is is mainly a story of losses. Like all similar work, but less than some, it has suffered during the last sixty years. The first is what may be called the aristocratic loss. Fewer of the men and women who have the highest advantages submit themselves now, than formerly, to the supreme tests that work for the pariah, and the children of the pariah impose when fully and faithfully done. As the discipline must always be more rigorous for them than for others, they are the best judges of their own responsibility. They do not perhaps know so well as those who miss them, what the cause has lost, nor realize so fully what they themselves have lost. When the children of privilege struggled through the many obstacles to deter them, in old days, they took premier rank, not on account of position, or possessions, but because they had endured more, as seeing Him who is invisible. They were never numerous, but their leadership, because of the force of character that secured it, was invaluable. With the naïveté that distinguished Ragged School Union writers in the formative period, the author of the philosophy of ragged schools declares that only two or three gentlemen *were able* to go low enough. The same may be said now, and the remark applied in a more general way. With the ladies it was and still is different. Yet the ranks thinned by death, have not been filled up. Still they will yet come to supplement and extend the efforts of the faithful few. Whenever that time comes, the Ladies' Auxiliary of the R.S.U. will afford them fullest scope. There have been other losses, due to changes in the religious life of the country, and to altered modes of living, and to a different distribution of middle-class homes in London and the surrounding neighbourhoods. But in spite of all, the number of teachers is higher than it used to be. There has been a temporary set back since the Jubilee of the London Union among the affiliated schools. It is sufficient to stimulate all to fresh exertions, but not bad enough to cause real anxiety. If the diagram in this chapter be consulted, it will be seen that there has been a gradual rise, from 1870 when the schools were supposed to become extinct. How have those numbers been augmented ? By the grateful services of those whom the movement has benefited, is the answer. Many of the scholars were dispersed beyond the seas, some to make comfortable homes in British Colonies to which they invited their parents to come and rest in their declining years, or like one whose interesting letter from British Columbia is before us now, to be public workers in the lands that adopted them.

This particular scholar, who is now forty-seven years of age, saw a paragraph in a colonial newspaper about the R.S.U. Diamond Jubilee. He has written to say, that with a family of nine children around him, he is hard at work paying off the cost of his farm, eighteen hundred dollars. He is President of his Trades Union for the fourth term, a member of the Trades and Labour Council, and is also engaged in promoting a co-operative society for Vancouver. To write a boastful letter has not been his object; it is to say that meals at the old ragged school saved him and his brother from starvation, and that but for the helping hand he had, he " might have swelled the criminal list."

But while some scholars went abroad, others stayed in London and have worked in the cause, inducing their children and their children's children to do the same. So it happens that a neglected cause has great reserves of strength.

Nevertheless all London work is now very complex, and must be scientific, and like every other Society the R.S.U. seeks for workers able to lead and guide. Here the words of Lady Laura Ridding, when pleading for women workers in the educational cause, may well be adopted for this work for the London child. " I believe there is no better recruiting ground than among the families and homes of the Church and other religious bodies. . . . I would urge on all to do their utmost to try and convince its ablest quiet-souled women that this work makes special demands on them, and to flood their consciences and intelligence with illumination."

If men have not been asked for specially, the reason is not far to seek. A youth once asked a shrewd old superintendent why he always appealed for lady teachers when teachers of the other sex were also needed. The reply was: "If I get them, the men will follow."

CHAPTER VIII

The Teachers—(*continued*)

" We go back to the grand discovery of Francis—say rather the interpretation of Francis—that the great sluggish, apathetic mass in which are born creatures of hideous mien and malign brain can only be moved by personal service."— SIR WALTER BESANT, *on the R.S.U.*

COMPOSED of such elements as have been described and subjected to influences that only the highest character, sustained by deepest faith, could endure, the staff of voluntary teachers in the ragged school movement became a great social force. In the ranks appeared some of the noblest men and women of the Victorian period, people whose influence for good was not confined to ragged children but affected also the higher strata of society. The majority, however, were people of humble station whose example would be unnoted by those who wield the pen, but nevertheless exerting a very precious influence upon many human lives. Here and there a chance reference in the writings of some great man who has gained in his own soul by knowing them, preserves the memory of one or two, otherwise they would now be forgotten. Such an one was Miss Mary Broom, of Gravesend, spoken of by the late General Gordon as " one of the best women in England. With little that was adventitious to aid her, and with daily duties to attend to, she spent hours every day in the lowest parts of the town ; gave her life for the up-lifting and salvation of a river-side population ; and contracted an infectious disease during her voluntary visitations, of which she died."

As representing the other sex we may take Roger Miller. Of him Lord Shaftesbury at his death wrote in his diary—" Here goes a city missionary at thirty shillings a week, and hundreds are in an agony of sorrow, I have lost an intimate friend. I have known men of a hundred thousand a year depart this life and every eye around, dry as the pavement."

No better argument could be adduced for the ragged school cause than the fact that great men of widely differing gifts have found in it a channel for the exercise of all their powers, and have at the same time found in their fellow workers of small resources and slender equipment inspiring companions capable of bringing blessing into their lives. Another phase is the satisfactory conditions for work that they found existing.

Is it conceivable that two such men as the late Professor Leone Levi and the late General Gordon, differing in their special gifts as widely as two men could differ, yet so similar in their impatient repudiation of everything checking their ideals, could work without friction with smaller men for a narrow interest ? The broad generalizing intellect of the jurist and the concentrated practical energy of the administrator embodied in two nervous sensitive men, found room in this cause, which is the " citizen's own." Had either of them, in seeking the space his great nature needed, touched an irritating barrier, there would have been a scandal. Much of their lives in both cases was spent in protest and suffering, a baffled beating of soul-wings against the bars of destiny. Work for the London urchin gave them peace and joy.

PROFESSOR LEONE LEVI, LL.D.

Professor Leone Levi, LL.D., Cavaliere of the order of SS. Mauritius and Lazarus and of the Crown of Italy, came from Italy to England in the very year the R.S.U. was started. He came as an agent for his merchant brother, who had large dealings in metals.

For a short time his restless and fiery nervous energy found a complete outlet in the process of " looking round." Our Protestantism with its sub-divisions perplexing to the foreigner, and a comparison of Judaism with Christianity occupied his leisure. The study of fiscal matters and practical business filled the day. In 1845, the revolution threatened in 1844, by all indications and prophesied by not a few, did not come. An economic change staved off the trouble for three years. Corn and iron fell in price. Changes that benefit a people may make private business difficult. They did so in this instance. The commercial crisis of 1847 emphasized Mr. Levi's troubles, dashing to the ground his hopes of expanding his brother's business for the time being. These difficulties, occurring as they did when he was between the ages of twenty-three and twenty-six were the making of the man. He appears to have had a marvellous capacity for mental work. His brain worked quickly and he was able to stand the strain of long hours of labour.

In the end he became a statistician for whom Lord Brougham, and after him Mr. Gladstone, entertained great admiration, and upon whose conclusions they placed the utmost reliance. The Liverpool Chamber of Commerce was his creation, but that alone did not satisfy him. He wished and worked for an entire alteration of all laws and regulations in this country that hindered trade. What the value of this man's work was to our empire, coming at the time it did, cannot be overestimated. Directly free-trade was sanctioned it was in the highest degree important to this country as a commercial nation that there should be no barrier of the legal kind to unrestricted commerce. As hon. sec. of the Liverpool Chamber of Commerce, he sent a circular letter to all foreign chambers of commerce to get the constitutions by which they were governed. He wrote *Commercial Laws, their Principles and Administration, together with Particulars respecting matters of Trade with the various Countries of the World.* Sixteen or eighteen hours a day at literary labour was a common thing with him. Omnivorous of information, he was continually in correspondence with the Chambers of Commerce of the world, asking for fresh facts. A valuable recommendation for the formation of associations for a national and international code of commercial law was due to him.

The Prince Consort was deeply interested in all his efforts, and wrote in 1851 to say what great pleasure it would give him to give all the help he could in procuring information from foreign Governments.

It is not necessary to follow his career further. His achievements brought him honours which never spoiled the man. The King of Prussia and the Emperor of Austria sent him gold medals. The Society of Arts gave him a valuable cup. His undisguised delight at every distinction had not the remotest connexion with personal vanity. In his vivid Italian nature were combined the artistic temperaments of Benevenuto Cellini and Raphael. He loved and admired fine work wherever he saw it. If it happened to be his own, the more ground for rejoicing, but he liked companions to share his pleasure. No one can read his brief unfinished autobiography without learning that he was a man making large demands on the sympathies of his fellows, giving in return more than he received, and carrying his friends with him in the joy of high achievement, at the same time without one self-magnifying thought.

He compels the reader of his life-story to feel with

him in the joys and anxieties he encountered. The chivalry of his gentle nature is exhibited over and over again, in the minute descriptions of his experiences in lodgings before his marriage. His indebtedness for kindnesses and attentions ministering to comfort on the part of his landladies and their domestics are to him obligations that can be only liquidated by a very full expression of gratitude. Every household of which at any time he was a temporary member entered into his hopes and intentions. His fellow-boarders and the servants saw him off to Windsor when summoned by the Prince Consort, Miss Neill, Miss Betsey, and Miss Ritchie, ladies of one of the houses where he had rooms at the time when he was to deliver a lecture to the Social Inquiry Society of Dublin, personated the three leading men he would meet upon the platform. To them he rehearsed his lecture. His all too brief auto-biography, interrupted by death, is full of charming domestic incidents which show how he revelled in human sympathy. When the Maclise Goblet and £100 was given him by the Society of Arts he could not rest till he had told some friend about it. It was an award in a competition among English, Scotch and American writers on Jurisprudence, and was given for his *Commercial Laws of the World*. He rushed from the Society of Arts in the Adelphi to his rooms in Doctor's Commons, but could not bear having no one to whom he could impart his joy that same evening. His friend, John Grant, was holding a Bible Class at a business house in Newgate Street. He went there and sent in a note asking him to come out for a minute or two, but his friend would not, and he adds " it was some time before I could have a disburdening of my full heart that night."

Some of the minor worries of this highly-strung man make the flesh tingle. On the Windsor visit he was behind time, and at the Castle had his nerves worked upon by passing in the corridors servants with luncheon dishes, and still further by the natural reserve and coldness of manner of the Prince Consort, but which he thought his unpunctuality had produced. In that condition he had at once to launch into his subject. The Prince was seated at one side of a long table and he was standing on the other side. The interview lasted an hour, he was not asked to be seated, and the Prince Consort had none of his son's power to put a man at his ease. In reality, Prince Albert was deeply interested.

Upon one occasion the Professor had to deliver a lecture at Birmingham upon a most intricate subject. He reached the London station just in time to discover he had left his manuscript behind and he had to buy a portable inkstand. In the train he made despairing attempts to scribble down some notes. As he alighted at Birmingham, in an agony of anticipation at the humiliation to come, the guard presented him with his manuscript. His faithful landlady had run all the way to the station, and had put it into the guard's hand as the train steamed out.

This lovable man began ragged school teaching in a little school in Bell's Square, Finsbury, afterwards continuing at another one in Golden Lane. It had been a coffee-shop, and was a very low-pitched dingy sort of place. At a later period he held a ragged school for Italian children in Saffron Hill. Like his fellow teachers, he came in for some pelting and general rough treatment, but the work appears to have been a source of great happiness to him.

General Gordon's biography is before the public, and has been dealt with very fully by able writers. Some particulars of his life at Gravesend, the impressions of his fellow teachers and a few letters that are characteristic of the man may however be new. Gordon has been said to have remarked that the six years passed at Gravesend was the most peaceful and happy portion of his life. His mode of life was simple in the extreme. Nothing superfluous was tolerated. His watch-chain was a knotted boot-lace, and when his housekeeper cooked eggs for his breakfast she was told she had better keep them for the poor. Yet, as it has been truly said—" To the world Gordon's life at Gravesend was a life of self-repression and of self-denial ; to himself it was one of happiness and pure peace. He lived wholly for others. His house was a school and hospital and almshouse in turn. The troubles of all interested him alike. The poor, the sick, the unfortunate, were ever welcome and never did suppliant knock vainly at his door."

Once a woman tramp called at his house and the General sent her out half-a-crown. She rewarded him by stealing his tunic and some coats from the hall. She was caught, but Gordon would not prosecute. However, she was wanted for another offence and was sentenced to a month's imprisonment. The morning she came out of gaol the General (he was colonel then) had her up to his office to talk over her future.

Upon one occasion the General had to get a brother officer of means to advance his pay to meet a pressing claim. His housekeeper had the bank-note in her purse and was in the hall ready to take the money, when a respectable neighbour came to him with a sad tale of an execution just put into his house. Immediately

GENERAL GORDON AND HIS "KINGS" AT GRAVESEND.

the bank-note was diverted from its destination to the relief of his neighbour's burden.

Mr. Penman, the superintendent of the Gravesend ragged school, wrote soon after General Gordon's death, the following—" He never left his class without a teacher. His thoughts were always about his lads. He invariably, moreover, took his part in the devotional exercises and regularly stayed after the teaching was over to our teachers' monthly prayer meetings ; with his right hand over his eyes, and his left hand supporting the elbow of the right, he would stand, and in his quiet humble way, speak with God. In all he did and said, he was marked among us for his deep humility and for a heart full of love and pity for the poor. He had a class of some fourteen lads in one corner of the schoolroom ; their ages ranged from twelve to seventeen. They were the very roughest and poorest we then had in attendance, but it was remarkable how entire was the control he had over them. Some of those lads he himself brought to the school ; their parents were mostly of no occupation, or in some way served the boats on the river. Several of the boys were employed on shrimp boats. He not only would teach the lads at school on Sunday evenings, he had them also at his own house every day in the week, feeding and instructing them. Four or five of the poorest and most miserable of the lads he kept in his home altogether, feeding and clothing them, they employing their time in the garden, in chopping wood and running errands. Three or four of them had scarlet fever while in his house. The Colonel used to care for them in their sickness, and would sit with them far into the night, talking to them and soothing them until they fell asleep."

The Rev. Wm. Guest, of Gravesend, who was a friend of Gordon's, gives this sketch of him—

" I have met him on regular visits which he paid to a poor lame boy who lived some distance from the town. He would, on errands of compassion, enter homes of infectious disease, where others hesitated to go. Constantly he visited the Union Workhouse and went laden with gifts of things needed by the children, or by aged paupers. He went among the sick in the wards, and would walk with the poor old men in the yard, without assumption or the shadow of condescension. After he left Gravesend, he kept up his gifts to the inmates—of tobacco for the old men who had used it. and I think of tea for the old women.

"A relative of my own cook was kept by him when the man was too old to work. There was one pensioner whom I visited during six or eight years after Gordon had gone from Gravesend, who was supported by him, who never spoke of him without a respectful affection most touching to listen to.

"I used to sit by this person as he delighted to talk of ' my dear Colonel.' I may add a fact or two in this case which illustrates the sympathetic minuteness of the General's attention. The man—who died a year ago (1884)—was a respectable, though poor clerk of a solicitor. He was paralyzed, and he told me that on the General's return one day to England from an important Eastern service, his very first work that same day was to find out in London the bedridden clerk. Discovering that the man was not in comfortable lodgings, the General ordered a conveyance, had him seated carefully in it, and went a considerable distance to place him in a suburban institution. As they drove up to the large building the countenance of the man fell. Quickly was the change seen by his benefactor, and in his prompt way he said—'What is it?'

" 'I have a feeling that if I go in there I shall not come out till I am carried out.' Without an attempt at expostulation, the General said—' Oh, then you shall not go!' And the driver was told to turn the horse's head. Lodgings were secured for him in Milton-on-Thames, near to my own residence. The man was intelligent and fond of reading. He liked to see the *Daily News*. An arrangement for its transmission had somehow failed. General Gordon on learning the fact during a visit to the man, went the very next day to the Horse Guards (I think) to secure a reliable person who was told to send it regularly, and of course at the General's expense. It seems a small thing but he knew, in his beautiful thoughtfulness, how much the daily paper would cheer a man who could not leave his room."

The letters we are privileged to print tell their own stories—

GALATZ,

March 5, 1872
(the day of your School treat).

MY DEAR MR. PENMAN,—

Thank you very much for your kind letter, February 24, which came here yesterday. I can assure you I do daily twice pray for the welfare of the school and teachers, and I often think of you all, and would like to come among you. You can scarcely imagine what it is to be in such complete exile as this place is ; for spiritual matters we have a service read by the Consul on Sundays, but there is not one to whom you can speak on the great subject, not but what I do talk over it sometimes to an Italian Catholic here who is a nice fellow, but who of course must think very differently from us. The place is a large, very ill paved, straggling town ; you have mud ankle deep in all the streets, the population cosmopolitan, and numbering many Jews, who are an evil-looking lot, and who are much disliked ; there are lots of Greeks. If you saw the Jews you would certainly wonder that they should have been, and are now, chosen people of God, and that our Saviour was of their nation ; they are the leeches of the country. The Roumanians are a thriftless race, and get into debt to them so that they squeeze the lives out of the people, and living on very little, never spending anything, they drain and exhaust the country.

One large town here is called the New Jersualem, from the number of Jews in it. My work is not hard, it is something like the Trinity Board's and Thames Conservancy Board's duties. The town of Galatz is built on the Danube, which is not wider than the Thames at Gravesend ; about thirty miles below this begins the Delta, a low, marshy tract of land through which the Danube splitting into three branches falls into the Black Sea. Though melancholy in the extreme, this tract has its villages, and inhabitants mostly refugees from Russia ; they are of different sects, some of them most peculiar, as Mr. Tilly will tell you to whom I have described them, but though the surroundings are very dull, and the swamps they live in are dreary enough, the people look happy and seem to have no greater burthens than those who live in better lands. You see the same careful, loving mothers, the same careless Russian Willie Websters running about as in Gravesend. The Lord's ways are all equal, and to Him they are as much valued as the greatest in the world, and thus the seeing them makes me think of your flock, and yearn for the time when He will bring us altogether as one people with one God, a great multitude whom no man can number, clad in white robes, with palms in their hands." These parts have been the battlefields of Russians and Turks for centuries, and before them of the Barbarian tribes and the Romans.   Many are the historical mementos ; as you go down, you pass Isakhta, where Solyman the Magnificent crossed the Danube to help the Poles against the Russians, 1728 ; and there is the tumulus which the Emperor Nicholas erected in memory of an escape he had from the bursting of a Turkish shell at his feet ; there at a little distance is Ismail, a decaying place, which Suwarrow took in 1789 from the Turks, after a great slaughter ; these and many other famed places are all along the river, now so quiet and deserted ; those whose bodies lie sleeping in these parts are long ago forgotten, and the remark that there was a great siege or a great battle is all that remains of their deeds.   These Russian Sectarians live quietly and happily under the Turkish Government, and far prefer it to their own Government ; the latter is an ambitious, evil one, and can never be trusted ; these people with their faults are not bad and would live in peace if they could.   You must give my kind regards to all my friends, the teachers, Miss Young, Mrs. Crook, Crowhurst, and all of them, and the boys and girls of the school.   I hope they are doing well, and will conclude, my dear Mr. Penman ; and to Mrs. Penman and the children I shall write again soon (D.V.). How does the Town Missionary do ?

Yours sincerely,   C. G. GORDON.

P.S.—Will you give my kindest thanks for the kind resolution sent me. Your kind letter gave me very much pleasure. How is Mr. Hilder? Kind regards to him, Mr. Guest and Mrs. Guest.

Galatz
5 March 1872
(The day of your school treat.)

My dear Mr Penman

Thank you very much for your kind letter 24 Feby which came here yesterday. I can assure you I do daily twice pray for the wel-fare of the school and teachers and I often often think of you all. and would like to come among you you can scarcely imagine what it is to be in such complete exile as this place is for spiritual matters we have a service read by the Consul on Sundays but there is not one to whom you can speak on the great subject. not but that I do talk over it sometimes to a Italian Catholic here who is a nice fellow but who of course must think very differently from us

REDUCED FACSIMILE OF A PORTION OF ONE OF GENERAL GORDON'S LETTERS.

GALATZ,
October 3, 1872.

MY DEAR MISS BROOM,—

Thanks for your two letters, which I received on my arrival from Constantinople. With respect to Fordham, I will give him £5. I cannot afford more, poor little chap. I have done what I can for him considering others. With respect to Mr. Cooper, I wish you would see him and show him this, and ask him if he cannot oblige me by abating the sum for Baldwin. He will, I think, do so, and the more so as he knows how many leaks I have for my money and how little it is to meet all the claims. Keep Arthur White, nice little chap, at school as long as he likes. Luke and Morris live in Passengers' Court, which I think you know. Glad Dr. Cressy is well. Keep on the pittance to Stockley, if she is not too proud. Kind regards to her. Sorry for her son's affliction. I do not know when I shall get home, for I am just back from the Crimea and have lots to do. Sorry for the lads of the Lott family, she was a nice woman. Will you keep their address for me; tell them I hope they are doing well. I send you a cheque for £20.* Of this there is £2 for Mrs. Warren for Clifford; £2 5s. 6d., for Mrs. Warren for Carter. My kindest regards to Mr. and Mrs. Warren, who, I hope, are well. £2 14s. 6d. for Mr. Lilly, with thanks for his nice letter. I wish you could help Chipperfield of Tilbury Station a little. I will write soon to Lilly; tell him I do not know about Mrs. Burton; her son is too young for War Dept. Vessels. How is Vine? Will you see what can be done for Mrs. Burton? I send this time you see £13. This must do for my subscription—Ragged School, and Xmas Dinner (which I think is a thing others can subscribe to), and Infirmary subscription, and anything else, for I have no more money this year. The Russians were very civil, but are rather sulky at their position; they do not like the Germans at all.

Kind regards to Mr. Penman, Fenwick, and all my

* At General Gordon's death a memorial fund for such purposes as this letter indicates was started and is still in active operation (see supplement).

friends.   How is little white-haired girl in your class?
Good-bye.

Yours sincerely,

With kind regards to your father, and sisters,

C. G. GORDON.

I hope Cooper will invest in Baldwin.

P.S.—I shall be afraid of coming to Gravesend,
for it will cost me a mint of money.

Private.

68, ELM PARK ROAD, CHELSEA.

2—3—81.

MY DEAR MR. PENMAN,—

Thanks for your kind letter.   I feel sure you know
I take the greatest interest in school and in your people,
and I may say I have never forgotten it; since I left
I have daily been in spirit with you and others I knew
there wherever I have been; but I could not come
down for several reasons; my last visit was too expensive and I cannot afford it just now.   How are Mr.
Crowhurst, Box, and all my old friends?   My kindest
regards to them.   With kind regards,

Believe me,

My dear Mr. Penman,

Yours sincerely,

C. G. GORDON.

SOUTHAMPTON.

7—3—81.

MY DEAR MR. PENMAN,—

Many thanks for your very kind note.   I have left
town for a time, and am very sorry I must decide not
to come down; you will not be angry with me about

this, but forgive it, and do not put it, my refusal, down
to want of interest in you all.

Believe me,

Yours sincerely,

C. G. GORDON.

This chapter has been devoted to four typical characters, to show how social extremes met, in ragged
school teaching and in what an atmosphere of fraternalism the meeting took place. In the same school
might be found a cobbler, and beside him a stock-
broker, Sir Robert Carden, a labourer and a
banker, such as Mr. Frank Bevan, valuing an exchange of greetings as one of the pleasures of the work.
If a list of distinguished teachers were attempted it
would convey no more than this, and such an attempt
would not be successful.

Reviewing the chapter it becomes noticeable that the
ladies are not fairly represented. To equalize matters,
may we be permitted to mention two who represent a
very important element in the teaching staff,—the
educated lady of means.

Mrs. Barker Harrison, better known by her maiden
name, Miss Adeline M. Cooper, worked in Westminster, and was the intimate personal friend of the
Baroness Burdett-Coutts. For thirty years she laboured
at the thieves' tavern that she and some friends
turned into a ragged school. And her labours were
not of the supervising order merely in that aforetime
" Citadel of Satan in the Devil's Acre." Like most
of the early workers she valued direct contact with the
children and the people. Standing by her open grave
her life-long friend, the Baroness, as she threw in
white flowers expressed the thoughts of many hearts.

" Many and many a year must pass before she will be even partially unremembered, and her good acts forgotten."

Mrs. Frank Bevan held memories of our sainted dead that are precious. At the opening of the offices in John Street, she contrasted the present with the past when she and her husband were teachers at Gray's Yard. The

MRS. BARKER HARRISON, NÉE ADELINE COOPER.

conveniences and comforts of to-day compared with the drawbacks of that period are all in the teacher's favour. There was a time when in many of the schools a teacher did well, before settling his or her seat, to see that they would be clear of the drippings of the tallow candles in the tin chandelier, the sole means of illumination. There was a time when not a few schools

had earth floors, and a good deal of money in R.S.U.
grants went for wooden flooring. Whether Mrs.
Bevan ever had any of the extreme experiences is
doubtful, but from her remarks on the occasion referred to it was clear that she had roughed it somewhat.   By these memories she was bound to the
cause, she told the workers, and by two other associations. Lord Shaftesbury, towards the end of his life,
said to her, " My days are numbered, and there is one
promise I would like you to make to me—that you will
stick fast to the Ragged School Union."

The other was a very similar experience connected
with the late Princess Mary of Teck.   One day, when
they were sitting together, she said—" Will you promise
me one thing ?   You know I am getting old and life is
uncertain.   I hope that you will continue your interest
in some of these associations, and she pointed to a long
list of names.   When Mrs. Bevan asked for further
instructions, she pointed to the name " Ragged School
Union," and said—" Never forget it."

The influential and the well-equipped in goods,
education and faculty were the few, the men and
women of moderate resources the many in this band.
But whatever their advantages or limitations they
were some of the earth's noblest.

There is, we think, an obligation resting upon those
who knew them, to keep inviolate a testimony
that may not be surrendered, the tradition of a
patriotic working Protestantism.   That this testimony
may be kept till saner methods of evangelical and social
service again prevail, is to be hoped for the well-being
of our country.

CHAPTER IX

The R.S.U. and Links with the Churches

" Let me speak through you to all in your parish or society, that there be no man or woman left among us who does not labour to make God's dear England kinder and purer, godlier and happier than it has ever been.

" Has not the care of souls been left too much and too long in the hands of the clergy alone, or nearly alone ? "—*The Priesthood of the Laity*—BISHOP OF TRURO.

DR. GUTHRIE, " THE APOSTLE OF RAGGED SCHOOLS."

THE great orator and statesman, Edmund Burke, in his *Reflections upon the French Revolution*, claimed that toleration was a marked feature of the Protestantism of this country. He added that " we tolerate not from indifference but from zeal." Had he lived a few years longer he could have strengthened that sentence by substituting the word co-operate for tolerate.

Without any forfeiture of principle on either side, ecclesiastics of the Establishment and prominent ministers of the various denominations have found it possible to unite in work for God and their native land during Queen Victoria's reign. It cannot be said that it was ever a large group, and it may have grown smaller in recent years through the action of extremists on both sides. Nevertheless, it can boast great names in the past, and possesses honoured representatives of the National Church and Nonconformity in the present day.

As indicative of the line of thinking along which this meeting takes place, a passage from the charge delivered to his clergy by the Bishop of Rochester last year, and an extract from *The Dissolution of Dissent* by Dr. Horton, Congregationalist, will serve as illustrations.

In reading the Bishop's charge, we note that he is the hundredth right reverend father in God to occupy the episcopal throne of Rochester. If a pious wish be not out of place, it is that Rochester and every other British diocese may each have another hundred bishops with similar liberality and courage to his lordship.

" There are two ways in which Christianity is manifested to the world : one the embodied way, through ' the Body or Society of His pledged believers ' : the other the diffusive way, by which influences from Him spread out without limit into the life and thoughts of men. In our Lord's own words one was figured by the net and the building : the other by the leaven. Both are essential and permanent. They ought to be entirely allied ; the embodied force ever acting with fresh leavening power as the influence of the Christian Society communicates itself to all the life around it ; the diffusive force providing ever fresh material upon which the Body can lay hold, and build up into itself.

" While the one force, the embodied Christian life, carries with it all the disfigurement and mutilation (much larger than we professing Christians recognize) caused by ecclesiastical and clerical and Christian narrowness, or laxity, or pretension, or bigotry, or divisions in the past, the other or diffusive force has unprecedented vogue and attraction. For amidst all the evil and materialism there never was a time when there was so much sentiment, philanthropy, corporate and mutual service, inspired by Christian influence, when there was so much broken light of Christian source, as there is to-day, or when it expressed itself with anything like so much freedom and variety.

" I find in this a very real help in analysing that with which we have to deal, viz., a time with so much re-ligiousness, and so little definite religion ; a time of real moral progress in so many ways, along with so much depreciation of those truths and practices of belief and worship and membership which to Christians em-body the great secret and centre of moral growth : a time alarming and yet tantalizing, too, to the believer, who finds, as it seems to him, so little of his belief, and yet so much of what should naturally spring from it, or respond to it.

" I think I observe a similar feeling on the part of one of our most thoughtful and distinguished Nonconformist neighbours in South London work, Rev. J. Scott Lidgett, Warden of the Bermondsey Settlement, ex-pressed in some words of the preface to his valuable book on *The Fatherhood of God* (T. and T. Clark, 1902) : ' Many are greatly perplexed by the seemingly rival claims of spiritual work, and of the motives of natural and generous sympathy. It is of great importance to seek a reconciliation between the two.' "

Dr. Horton holds a position among the Independents which imparts special value to his words, when re-garded as representing patriotic dissent. He has been chairman of the Congregational Union and holds high office in the Free Church Council. Referring to the dissenting churches he writes—

" If, of course, any one of them nurtured the pitiable delusion that it and it alone constituted the Church of Christ, a kind of religious mania to which churches, like individuals, are liable, it would have to be left out, (from a scheme of co-operation of Anglicanism and the sects).

" But when the Anglican Church had set the example of the wider and juster interpretation of the Church, it is doubtful if the small and exclusive sects would hold out in their infatuation.

" But the future of our country and of our race will be sufficiently secured, if those who agree in regarding the New Testament as the sole authority in religion, outside and beyond which nothing should be maintained as necessary to salvation, can come to such a spirit of practical unity and co-operation, that they work together in the vineyard of Christ." [1]

In spite of the controversies that have divided and still divide English Protestants, a practical and solid achievement in more than one direction can be shown as the result of the united action of men who were, and are, members of differing communions. The work of the R.S.U. is one of the products of such unity. The concord in this instance is the more remarkable because the training of children is the one subject upon which the Churchman and the Dissenter are supposed to be irreconcilable. Ragged school men find it difficult to be dogmatic, however heedful to sound doctrine they may be, or definite in their convictions, and zealous in supporting them. Even for members of the Romish

[1] *Dissolution of Dissent*, p. 125 (1902), A. H. Stockwell, 2 and 3, Amen Corner.

Church a warm appreciation has arisen, when, in times of epidemic, they have found themselves working side by side with priests rendering a whole-hearted service to the poor. An appreciation that is not concurrence of view has a broadening effect. They remember the ragged school men who were Catholics, Cardinal Borromeo at Milan, Savonarola at Florence, Clement XI, who built a reformatory for boys at Rome.

They cannot forget that it was a book from the pen of a monk that shaped the character of their fellow-teacher, General Gordon.

In the same way a profound respect and liking arises for the earnest and philanthropic Hebrews whom they find at work in the slums. These are two extreme instances of many of the good men the ragged school teacher meets and is compelled to admire. A certain disposition of mind is induced, which Lord Shaftesbury, who was himself an illustration of it, described in one of his speeches at Exeter Hall. " It is a very blessed thing, again in reference to the times, that there is this power of union among those who differ upon other matters ; and I will appeal to all my friends here—to my dissenting friends on the one hand, and my friends of the Church of England on the other—and ask them whether they will not concur with me in the sentiment I now utter, that the ragged school movement has contributed singularly to soften the asperities that existed between them ; and whether they do not now find a deep satisfaction and a holy joy, not only when they come together on the same platform here, but when they come together in the same school and under the same roof, in teaching to those around them the great and inalienable and eternal truths of the common religion they profess."

The ultimate result of these friendships was an experience fruiting in a conviction not unlike that which Professor Blackie gives as one of the great lessons of history, that " the best form of church government is a strong establishment qualified by a strong dissent." [1]

This was not quite the ragged school position, but it very frequently arose out of it. That position was outlined very clearly by Lord Shaftesbury upon another occasion when he said—

" It is the principle that for this great end shall be combined all who hold the great leading doctrines of Christianity ; that in this matter we will know neither Jew nor Gentile, Church of England man nor Dissenter ; but we will only know the man who seeks to promote the honour of the Saviour, by making Him known to those sitting in darkness. That is our principle. And see how this year, 1856, we have tested and proved it. In one of your pulpits you have the Archbishop of Canterbury preaching on behalf of this Institution ; in another of your pulpits you have a Nonconformist minister, like my friend Thomas Binney, preaching in support of the same cause : the great Nonconformist and the great temporal head of the ecclesiastical Church of England being joined hand in hand in the furtherance of this noble undertaking. That is an achievement worthy of the days in which we live."

It will be fitting that these two great names shall head the list of representative Churchmen and Dissenting Ministers who have been friends of the R.S.U., and sufficiently in advance of their times to perceive that London'could only be effectively dealt with, either from the evangelical or philanthropic point of view, by a joining of forces and by a use of all worthy expedients.

[1] *What Does History Teach ?*   p. 120.

Archbishop Sumner was a small boy in a country rectory when the French Revolution took place. It is not unlikely that the conversation of his father and mother upon the shocking excesses that the mob, so long oppressed and neglected, were committing in Paris, may have impressed him. As a man of thirty he may have read Robert Hall's pamphlet on *The Advantages of Knowledge to the Lower Classes*. There was an extraordinary intensity of energy in the cause of religion and education in this man. Surmise as to the origin of the impulse is irresistible. That activity which caused Sir Robert Peel to mention him in terms of warm admiration in the House of Commons in 1843, and which had as its product the opening of upwards of two hundred churches and schools during his Chester episcopate may well have had its mainspring in a strong impression gained from such a passage as this.

" Nothing in reality renders legitimate governments so insecure as extreme ignorance in the people. It is this which yields them an easy prey to seduction, makes them the victims of prejudices and false alarms, and so ferocious withal, that their interference in a time of public commotion is more to be dreaded than the eruption of a volcano. . . . Look at the popular insurrections and massacres in France. . . . Who were the cannibals that sported with the mangled carcases and palpitating limbs of their murdered victims ? They were the very scum of the people, destitute of all moral culture, whose atrocity was only equalled by their ignorance, as might well be expected, when the one was the legitimate parent of the other." [1]

Be that as it may, Sumner was a most active man in

[1] Robert Hall. *The Advantages of Knowledge to the Lower Classes.*

work among the poor.   At twenty-two he was a schoolmaster at Eton.   At thirty-eight rector of Mapledurham,
near Oxford, and not till he was forty-eight was he made
a bishop.   This experience and slow preferment ripened
him so that as a bishop he was an unspoiled man.
Against Romish doctrine he never failed to use voice
and pen.   Because of this trait the Duke of Wellington
preferred him to the See of Chester and made one of the
few mistakes of his life.   He expected that he and his
brother of Winchester would vote against Catholic
Emancipation, but they did not.   They happened to be
two Englishmen who felt that Protestantism would not
be weakened but buttressed by fair-play.   Queen Victoria and Edward VII seem, both of them, to have
thought likewise.   Their exchange of courtesies with
the Pope were the first national tributes paid to Catholic
patriots since England became a Protestant nation.
Yet it was a Catholic admiral, Lord Howard of Effing-
ham, who defeated the Armada, and in our own day
we have seen the Duke of Norfolk, when forced to
choose, deciding for his sovereign against the reigning
pope.[1]

By voting for the removal of disabilities, Bishop Sumner strengthened his witnessing to the testimony that
might not be surrendered, and addressed his clergy in
vindication of the vote.   Had he been an opportunist
seeking promotion he would not have crossed the Iron
Duke in this way, nor would he have repeated the
offence when the Reform Bill came up for a second
reading.   His experience as a country rector and bishop
of an agricultural see made him a useful man upon the
Poor Law Commission of 1834, when he was fifty-four
years of age.   At the ripe age of sixty-eight he became

[1] In the ecclesiastical titles controversy.

Primate, in which capacity he earned the criticism of Wilberforce, " Good, gentle, loving and weak." There is no question about any of these four adjectives except the last one.

Dr. Binney was a man whose greatness was so much a matter of personality and leavening influence that there is not much of an impressive character to point out to generations succeeding his own. But he would have a larger monument than many a man who has written a great book or founded a national institution if it were possible to translate unseen forces into some visible equivalent.

At the King's Weigh House Chapel he was the centre of a marvellous influence upon the commercial life of London at the time of its greatest expansiveness. Hardly another man has had so large a share in the shaping of modern nonconformity. He said some hard things of the Church, at times of exasperation, but he had much in common with Churchmen. It was this very sympathy with much that is dear to them that increased his power as an apologist for dissent.

Born in 1798, his early youth was spent in that stern, bare and bigoted environment that nearly two centuries of unfairness and injustice had produced among Puritans. He was a redoubtable champion of liberty of conscience, because he was perhaps the first advocate to " attemper with religious principles and feelings the merely political aspect of Nonconformist disabilities." By thus elevating the Nonconformist argument he gave it power. But Dr. Binney, in so far as he was controversial, was so in spite of himself. Large in every aspect of his being, he was a genial nature-loving soul, into whom the crabbed and the sour could not find entrance.

His great contribution to free church life was not unlike a service rendered to the Establishment by the
Tractarians. All who have the patience to read this
book are likely to deplore some of the results of the
Oxford movement, but none will deny that the restoration of the decencies of worship, its bye-product, was a
gain. Dr. Binney did something similar for historic
puritanism. The average Churchman knows as much
of the oppression that Dissenters have had to endure
as an Englishman does of the past treatment of Ireland. If both histories were carefully read and submitted to fireside tests the nation would gain. Not
knowing otherwise, the Churchman attributes the narrowness of the old conventicle to the position of protest. But the first Puritans were cultured men, who
loved " the high embowed roof," " the storied windows
richly dight," and the pealing organ of the cathedral,
and knew what it was while listening to " the full-
voiced choir " to be " dissolved into ecstasies " and
assisted thereby to a consciousness of a present heaven.

Dr. Binney restored the Dissenter to the Miltonic
type. Dr. Henry Allon, in a biographical sketch,
wrote " that many of Mr. Binney's natural preferences
and sympathies would have led him into the Established
Church, his aesthetic tastes in worship and his shrinking from any position of antagonism especially. He
was one of the least extreme and violent of any of
the Nonconformist ministers of his generation."

Our brethren and cousins in the colonies and the
United States have the advantage of reviewing the
historic controversies attendant upon our progressive
Protestantism at longer range. Not only do those
Anglo-Saxons abroad, who cannot regard Anglican-
ism in its present expression as being their ideal of the

Christian Church, far outnumber those who are its members, but the Episcopalians themselves are less rigid than in this country. An instance occurred when Dr. Binney visited Australia. The Bishop of Adelaide corresponded with him, discussing the possibilities of an interchange of preachers in Nonconformist and Church pulpits. Almost simultaneously the bishop received a memorial from Episcopalian laymen, asking that Dr. Binney should be invited to preach in the cathedral. It was signed by the Governor of the Colony and Ministers of the State.

Another apostolic man, the successor of Dr. Sumner in the Primacy, was Archbishop Tait. How the heart warms towards him when tracing his labours of love. Open-air preaching by men whose powers gained for them a hearing was more common then than now. Bishop Tait was indefatigable in this trying form of ministry. He would go from the House of Lords down to the docks to give parting counsel to a shipload of emigrants, or speak to a crowd of omnibus drivers in a yard at Islington. At another time it would be to meet costermongers at Covent Garden Market or to address railway porters, using a railway engine for a pulpit, or yet again a colony of gipsies at Shepherd's Bush. Our connexion with him is that he thought it among the duties and privileges of his office, after leaving Convocation, where Church Discipline was being discussed, to go down to Golden Lane and in a little stuffy school deliver an address to ragged school children.

One of the fathers and founders of this movement, as also of the London City Mission, was the Hon. and Rev. Baptist Noel. Originally trained for the bar, he afterwards took holy orders, and in 1827, when twenty-nine years of age, was in charge of St. John's Chapel, Bedford Row, where he had among his congregation the leading spirits of the " Clapham " philanthropic and reforming group. He was one of the first to draw public attention to the sad spiritual condition of London in a letter to his bishop in 1835. This was published and had many fruitful results. He was forty-three when he published his anti-Corn-Law tract, " A plea for the poor," and the same year was made one of the Queen's chaplains. After serving upon a Government Commission on the condition of education and helping to set on foot the Evangelical Alliance, an incident occurred which changed the whole course of his life, as well as of other Churchmen, though the direction was not in their case the same. The Archbishops of Canterbury and York having ruled that it was not essential that a clergyman should believe in baptismal regeneration, he resigned his living. Mr. Noel joined the Baptists, other clergymen turned to Rome. Though severing his connexion, at the dictates of his conscience, when fifty years of age, he retained his " admiration for many of his beloved and honoured brethren in the Establishment," and would never have anything to do with the Liberation Society.

His preaching was as popular and his congregation as influential as before taking that step, which must have caused him so much pain. He became President of the Baptist Union in 1855 and 1867. But whether as a clergyman or Baptist minister he was always the warm friend and practical helper of ragged schools.

In a later chapter, when dealing with Exeter Hall memories, some of the clergy and ministers sharing in this work will be mentioned, but here only a few typical worthies can find a place.

A never-to-be-forgotten service was that rendered to the cause by the late Dr. Billing, Bishop of East London. As Rector of Spitalfields and rural dean he had become thoroughly conversant with the work. The occasion was soon after the death of Lord Shaftesbury. There was a general disposition in the public mind to regard the work as one of the byegones of history. The bishop preached in Westminster Abbey, and in doing so gave not the history but the up-to-date work then being done. No advocate ever marshalled his facts better. Leaving till last the most telling fact of all, the unbought labours of an army of devoted men and women, he told the congregation from his own knowledge where some of them could be found in the precincts of the Abbey itself. Then, leaning over the pulpit, he said—

" At the present time there are from three to four thousand of these teachers around us. Would you like to have that band disbanded ? Would it not be a serious loss to the Metropolis and to the country ? " The reminder at the time it came was of great value.

Dr. Guthrie's words and works receive such ample notice in this volume that we shall here rest content to do no more than link him with the liberal men, as shown in his sketch of proposed church-work in Edinburgh in 1867 : " Let the ministers or representatives of the different denominations within the city—Episcopalian, Baptist, and Independent ; United Presbyterian, Free Church, and Established Church—meet, and form themselves into a real working evangelical alliance. Agreeing to regard all old divisions of parishes with an ecclesiastical right over their inhabitants as nowadays a nullity—and, so far as these are preventing Christian co-operation and the salvation of the people,

as worse than a nullity—let them map out the dark
and destitute districts of the city, assigning a district
to each congregation. Let every congregation then
go to work upon their own part of the field, and giving
each some five hundred souls to care for, you would
thus cover the ' nakedness of the land.' "

There has been in the past and there still exists a
group of divines, themselves immersed in the work.
Not only did they preach sermons, and speak at meetings on behalf of it, but they encouraged their hearers
to engage in it, and to find the sinews of war for causes
in the poorer districts. For these their churches in-
curred definite permanent responsibilities. In some
instances more than one mission was undertaken. As
one of these ministers said, " a ragged school is worth
ten spires." The late Dr. Henry Allon, of Islington.
the late C. H. Spurgeon, and the late Dr. Newman Hall
may be regarded as representative of the group. It
was Dr. Allon who said that he " had seen more
religious romance in connexion with this community
than in his entire religious experience."

Between Dr. Hall and Lord Shaftesbury there was a
close friendship. Readers of the biography of Newman Hall will remember with what misgiving and shy-
ness the Earl attended that remarkable tea-party at
which bishops and dissenting preachers talked over
their differences, and his share of the surprise all seem
to have had in the discovery of the large amount they
had in common. Dr. Hall, prince of tract-writers and
open-air preachers, was a friend of the R.S.U. throughout his London ministry.

With Spurgeon it was the same. Every year he met
the ragged school teachers of London and addressed
them. He was one of the men from whose friendship

Lord Shaftesbury derived comfort and strength. He wrote of him—

" There is no man in the country whose opinion and support in such matters (the service of the poor) I prize more highly than those of my friend Mr. Spurgeon. Few men have preached so much and so well, and few men have combined so practically their words and their actions. I deeply admire and love him, because I do not believe that there lives anywhere a more sincere and simple servant of Our Blessed Lord."

Dean Farrar at Margate preached a most eloquent sermon on behalf of our Cripple Mission, and is one of the men whose memories are dear to us.

There are two great preachers whom we mourn, for whom a talented secularist, George Jacob Holyoake (Chairman of the Rationalist Press Association), entertained a profound respect, and with whom he enjoyed a real personal friendship. Without changing his views, he knew them for what they were, genuine Christian men. The Rev. Hugh Price Hughes and the Rev. Joseph Parker.

Mr. Hughes, whom he calls " the Hotspur of the Pulpit," wrote, in his opinion, " nobler words in testimony of the possible morality of Atheists than any other Wesleyan ever did. *The Atheist Shoemaker*, contains the first historical instance of the Christian concession of ethical heresy." He honoured him for his efforts to render Christianity ethical.

With Dr. Parker he had a closer tie. At a time when, as Mr. Gladstone regretted, most preachers relied in the defence of the truth upon " reticence and reviling," Dr. Parker met Mr. Holyoake for a three nights' discussion at Banbury. Those who attended witnessed that rare sight, two theological duellists absolutely fair to each other.   Neither gave way, but they became firm friends ever after.   When the *Daily News*, years after, started a fund for the purchase of an annuity for Mr. Holyoake, £5 promptly came from Dr. Parker, accompanied by a letter to be printed in support of the proposal.   At Dr. Parker's death Holyoake's panegyric of the great master of " public speaking and debate," to whom he had dedicated a book with that title, was so appreciative, that his rationalist friends wondered.   Fifty years before he had written words of praise of Dr. Binney, whom he found more satisfying than John Angell James, of whose church he had been a member.

In explaining his position afterwards it was clear that he had not changed.   " The first duty of a man," he wrote, " is the maintenance of his own convictions. The next is respect for those of his neighbours."

Hugh Price Hughes and Dr. Joseph Parker were both friends of the R.S.U.   When the shadow of death was already upon Mr. Hughes, this overwrought man was ready to consider how one of the Sunday afternoons at St. James's Hall could be utilized to the best advantage for pressing its claims, and his last illness and death alone prevented the completion of the arrangements.

With Dr. Parker our link was the cripple interest, and details will be given when the part of the book dealing with them is reached.   Some time ago an enterprising publisher conceived the idea of collecting opinions on postcards from various divines having home and foreign interests, upon the question : " Where is Christian effort most needed."   Dr. Parker's reply was—" One mile radius from the London Stock Exchange as a centre."

With this view we concur, if allowed an extended radius.

The Archdeacon of London is an old and valued friend. His testimony is as hearty now as it was years ago, when through the Baroness Burdett-Coutts he first became acquainted with the work. A portion from a speech of his will fittingly close this chapter.

" Those who have studied the matter know that ragged school institutions have conferred the utmost benefit on the country, and that not only on the children themselves, but also on those who have followed your example in giving the benefit of free education. You were the forerunners in this as in many other forms of discriminatory benevolence and philanthropy. But I am aware that all this may be conceded frankly by some who still maintain that, great as the benefits of ragged school work have been, they are not necessary and important now. With such I join issue at once, and ask them if they have considered the rapid growth of London ? Do they bear in mind that the population is increasing at an enormous rate, in leaps and bounds, and that the Metropolis is growing with such prodigious speed that all the ordinary agencies of church and chapel put together are wholly insufficient to cope with the difficulties they have to encounter ? The population grows faster than our machinery for spiritual work can do. Moreover, where there is such a large and varied population as is to be found in this province of bricks, depend upon it there will always be amongst these five millions, whole areas occupied by the poor, thriftless, shiftless classes many of whom may be classed as drunkards, convicts, criminals of all kinds, and, apart even from the respectable poor, the children of these people need your attention and tender care if they·are to be saved from growing up like their unhappy parents. Not least among the national benefits conferred by the R.S.U. is the opportunity it has given for fraternization in social work to men of differing creeds."

THE LATE MRS. PARKER'S LITTLE CRIPPLE FRIEND.

CHAPTER X

The Work Matured

Period I.   1844–1851

" We have devised and organized a system of prevention,
by which to stop crime while it is in the seed, and sin before
it has broken into flower and desolated society."—Lord
Shaftesbury, 1851.

THE founding of the Ragged School Union, considered in relation to its full meaning as a present
day and future social force, is not a proprietary privilege,
but a partnership.   There were four collaborators, of
whom one survives, and he was the earliest worker.
Mr. S. R. Starey was the man who coaxed, argued and
cajoled the leaders of twenty Sunday ragged schools
into the view that there was some gain to be expected
from combining.   To bring them together he had
some labour apart from that expended upon persuasion.
Antecedent to *founding* a union there needed to be a
finding of schools.   This he effected by going into poor
neighbourhoods, making friends with children, and asking if they attended Sunday schools.   Then, when confidence had been gained by the bestowal of coppers, he
was led to some little school to whose officers he was
able to explain his purpose.   " His was the first name my
eye ever rested upon as engaged in the work of ragged

schools," said Lord Shaftesbury, in 1859; "and from
that hour to this we have been associates, and he
has lived to see the schools in London rise from four
to 140."

When he had something tangible to offer, Lord
Shaftesbury was asked to head the amalgamation. He
did so, and brought with him all his child-championing
prestige, and by his personality alone, before he had
done a stroke, widened the outlook enormously. The
other two men who completed the quartette were Mr.
William Locke and Mr. Joseph George Gent. Mr.
Starey's contribution of effort, so far as London is
concerned, was not continuous, so may be dealt with
now. To give the work visible form and place it under
a great leader was not all he was destined to do before
he left London for Nottingham. In 1854, Lord Shaftesbury was able to say of the Ragged School Union, "I
rejoice in it, because it is a great lay society in which
the laity come forward not only to claim, but to exercise, their great and inalienable right. They bow with
deference to the clergy; they rejoice in the advice, in
the counsel, in the protection, as it were, of the ministers of religion; but the laity do claim, and, claiming,
they will assert, and asserting, they will exercise their
inalienable right, not only to read, but to teach the
Word of God." Ten years previously he would not
have said so much. A London clergyman advanced
the proposition that he had a right to be consulted
before a ragged school should be started in his parish,
and that, should he object, his veto should be final.
Lord Shaftesbury was a Churchman, and thought the
clergyman was right in his contention. It was a point
that could not be conceded; and Lord Shaftesbury,
before he had well begun, felt he must resign. In a

personal and private interview Mr. Starey won his lordship to a different view. Laymen had not lost

SEVEN YEARS' INCREASE IN THE NUMBER
OF AFFILIATED SCHOOLS.

1844	5	6	7	8	9	50	-	
							■	110
						■	■	105
						■	■	100
					■	■	■	95
					■	■	■	90
				■	■	■	■	85
				■	■	■	■	80
				■	■	■	■	75
				■	■	■	■	70
				■	■	■	■	65
			■	■	■	■	■	60
			■	■	■	■	■	55
			■	■	■	■	■	50
		■	■	■	■	■	■	45
		■	■	■	■	■	■	40
		■	■	■	■	■	■	35
		■	■	■	■	■	■	30
	■	■	■	■	■	■	■	25
■	■	■	■	■	■	■	■	20
■	■	■	■	■	■	■	■	15
■	■	■	■	■	■	■	■	10
■	■	■	■	■	■	■	■	5

EACH COMPLETE BLACK SQUARE
REPRESENTS FIVE INSTITUTIONS.

their rights because ecclesiastical conditions in the fourth century had seemed to give the clergy an opportunity to wrest them from their grasp. Robert Raikes had brooked no clerical supervision or control, although he taught the Church catechism and took his school children to church. Hannah Moore took the same position, and, though a devout Churchwoman, risked the penalties of an ecclesiastical court to maintain it. In fine, Mr. Starey's defence was based upon the same argument as that advanced by a Church layman of our own day : " The clergy are not despotic chieftains of a local clan, but Christ's Ambassadors and Ministers of State for His world-wide kingdom, whose ' equality, liberty, fraternity' are righteousness, peace and joy in the Holy Ghost." [1]

The earl yielded, and thus the nearest approach to a "religious difficulty" the movement has known vanished into thin air. Not long afterwards, for the first time in his life, he presided at a Dissenters' meeting at Vernon Chapel, King's Cross.

When Mr. Starey went to Nottingham he took the same position with Archdeacon Davis, afterwards a firm friend, with respect to a ragged school he founded there. The Archdeacon wished the name to be Trinity Church Ragged School, but Mr. Starey named it after the town. This attitude has never caused friction within the movement since.

John Macgregor was able to write in 1854 :—
" Here we meet on the broad platform of Scriptural education, and all distinctions are forgotten which could ever interfere with our object ; and though far from being less anxious to uphold the various com-

---

[1] *The Responsibility of the Layman in the Church.* J. H. Cockburn, Barrister-at-Law ; Lay Reader, Diocese of York, S.P.C.K., 1901.

munities we are attached to, our faith is thus declared to be one, and our hands are knit together.

The beginnings of the Ragged School Union were seemingly insignificant. On April 11, 1844, four men met and prayed about the matter at a private house just off the Gray's Inn Road—No. 17, Ampton Street. They were Mr. Locke, a woollen-draper ; Mr. Moulton, a dealer in second-hand tools ; Mr. Morrison, a City Missionary, and Mr. Starey.

At this little gathering the following resolution was framed :—

" That to give permanence, regularity and vigour to existing Ragged Schools, and to promote the formation of new ones throughout the metropolis, it is advisable to call a meeting of superintendents, teachers and others interested in these schools for this purpose."

A meeting was accordingly held at a school in Streatham Street, St. Giles ; but the first public annual meeting was held on June 10, 1845, at the old concert hall in Store Street, Tottenham Court Road. The first reports are largely devoted to the discoveries by City Missionaries of the depravity and ignorance of the people. In this there is a recognition of the schools that have been working for some years, one in particular with an average attendance of 250, through which no less than 5,783 children had already passed. The germ of the day school is seen in the regret that as yet the infant society has no money for daily teachers. The great advance of the movement through the birth of the Union is indicated in the definite formulation of the basis of the work : " The grand fundamental doctrines of the Gospel alone." A pamphlet, called " The Perils of the Nation," is quoted in the first report as asserting that there are 100,000 untaught children in London, and 50,000 juvenile paupers in the workhouses.

The first journalistic help had already come from *Chambers' Journal*. That magazine was endeavouring to arouse interest by a series of articles.

None of the schools, not even the largest, seem to have had 300 scholars, yet one school had forty-five children who were, or had been in jail.

No less an enterprise did the Ragged School Union introduce to an astonished public than the fitting up of a school for 150 children at a cost of £35, more than half its first year's income, but it seeks to conciliate the critical with the assurance that it will only take £6 annually to run.

Another gain to the cause beyond what has been already mentioned was the publicity the first report gave to the difficulties of the teachers. The committee hoped that something would be done for a school, held in a room fifteen feet square, into which from fifty to sixty children and ten teachers were crowded. Some sat on the hob with their heads partly up the chimney. Such were the chief points in the first report. After that a quick growth is noticeable. In a very few years great strides were made. Lord Shaftesbury, just before he took up this work, had been enfranchised for service in a painful way. His opponents had at last brought it home to him that agricultural labourers' children had a case against landowners as well as factory children against manufacturers, and that on his father's estate things were as bad as anywhere.

He made a speech in which he said " he did not care to defend, while he did not wish to blame." For this he was turned out of his father's house. But that very fact brought him up to a definite point in his experience.

He was now the pledged champion of all poor children.
He was also freed from parliamentary duty soon after,

SEVEN YEARS' INCREASE IN THE NUMBER OF
VOLUNTARY SCHOLARS.

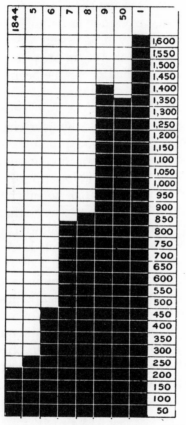

EACH COMPLETE OBLONG REPRESENTS
50 TEACHERS.

and during a brief period of liberty helped the cause
with his pen in the monthlies and quarterlies. Things

seemed past the worst. There was no longer the hopeless tone in the utterances of public men such as found expression in the words of Doctor Arnold, of Rugby, just before his death in 1842. He said " That all the worst evils of slavery and heathenism are existing among ourselves," and yet for him there was " the bitterest of all griefs, to see clearly and yet be able to do nothing." The country was really progressing. Sir Robert Peel had brought in the Bank Act, in 1844, to guard against financial troubles. Then came the beginnings of Free Trade in 1846. But as a nation we were plunging in railway speculation. The cost of production was greatly enhanced because the system was being " rushed " by speculators and promoters.

From 1845 to 1847 there was an enormous sinking of money in railway building, amounting to no less than £90,000,000. An investment of so much, in works of public utility but slow return, was more than the finance of the country could stand. Followed as it was by speculation and then bad harvests in England, a failure of the potato crop in Ireland, and a short cotton crop in America, matters were well nigh as bad as they could be. Raw materials were dear ; prices of necessaries rose two and threefold. Workers were discharged on all hands in England. Millions in Ireland were starving. Fortunately, wheat dropped from 102s. to 48s. a quarter. Though tens of thousands of workpeople were starving in the winter of 1846, yet a departure from the provisions of its charter by the Bank of England in the issue of more paper currency than sound finance allows, together with the fortunate discovery of gold in California, enabled the country to quickly recover. But the matter did not end here. Paris, Amsterdam, Frankfort and New York felt the counterstroke. A revolutionary movement followed on the Continent. The Pope was chased from Rome, the Emperor of Austria from Vienna, the Italian princes from their duchies, and the German rulers from their principalities. In Poland, Naples and Sardinia, too, there had been sanguinary struggles. This terrible wave of revolution that began through an English commercial crisis swept Europe first and then approached these shores. It seemed as though the dreaded Day of Destruction had come at last. But just as the wave curled to the break, the mighty onrush of its deep currents was caught and broken by unseen groynes and breakwaters, and its surface broke into the comparatively harmless spray of the Chartist riots. There are still living, men who think it was a shower of rain, and the special constables that saved us. It was probably the effects of the eighteenth century revival of religion, together with corn-law repeal. The middle and artisan classes were disposed to think, and though for a time there had been an alliance between Free Traders and Chartists, when the news of the excesses of the French working-men reached this country all hopes of combined action were gone. The physical force party were deserted. Unled and unsupported by organizing brains their ranks melted at the first collision. Economic prosperity following immediately afterwards, the keen edge of discontent was blunted.

The collapse of Chartism was so little expected that explanations of all kinds were offered. Lord Shaftesbury thought it a by-product of the ragged school movement and its influences in the great towns of the country. At the annual meeting in 1849, the late Duke of Argyll gave expression to the haunting fear that was in the minds of many of the aristocracy and people of wealth--

" There is one ground upon which these ragged schools have been recommended—the safety of our own Society. We have been passing through one of the greatest crises in the history of the world.   Thank God, we have hitherto passed through it safely, and I trust we may pass through what remains of it safely too.   Those who were on the continent of Europe during the convulsions of the past year, and those who are in the great cities of the continent at the present moment will tell you that it is astonishing and mysterious where those creatures of misery and crime that haunt the streets during every political revolution can come from ; they will tell you that they never saw such faces in quiet times, and that they know not whence they came.   I have heard some say that.such faces could not be produced in England ; but I advise you not to believe this too readily."

The earl had in his speech, which he was making when the duke arrived, been very emphatic in his praise of the schools.   " I do not scruple to say that the existence of these institutions, aided by the frequent visitations—by the increased intercourse of the poorer with the wealthier classes—mainly contributed in the past year to keep this metropolis in peace, while the whole world around us was in the throes of convulsion."

Although we may be of opinion that this was an over estimate at such an early date as 1848, yet the very fact that it could be said at all and be received with applause by a middle-class audience of thousands is significant.   It shows that in five years the work had gained acceptance in the public mind as a social force. The President was in good form that night, his opening remark being that the Institution was " now about to take its just and proper footing—just and proper

indeed, if that deserves the claim which is directed to
all that is great and good in humanity and religion."
He had every reason for his hopefulness. There had

SEVEN YEARS' INCREASE IN THE NUMBER OF
SUNDAY SCHOLARS.

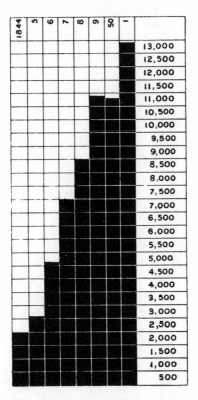

	1844	5	6	7	8	9	50	1	
								■	13,000
								■	12,500
								■	12,000
								■	11,500
					■	■	■	■	11,000
						■	■	■	10,500
						■	■	■	10,000
						■	■	■	9,500
						■	■	■	9,000
				■	■	■	■	■	8,500
				■	■	■	■	■	8,000
				■	■	■	■	■	7,500
			■	■	■	■	■	■	7,000
			■	■	■	■	■	■	6,500
			■	■	■	■	■	■	6,000
			■	■	■	■	■	■	5,500
			■	■	■	■	■	■	5,000
		■	■	■	■	■	■	■	4,500
		■	■	■	■	■	■	■	4,000
		■	■	■	■	■	■	■	3,500
		■	■	■	■	■	■	■	3,000
		■	■	■	■	■	■	■	2,500
	■	■	■	■	■	■	■	■	2,000
	■	■	■	■	■	■	■	■	1,500
	■	■	■	■	■	■	■	■	1,000
	■	■	■	■	■	■	■	■	500

EACH COMPLETE SQUARE
REPRESENTS 500 SCHOLARS.

been an extraordinary financial advance. The sub-
script.ns had increased nearly fourfold and the

donations nearly sixfold in one year. Her Majesty and the Prince Consort had given £100 ; the Government were paying all expenses for 150 emigrant children ; and the Lord Mayor held a meeting at the Guildhall to provide funds to build a central refuge. Lord Shaftesbury for a little while had the ear of Society until, in 1850, by opposing Sunday labour in the Post Office, he made himself " the most unpopular man in the kingdom." The Sovereign had always been friendly, but now he was regarded as an adviser in social matters by the royal pair. " The Queen has sent for me to talk over the condition of the working people " is an entry in his diary just after the Chartist riots.

A morning's walk and chat in the grounds at Osborne resulted in a visit in full State to the rookeries of the Dials by the Prince Consort to inspect some of the worst dwellings for himself. From that time onwards the subject of industrial dwellings had the deepest interest for him, an interest which his son as Prince of Wales inherited. 1849 was a terrible year for the street-trading classes, not only because of the ravages of cholera amongst them, but also because few people would buy of them for fear of the disease. The primitive drainage of that time and the defective water supply have already been referred to ; another cause of sanitary evils was the window-tax. It was 8s. 3d. a window. It made an annual difference of £5 1s. on a twelve-roomed house, if the builder provided for a draught of air through the rooms of each storey.

A witness before the Health of Towns Commission, 1844, said : " If the Commissioners would examine personally the houses in which the poor live in the close courts and alleys of the metropolis they would be surprised at the number of dark staircases and filthy holes which, although on upper floors, are quite as ill-ventilated and unfavourable to health as the cellars of Liverpool." Yet the teachers, well aware of the risks they ran, not only continued their work, but induced others to join them, in 1849. By the next year the voluntary teaching staff showed the most remarkable

BOOT-BLACK.

increase it had known since the beginning. There was an increase of one-third.

Meanwhile the various agencies for dealing with the physical condition, moral training and industrial equipment of the children, and the operations for bringing influences helpful to growth into the atmosphere of their family lives were coming into existence, and in the most advanced schools being brought to a high state of efficiency. Throughout the movement the idea had emerged by 1851 that a ragged school was an all-the-week-round work, something that first enveloped young life as a preservative and then permeated it with a stimulating love. By 1851 the Ragged School movement was matured, the last operation of the first septennial period being the launching of the shoe-black brigade. That simple link connects us with the ideals of the Royal Family in the middle of the nineteenth century, so pathetically similar to those of the Czar and Czarina of our day. The Queen and Prince Consort hoped as much from their Industrial Exhibition as did the Czar from the Peace Conference at The Hague. There was a real expectation that wars might be no more. The disillusionment of the Crimean War was parallel to that of the present year. But war was not in sight in 1851. All the obstacles to the Exhibition had been surmounted; the *Times* had thundered against, and *Punch* made fun of the idea in vain. The opposition was so great and so influential that " nothing but a great success could have saved it," and that success it had. The presence of the shoe-blacks at the opening of the Great Exhibition was the occasion of an eloquent reference to it at the annual meeting by a Nonconformist minister, which makes a fitting conclusion to this chapter :—

" That beautiful spectacle—where our Queen was present, enshrined in the affections of the people— better than bayonets—with the chief minister of religion, the noblest prelate that ever wore a mitre—I say that spectacle will not be new, but will be reflected and repeated in innumerable parts of the land ; and it will show to us that if this Christianity of ours ascends till it lends its charm to her who sits upon the throne, and

consecrates the opening of that great commercial and
artistic display—it at the same time descends into the
cellars and brings out of those subterranean mines
gems that will match the brightest in the diadem of
Queen Victoria."

CHAPTER XI

The R.S.U. and Education

" The eels which are in the mud the Government have been trying to catch with nets, and they have caught nothing but the fish that swim. The conductors of ragged schools alone have gone into the mud, and they have caught the eels."— SIR THOMAS CHAMBERS, Q.C., 1861.

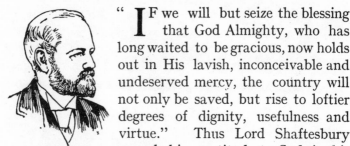

QUINTIN HOGG, FATHER OF POLYTECHNICS.

" IF we will but seize the blessing that God Almighty, who has long waited to be gracious, now holds out in His lavish, inconceivable and undeserved mercy, the country will not only be saved, but rise to loftier degrees of dignity, usefulness and virtue." Thus Lord Shaftesbury records his gratitude to God, in his diary, for the reception accorded to his speech in the House on February 28, 1843.

He had made a comprehensive claim for the children's rights at the hands of the nation, in a moving oration that for a time turned his enemies into friends.

On this date he had moved an address to the Crown praying Her Majesty " to take into her instant and serious consideration the best means of diffusing

178

the benefits and blessings of a moral and religious education amongst the working classes of her people."

Many of the public men of the day were ready and willing to do something in the matter. Attempts indeed had been made by successive Governments but any proposal of an effective nature invariably raised " the religious question," and had to be abandoned.

On the crest of the wave of genuine emotion that the Earl's speech produced in the House of Commons and in the country, an educational measure for factory children was introduced by the Government.

Everything promised well at the moment, and the Earl seemed justified in his hopefulness.

The condition of education was indeed a scandal, ten years previously the numbers of those who could read or write being only one in fourteen of the whole population, as against one in three in New York, one in six in Prussia, one in seven in Switzerland, and one in nine in Holland. Little had been done to alter this state of things in the meantime.

The Committee of the Privy Council on Education had indeed been formed two years after the Queen came to the Throne. It did not come into being, however, without violent opposition from the Lords, but the Queen would not agree with them. This small step in the right direction had been taken, and the annual grant for education had been brought up to the magnificent sum of £30,000 in the same year that £70,000, was voted for the royal stables. By 1844 no further progress had been made except that the grant had been increased to £40,000, the Budget for that year amounting to £55,000,000. This money was divided in no very ideal fashion between the two sets of voluntary schools, British and National, Unsectarian and

Church of England respectively. For these we may not be ungrateful, for apart from the Sunday school they were all the country had, and they did a good and useful work. Yet it must be confessed that they were deplorably inadequate. The provision made by the two school societies for the training of teachers was of the slightest, and the pay was so small that the best teachers left the profession. The Sunday schools being much more numerous, and free into the bargain, supplied a great want in a very limited way. One lesson a week in reading could not mean rapid progress, even for the brightest. Writing was regarded in many of them as too secular an occupation for Sunday.

An impression gained ground in Chartist times that nothing would under any circumstances be done in the matter of education by the State.

Lord Shaftesbury had abundant grounds, therefore, for rejoicing in the prospect of schools for factory children. But his satisfaction was premature. The old difficulty presented itself again. The Sunday School Union organized an agitation which caused the Government to withdraw the Bill. So within four months of that hopeful entry in the diary he wrote again—

"Another failure then, and yet I am not disheartened. A few thoughts and regrets may be given (and pardoned) to those miserable thousands, who might have been brought within the pale of physical and moral regeneration. God be their helper."

Although he was a Churchman, and therefore unlikely to view the protest of the dissenting party quite dispassionately, especially as it had been the means of depriving poor children of a great blessing, he had a shrewd idea that there was something to be said perhaps in defence of the wreckers.

DAY SCHOOL SCHOLARS, 20 YEARS' INCREASE PRECEDING
RECORD YEAR.

1849	54	59	64	69	
					25 000
					24,000
					23,000
					22,000
					21,000
					20,000
					19,000
					18,000
					17,000
					16,000
					15,000
					14,000
					13,000
					12,000
					11,000
					10,000
					9,000
					8,000
					7,000
					6,000
					5,000
					4,000
					3,000
					2,000
					1,000

EACH COMPLETE BLACK SQUARE
REPRESENTS 1,000 SCHOLARS.

Note—Evening class figures not yet dissociated from day
school figures.

Sir Robert Peel, an earnest friend of education, wrote him—" It is but a sorry and lamentable triumph that Dissent has achieved." But the Earl's reply was a guarded one ; it indicated suspension of judgment, while it went right home to the heart of the subject.

" Wherever the fault lay, one thing was quite clear —that the really suffering parties were the vast body of neglected children who, as present appearances went, were now consigned to an eternity of ignorance."

But as this door closed, another opened. It was not through the factory children of the north, but the slum children of London and the great towns that the experiments that ultimately resulted in a national system of education were to be made. Just after his great disappointment, Lord Shaftesbury became acquainted through an advertisement in *The Times* with the first school that was called a ragged school, that is to say, the words a school for the ragged were abbreviated into ragged school. He was soon afterwards asked to be president of the few whose conductors thought there might be some gain in combining, and then the rapid evolution of the educational side began, as already described.

In a very few years the united labours of these schools presented a phenomenon of much interest to the thoughtful. A system of elementary education giving good results was in action, among the most unpromising of the juvenile population, among a class that most people thought quite hopeless material.

To understand how this would be viewed is not easy in the year 1904. Sixty years ago there was a large body of opinion opposed to anything and everything likely to benefit the masses, having its origin in fear

of the people. Lord John Russell's statement in
regard to the Reform Bill, that it was a final measure,
makes amusing reading now, but it shows what appre-
hensions he had to allay. The midnight visit to a
church belfry by the Tennysons to furiously ring the
bells when it had passed, indicates how important they
regarded the victory. This reactionary party was
still very strong for many decades later. The wars
with France were England's official protest not merely
against the excesses that disfigured the Revolution,
but against its essential teaching. That lesson was
that the people of France had determined that three
per cent. of the nation should no longer use the other
ninety-seven for their own benefit, and oppress them
in doing so.

Those who doubted whereunto this might grow,
wished the people kept ignorant. Some of our best
men—poets, preachers, and one or two statesmen—
hailed the coming of man into his own which the
nineteenth century exhibited, with delight. To Cole-
ridge it was " Slumbering Freedom roused by High
Disdain." Wordsworth shared the feeling, but with
more restraint, while Burns taught men of British
blood to dare to be poor. Robert Hall, the Nonconformist divine, justified the French and appealed for
educational provision for the English working-classes.
Lord Brougham and Sir Robert Peel did all they could
to prepare the nation for great economic and social
changes along the same lines. Though it was an
influential group who took this attitude it was not a
large one. The governing and moneyed classes generally would endorse the sentiments of one of the London
newspapers upon Mechanics' Institutes when they
were founded. It said " that no better scheme, for

the destruction of the Empire, could have been devised by the author of evil himself." We are not surprised, therefore, that many working-men, in a confessor-like spirit, did educate themselves to a very high standard. Chartism took the form of a defiant self-culture with not a few, just as Bible-study gained a stimulus at one time from State prohibition.

The spirit of the period may be gathered from a newspaper advertisement—

" Wanted, a servant as valet and groom ; he must be a small, clean, civil man, and near forty, as a remarkably steady man is required ; one who can neither read nor write, and a Scotchman who does not drink preferred."

It was under such conditions that the public were asked to support an educational provision for the children of the poorest and most disreputable classes in London.

It is not possible to gauge the standard of education given in the schools. It could not be fairly brought into comparison with anything we have to-day. It had its own conditions, and the masters, mistresses, and monitors did wonders, all things considered. The nearest approach to a standard for measurement would be the output of the British and National schools at the same periods. Such things as are to the credit of these schools exist chiefly in the memories of people of advancing years among the working-classes, who stoutly aver that a better education for a poor man's child was given in them than in the Board schools of the present day. Allowing for their partiality, it may be in a degree true. The absence of school appliances kept the scholars concentrated on fewer things. Those subjects in which they were well grounded have been practically the only ones they have needed in the business of their narrow lives. There was as well an outlook on the world and human duty in relation to it, which was a very valuable part of the teaching. This has in a measure been lost, or at least been less emphasized, in the teaching of children during the past thirty years.

The ragged school would be a grade lower than either British or National, both as regards apparatus

GEORGE YARD RAGGED SCHOOL, WHITECHAPEL.

and the acquirements of the staff, but quite as good a rudimentary education might be given, and probably was given in them. It is observable that wherever one of the old educational ragged schools used to be, the adults of the locality were not in the least behind their boys and girls of fifteen or sixteen in educational attainments.

Just at the present time, criticism of the National schools is very general, but it should be remembered that up till now their supporters have been relieving the taxpayer of part of his burden. One of the many controversialists endeavouring to make a case for a particular view on education prints the following : It is given as a piece of work done in a National school by a child of average intelligence in an inspected school in 1855, as a reply to the question : " What is thy duty towards God ? "

"My duty toads God is to bleed in Him, to fering and to loaf withold your arts, withold my mine, withold my sold, and with my sernth, to whirchip and give thanks, to put my old trash in Him, to call upon Him, to onner His old name and His world, and to save him truly all the days of my life's end."

But this could not be a fair sample of composition among the working-classes in 1855. If it were, the following would not have appeared in *Household Words* in 1855. The bad spelling would not be humorous in general. Besides all which, the writer admits he left school early, and it is clear from his age that his school days must have been spent somewhere about the year 1815.

"SIR,—

" I have seen an advertisement for a Master and Matron for the Workhouse. Now I mean to try for the Job if you think Sir, that I can manage the buisness I will leave it to your judgement wether I can do, and whether is it any use for me to try because there will be many otherers I supose now you see my hand writeing it is rather bad and you can ges wat I can tolk of englis as for irish let me a lone for it I am 48 yeare of age and my wife is 46 shee can so and net and she had far beter educasion than I ever had, I was a

farmer for 30 years in the same farm that my Father
and Grand Father was, payd all the rents in the dwe
years, I sold all my stock for America and went to
Liverpool and my wife went poorly and we put back
her i am now doing nothing as for a caritor I dont
now what to say I am a member of the calvin methodist
church and was chost as a Diacon 15 yeare ago, and I
wel poove oll wat I say and will put £200 down for my
honesty. I have no acwintance with your gwardians
a tol   I wil leve it to you   I have a couson I dont now
whether he belongs to your Uunion or not, all that I
am afraid is of making the acconts yp   I can work
single rul of three but I ama afraid of Practice,

"Now Sir i wil leve it to you, and if you please show
this to som of the Gwardians.   I dont now the names
of either of them.   Be so good as to send me few lines
wether you think better for me to try or not and you
think there will be   sum   chance I will Come to the
milling on the 10th of this month

                    "I am your obedient Sarvant

                                   .   .   .

    "Direct as follows . . .
    "oll wat I say is in ernest, and in my own hand
writing and my own words and Langwage   Look
inside for the Stamp."

To use the previous quotation as an indictment of
the teaching given, would be as unfair as to regard the
facsimile frontispiece of Miss Honnor Morton's pamphlet, *Consider the Children*,[1] as a sample of the general
output of the School Boards.   Miss Morton, formerly
a member of the London Board, says this autograph
performance—

    "Our frontispiece is only a specimen of what girls in

    [1] *Consider the Children.*   Brinsley Johnson, 1904.

the fifth standard, just leaving school, can make of a song in which they have been no doubt thoroughly trained—

> They scour the coin blossams
> And boiled them away

is a cruelly suggestive paraphrase for—

> I culled the coy blossoms
> And bore them away.

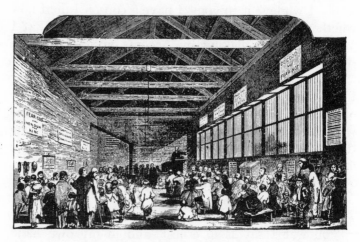

GRAY'S INN LANE RAGGED SCHOOL.

This kind of thing is still possible after the education authority in London has been thirty years at work, having had at its disposal of late years more money annually than the entire national Budget for all purposes of such countries as Denmark, Norway, or Switzerland amounts to."

It cannot be claimed that a great number of ragged school masters and mistresses held high certificates. Their work did not demand them. The qualities they needed were of a different order than extreme educational proficiency. At one of those junctures when superior persons suggested that all the children in ragged day schools should be sent to the National schools of London, Canon Cadman, who knew and was interested in both, came forward as defending counsel for the ragged schools—" The National school system did not suit the case of those whom ragged schools sought to benefit," he said. As between the two there was this difference in all-round appliances for touching a wild and much-tempted nature, and also catering for the family of which he was a member.

National School.	Ragged School.
A Day School.	A Day School.
A Sunday School (not always).	A Sunday School.
	Sunday Evening Service (for youths).
	Band of Hope.
	Clothing Club.
	Drum and Fife Band.
	Adult Services.
	A Prayer-Meeting (in the week).
	An open-air Service.
	Mothers' Meeting.
	Mothers' Bible Class.
	Temperance Meeting.
	Provident and Benefit Clubs.

It would be a well-organized school that contained all these, but all schools would have some of them, and most would be aiming to possess these agencies.

The following are a few of the Canon's points—" The rope which the National school let down the mine was not long enough to reach the bottom."

" Some ragged schools were feeders to the paying

schools. He knew one that in a very short period sent seventy-five children to a school of higher grade."

Moreover, "he could produce ragged school-children who were able to read as correctly, and with as true emphasis, if not better, than some of the children who were taught in National schools." In addition to this, the common elements of education, such as reading and cyphering, were also imparted.

These early teachers taught well all that they had the chance of teaching, but as they had to adjust their lessons to terrible conditions of child-life, it had to be judged by the surroundings. Sir Thomas Chambers sketched one of these pupils, without an exaggerating touch, as "a wild lad, perhaps without father or mother, without home or hope, in the streets of London, untutored and savage, not used to restraint, abhorring to be under cover for an hour together, yet brought to school," and he very properly asked, "where was the Government agency that could work a miracle like this, next only to a miracle of creation."

The largest factor in the work was the unseen one of moral support, stimulus, and discipline, for a hard battle.

This work continued and was necessary till 1891, when school fees were abolished, and the School Board had gradually been able to assimilate the scholars with those they had.

A little incident that Dr. Guthrie records as occurring in a Scotch ragged school illustrates the kind of influences the children came under, and how valuable they were in forming character.

"We'll stop if you'll no *lick* us, Sir,—if you'll no gi'e us *palmies*."

" Boys, were you ever punished before ? and why ? "

" Because we deserved it."

" And don't you deserve it now ?   Take it, and be done with it."

After trying them in this manner for some time, without any success, Mr. Gibb addressed them in a

DIAGRAM REPRESENTING THE NUMBER OF SCHOOL-
MASTERS AND MISTRESSES EMPLOYED 20 YEARS AFTER
THE SCHOOL BOARD CAME INTO EXISTENCE.

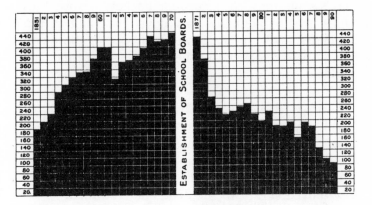

EACH COMPLETE BLACK SQUARE REPRESENTS 20 PAID TEACHERS.

farewell speech, suited to the taste, and calibre, and character, of those he spoke to, saying,—

(It should be explained that these four boys were the ringleaders in a school rebellion, and were about to receive the punishment that a law of the boys' own making assigned.   Stampedes of the entire school frequently occurring, something had to be done.)

" Well, then, boys, I think I have done ;—I can do nothing for you ;—I dare not let you pass.   You are going away, and it may be that I will never see you more. Perhaps I will see you rich and respectable men. Perhaps I will see you masters of a fine shop, standing behind the counter, with your hair nicely curled, and dressed like gentlemen. Or, may be, when I am an old man, and walk leaning on a staff, I will see you rolling by in a fine carriage, drawn by two grey horses, attended by grand servants, and a beautiful lady seated by your side ; and when you see me, you will say, ' Look, there's the ragged school master, that used to lick us when we were laddies : here, Mr. Gibb there's something to keep your pocket.' Now, these things may be ; but ah ! my boys, I much fear that if ever I see you riding, it will be in one of those dark gloomy carriages, with the locked door and iron gratings, conveying you—you know where to ! "

" Yes, Sir."

" And is it not likely, if you go away from the school, that you will be obliged to sink to begging again ? And then your next step down will be to stealing ; and down and down you go."

After shaking hands all round, weeping bitterly, they moved slowly to the door—but returned.

Lord Shaftesbury on one occasion displayed to the audience at an R.S.U. meeting a long strip of paper measuring seven feet. It represented the sinister record of a convict. It was a list of his offences from the age of ten to thirty, when he expiated his crimes by being hanged at Norfolk Island, His lordship's comment upon it may fittingly bring this chapter to a close.

" All this was the work of one single man, one man alone thus distressed and ravaged society. I say that if it had been instrumental in saving society from but a dozen such men as that—and I believe it has saved

Society from hundreds and thousands—the ragged
school system would have earned the prize and gratitude of the Statesmen that do rule, and of all the
Statesmen that shall be called to rule, the destinies of
this mighty Empire."

PORTRAIT OF MR. R. J. CURTIS.

CHAPTER XII

The R.S.U. and Industrialism

"One poor fellow said to me—' We have not a chance, sir.' "What tradesman will take them into his shop, or what mistress into her kitchen ? They are shut out from all honest employment. They will not starve ; they must steal. Society, having first neglected, now shakes off the drowning wretches : they sink, and no wonder."—*Seed-time and Harvest*. Dr. Guthrie

"**I**NTELLECTUAL teaching is feeble in the work of reformation," says John Macgregor in his book entitled *Ragged Schools : their Rise, Progress, and Results*. " The hand and the eye must be taught to work as well as the head stored with book-learning, and a school which has no Industrial Class leaves an essential part of the engine of improvement unemployed.

" In fifty of our ragged schools of London there are Industrial Classes (1855). The number of children employed there is about 2,000 ; but their example and influence is extended through five times that number of scholars, and generally they impart a healthy tone to the institutions themselves.

" Boys are instructed by masters in tailoring and shoemaking, making and mending the clothes of their school, or the articles made are sometimes sold at low prices. Wood-chopping is another employment in which many are engaged, and the faggots thus prepared for firewood are bought by those interested in the school."

Horse-hair picking, carpentry, matmaking, knitting fishermen's nets, paper-bag printing, and ornamental leather work are referred to as being occupations of

IPSWICH.   MAT-MAKING.

the scholars at this time. For the girls there was sewing, knitting and embroidery.

The workers were hard put to it to find openings in life for these children. It should be remembered that an enormous economic change has taken place. Whereas it used to be difficult to get work for children leaving school, it is now different. It is the adult over forty who feels industrial pressure now.

In the old days it was rightly considered that the entire work was a failure unless a start in life was secured. So any and every means were tried.

One of the avenues to industrial life was boot-blacking. The Shoeblack Brigade was started in 1851 at the great international exhibition. The year 1854 saw the formation of two other Shoeblack Societies, the East and South London, and in 1857 the movement had further spread, and the North-West London, West Kent, West London, Islington, Notting Hill, Kensington, and Stratford Societies had sprung into existence. All these were founded for the employment of scholars from the ragged schools in London and its vicinity, and were based upon the same principles, and governed in the main by the same rules as the original, and as it is now called, the Central Red Shoeblack Society.

The conditions of London labour having so changed, the object of these societies is changed also. The aim is now to provide discipline and instruction for those who are getting their living in the streets and who, but for these societies, would have no instruction or control at all.

One result is the provision of a home for the homeless boys, and a Sunday school, as well as a regular week-day evening instruction at their premises.

In 1874 the Central Reds obtained a building lease in Great Saffron Hill, Farringdon Street, and a home was built at a cost of £4,000. It was opened by Lord Shaftesbury. The schoolroom holds 100, and there is sleeping accommodation for 44. Apart from the superintendent's apartments, there is a coffee-room, bath, and gymnasium. The rest of the boys employed, return at night to the homes of their parents or friends.

Upon entering, the Society provides uniform and outfit ; renewals of these are paid for from his earnings. The boys rise at 6 o'clock in the summer and 6.30 in the winter.   Then breakfast follows after prayers, and

IPSWICH.   YOUNG FIREWOOD SELLERS.

the lads disperse to their stations.   During the day the superintendent and his assistants get round to the stations to see that the boys are on duty.   A temptation to the lads is to relieve tedium by extra meals. At 5 in the winter and 6.30 in the summer the boys come home and hand over the day's takings. A daily account is kept with each boy, and the money is applied upon the following system : He keeps sixpence for dinner, the rest is divided into three equal parts—one-third the boy retains in addition to his sixpence, one-third is kept by the Society to meet the boy's expenses at the home, and the rest is banked for his future benefit. If his earnings any day fall below sixpence the difference is charged against his banking account. If they habitually do so he is discharged. The stations, of course, vary in money-earning opportunities. In the course of years their value has been gauged and they have been classified in three divisions : twelve of the best in the first division, fourteen in the second, and the remainder in the third. The boys are also classed in three divisions, and he has three days at each of the stations in. his division. The incentive to good behaviour is promotion to a higher division, where the takings are more.

The punishments are—

1. Fines for late hours, absence from the station or other misbehaviour.

2. Degradation from one division to a lower one for a limited period.

3. Suspension from work for a fixed time.

On the other hand, the rewards consist of—

1. Promotion from a lower to a higher division.

2. Monthly prizes of sums from 2s. to 3s. to boys who earn over a certain sum according to their division, also a prize of 1s. for the boy who earns most in each division. The school is under Government inspection, and receives a Government grant. The schoolmaster has held his present post for upwards of thirty years. On Sundays the boys have dinner at the home and go

out in the afternoon.   A morning and evening service is conducted by the superintendent and friends.

As the boys grow older they are launched in life, when the banking accounts prove very useful.   The uniforms of all the societies were—

Central London,	Red.
East London,	Blue.
South London,	Yellow.

YOUNG EXPERTS WITH THE NEEDLE AND THEIR INSTRUCTRESS.

North Western,	White.
West Kent,	Green.
West London,	Purple.
South Suburban,	Red, green facings.
Islington,	Brown, red facings.
Kensington,	Brown, purple facings.

The great names in this movement were Macgregor, Fowler, Snape and Ware.   About the same time as the Shoeblack Brigade started, efforts were put forth in other directions to give employment.   The abominable condition in which the corrupt vestries of that day

allowed the streets to remain, gave ample scope for the
sweeper. Twenty boys, under the title of broomers,
were employed one winter in the streets to clean down
the fronts of shops. The grant in aid only came to £1,
for the wages were £83, and the earnings from shopkeepers £82. But street-work needs supervision, and
in this case it was not possible to give it. From the
refuge in Dorchester Place girls used to go out to clean
steps and were called "steppers." "Messengers"
recruited from our schools were employed in the City
and West End, and were responsible for value of
parcels up to £3. Private firms, as well as the Electric
Telegraph and Crystal Palace Companies employed
them. In 1856 the Southwark Board of Guardians
employed seven boys as road-cleaners, selected from
South London ragged schools. They were attached
to the Shoeblack (Yellows) Brigade. They were clad
in reddish-brown jerseys with red collars ; a cape of
oilskin and a water-proof cap completed the uniform,
except for a red badge worn on the right side of the
breast, upon which the lad's number and the words
"public sweeper" appeared, worked in white beads.
Alderman Sir Robert Carden at the same time gained
permission to substitute boys from City ragged
schools to supply the places of City crossing sweepers
discharged for misconduct. From these sweepers in
direct descent are the street orderlies of to-day. Out of
another effort to provide children with work sprang
the house-boy brigade. But there are a great many
drawbacks to street occupations for poor children, so
gradually these were abandoned.

In 1847 a Juvenile Refuge and Home of Industry
was opened under the auspices of the R.S.U.,
at Old Pye Street, Westminster. It began with a

dozen boys, increasing to fifty. These were for the most part children of drunkards, . who kept body and soul together by begging and stealing. Some had been used in the disposal of base coin. Some were found to sleep at nights in sawpits, on staircases, or under the ruins of an old arch. Provision was made for eight to sleep on the premises.

Very soon a great change was seen in the appearance

CARPENTERING CLASS.

and character of these lads. The neat clothes they wore had been made by themselves, and they were hopeful and bright. The day's routine was as follows :

From 6 till 9, cleaning up by the resident lads and breakfast.

9. School opening and admission of the other boys.

9 to 9.30. Scripture, singing and prayer.

9.30 to 11.   Reading, spelling and singing.

11 to 12.30.   Arithmetic and writing.

12.30 to 1.   Dinner—bread and soup for fifty boys.

1 to 2.   A game in St. James' Park.

2 to 5.   Trades—tailoring and shoemaking.

5 to 5.30.   Tea—a piece of bread.

5.30 to 8.   Singing, geography, etc., and Scripture reading.

This enterprise, so far as it went, was in itself satisfactory, but as an object-lesson to the schools it was very valuable. It stimulated the activity of the teachers in getting the children launched, as did also the emigration efforts. The placing in situations was, after all, the best phase of this operation, because of the much larger numbers provided for. Also because institutional training for business is never quite the same as living in the work-a-day world. Institutions of any kind have also this difficulty. A market for imperfect work is not easily found. If the trades are worth anything to learn, the work of learners is poor for a long while. In a large firm the work of apprentices goes in with and is masked by the work of the men, but when all are learning the output is unmarketable. No charity could stand the expenses for very long. It accordingly gravitates to this, that the trades taken up are those which have to do with the production of goods the institution uses in quantity, or else simple industries are engaged in that are profitable, but for which no skill is needed.

It must not be forgotten, however, that the *old* problem had more than one aspect. A habit of settled living and continuous industry in the scholar was a very difficult thing to inculcate. Without it, he or she would not keep any place a week. So that, regarded from that point of view, wood-chopping and horse-hair picking would be valuable pursuits. But all these direct industrial enterprises had the value of demonstrating to ragged school friends that if all previous effort were not to be thrown away the children must have a start in life. One embarrassing thing in con-

TURNERS.

nexion with writing a book such as this in more than one direction is the absence of figures. Volunteer workers giving all their leisure to the children avoid clerical work as much as possible. Some figures they must report to qualify for grants in aid. Those are available. Outside are many matters of interest upon which very partial information is given. The securing of employment for children is one of these. Reporting this is just one of those things which a school officer may regard as a counsel of perfection, but by no means compulsory. Scientific calculation is therefore impossible, but we have data sufficient to show that a very extensive work was done. The figures of recent years do not mean as much as earlier ones, though they may be actually larger. It is no longer a feat to get a child a situation. The children are not so rough and wild, and there is a demand for youthful labour. It would be fair to take the years 1857 and 1858. In 1857 1,260 were placed out, and in 1858 1,320, but the report for the latter year says that the numbers not given in would perhaps be 1,500 more. So that in two years nearly 4,000 were put in the way of earning a livelihood in London.

Emigration was a very important feature of the work. When the pressure of the obligation to dispose of our surplus population was more keenly felt than now, there was quite a craze for a time to send young people to the Colonies.

Lord Shaftesbury obtained a grant in Parliament for a free passage and outfit for 150 scholars to Australia. The next year he was unable to get the grant renewed, although the results had been most satisfactory, so a public appeal was made and the emigration effort has ever since rested upon private philanthropy. The qualifications for a young emigrant were sound health ; regular attendance at school for six months ; ability to write a sentence from dictation ; to work the four simple rules of arithmetic ; to read fluently ; to repeat the Lord's Prayer and the Ten Commandments ; a certificate of four months' attendance at an industrial class or proof of knowledge of a practical occupation.

The last direct industrial agency on the part of the R.S.U. was the rag-collecting brigade. With

SCHOLARS' GOOD CONDUCT CERTIFICATE BEARING THE KING'S SIGNATURE AS PATRON.

efficient superintendence this might have become an important agency.   It foreshadowed one of General

Booth's proposals in his *Darkest England and the Way Out*. This agency working by means of eight trucks and forty boys at household salvage, in 1863 paid away £770 in wages.

Obtaining situations for children is one thing, inducing them to keep them is another. The institution of a prize and certificate for twelve months' steady conduct in the first situation has done a vast amount of good. When the illuminated certificates bore Lord Shaftesbury's and the Secretary's name only, they were valued, but when her late Majesty Queen Victoria added her autograph they were greatly prized. King Edward's signature is upon them now.

This narrative of ragged school work, as far as it has gone, has introduced the reader to the children, the teachers, and the agencies employed in a reforming, crime-preventing, and educating work inspired by religious zeal. There are no other broad features to exhibit that belong to what may be called the historic period. That period closes when school-fees were abolished in London Board schools. After that we have a modern period, exhibiting the same spirit, but with some entirely new manifestations.

Much that is still needed is retained of the old work, a little has been dropped, but much has been added to suit new needs.

All divisions of time in history are arbitrary, but there is a convenience in it. Now that the pith of the story of our historic period has been told, we are free after a cursory glance at the extension of the system throughout the country to glance rapidly over the years of that period. These become naturally subdivided into the group of years when the work was taking shape: From 1844 to 1851, a second period of scarcely ruffled progress up to 1870, then another twenty years of gradual adaptation and change. After that there is a conscious facing of modernity and an attack of new problems that is still proceeding.

CHAPTER XIII

Extension of the Ragged School System

This Institution has differed in one respect from other Institutions, inasmuch as it had no period of infancy, but has sprung at once into manhood ; and the number of those schools which are being established in the metropolis, show the strength which has been imparted to them by the formation of the Ragged School Union.

These schools have been established, not only in the metropolis, but in many of the manufacturing town.

THE LATE RIGHT HON. LORD KINNAIRD, 1851.

THERE are not wanting among us friends who sigh that the ragged school interests and the specialized institutions that have had their origin in ragged schools have ever been scattered. In conversation with them it sometimes leaks out what their daydream is. They would have dearly liked to see as an outward and visible expression of the power and magnitude of a missionary impulse, a sky-scraping building wherein the offices of all these now independent agencies were contained.

It is a little mortifying, it must be confessed, to meet, as one now does occasionally, with people who never heard of ragged schools. How different it might have been had our fathers been more business-like, say the friends referred to. Yes, it might have been a gain in some things, to be more prominently before the public

but it is far from doubtful whether the best has not
happened.

In spite of the fascinating vision of a National Waifs'
Mission House, an acquaintance with enthusiasms turned
into businesses inspires misgivings. " But think ! " say
they, "how well it would have advanced the interests
of the cause to take a friend into a place like that.
You push open a pair of handsome swing-doors and
there to the right and left and on every floor are offices.
Here is the Central Office of the London Union, we will
say, and on the ground-glass panels of the door are the
names of towns for which the office is also a bureau.
Then to the right are the offices of the Reformatory
and Refuge Union." As our friend's fancy warms, he
pictures a handsome suite, a whole floor in fact, given
up to Dr. Barnardo and his secretaries and clerks.
Another for the National Refuges ; another for London
Polytechnics, and so on. In the corridors are models
of training ships and country homes, in the hall a
splendid replica of the Westminster Abbey statue of
Lord Shaftesbury, paid for with shilling subscriptions.
Committee rooms, always in use, are on every floor.
Up and down the stairs and along the corridors
secretaries and clerks hurry with papers and ·lists of
agenda.

Had such centralization been maintained as to make
this possible, it would not have been to the interest of
the work. The social side would have been cramped
or the religious side secularized. As it is, the institutional branch of the movement went off to make its
own experiments and meet its own needs, and the group
dealing with children, maintained by parents but
nevertheless subject to hardships, difficulties and special
temptations, adapted themselves to changing social

conditions. The influence of this movement has been world-wide. America and Europe are debtors to it.

Those who had undertaken the entire support and training of children were less able to utilize honorary labour. But no deadening officialism crept in among them. The Biblical injunction has been obeyed, and " the things of others " have been looked upon with interest, as well as their own special work. A ragged school teacher wrote to Dr. Barnardo, one of the busiest of these men, not very long ago for a little information for a private purpose. He sent a reply, from which the few words that will be quoted may be regarded as expressing the fraternalism generally existing. " The cause of children is dear to all lovers of children, and any knowledge any of us possess is probably not an original acquirement, but more or less derived from others. Whether it be so or not we are each one of us debtors to everybody else doing similar work, and I shall be glad to give you what aid I can." It is in the same spirit that the secretary of the National Refuges kindly placed at our disposal for this book such originals, books and blocks as he had, bearing upon the subject. A voluntary offer of that kind has much disinterestedness of meaning, when officials have to be constantly on their guard lest funds be diverted from their own charities. An association of sentiment may be mistaken for a business connexion, whatever pains be taken to make things clear. The trait is exhibited right through the history. London borrowed from Aberdeen, the English provincial towns borrowed from London. Freedom and the diffusion of light made the work grow. When reformatories and refuges and industrial schools increased, there was no worldly thought at the R.S.U. that such a connexion was a valuable asset for money raising. They were formed into a separate society and launched forth upon the world with blessings.   When the Desti-

MAP OF THE BRITISH ISLES, SHOWING THE TOWNS TO WHICH THE RAGGED SCHOOL SYSTEM HAD SPREAD IN 1851.

tute Children's Dinners Society was started, the R.S.U. office was lent for a meeting, and the magazine to gain subscribers.   So it has been with many another scheme.

In consequence, where the R.S.U. might very early have possessed all the circumstance of pride and power attaching sometimes to a considerable work, it lost some attention when it seemed to need most aid. Two small rooms, two men and a boy were all that the world saw until a very short time ago. Considering that the conditions under which charitable institutions gain support are not unlike those of a family of beggars, who may lose by being seen on speaking terms in the street, the solidarity between the R.S.U. and its affiliated schools and the R.S.U. and institutions having a ragged school origin is very remarkable. John Kirk has done much to foster it, but nevertheless it is against nature, so should be looked upon as a sign of grace. In the report for 1846 when the R.S.U. was feeling how difficult it is to work with inadequate funds, there is this characteristic of looking upon the things of others with a desire to help, displayed. " Applications for information have lately been received by the Committee from various parts of England, and in various towns ragged schools have already begun. In Birmingham there was one opened nine months ago in the neighbourhood of Windmill Hill, in a loft over a blacksmith's shop, when eighty shoeless, stockingless, tattered and dirty children were admitted." The Rector sent a report to the R.S.U. with an acknowledgment that the idea was taken from its work.

At Nottingham Mr. S. R. Starey had commenced another after he left London and ceased to be Hon. Sec. of the R.S.U. A report sent to Croydon caused another school to be formed there.

The Windsor Ragged School was formed the same year in a shed, with an earth floor, by a chimney-sweep, whether as the result of London influence does not appear. Manchester and Liverpool at the same time showed signs of following a good lead.

In 1847 it is recorded with satisfaction that the comments on the reports of the leading journals (and possibly the articles in the Quarterlies) had caused numerous applications to be made from persons in various towns in England, Scotland and Ireland. Amongst those towns that had turned the information to account were Bristol, Bath, Manchester and Liverpool. The Committee had " endeavoured to stimulate all such movements in every possible way, and had replied to hundreds of letters from all quarters for information on the subject."

By 1850 the Committee had come to the conclusion that the plan that they had been considering of employing a travelling agent to help provincial friends to start schools must for the present be deferred, and that they must " confine their efforts, for the present at least, to the Metropolis and the suburbs." " This determination will not prevent," the report continues, " their helping their country friends, *as hitherto*, with all needful information, and where actually of service, a deputation also, to assist in carrying out fresh efforts." There are indications in the country reports that deputations went down to lend a helping hand when required. Judge Payne, Mr. J. G. Gent and others are mentioned in the early Ipswich reports as present at meetings on this service.

Apart from the towns already mentioned, by 1851 the system had spread to Southampton, Portsmouth, Sheffield, Birmingham, York, Newcastle, Hull, Nottingham, Brighton, Cheltenham, Windsor, Plymouth, Edinburgh, Glasgow, Dumfries, Perth, Dundee, Aberdeen, Isle of Man, Ipswich, Dublin, Belfast, Cork, Waterford, Gravesend, Bideford, Guildford, Norwich, Whitehaven, Jersey, Dover, Luton, Margate, Chester, Woolwich and Reading. Liverpool had twenty schools.

It would be interesting to know to what extent, if any, the London work affected all these. With regard to some of them there can be no doubt that they were independent of it, the Scotch towns especially. Aberdeen was their Mecca, as it was ours when the ragged school had taken its complete form.

Still, Edinburgh learned something from London, if it was only what to avoid. Even at that, there is an obligation to the London capital. By 1853 the report of the London R.S.U. sometimes had extracts of the provincial reports.

The Cheltenham effort is there described as being concerned with some sixty of the roughest lads of the town. It had been suggested " because it had been tried and proved successful in several other large towns throughout the empire." About two dozen boys were all who could be coaxed to church because of the con dition of their clothes.

At Dumfries and Maxwelltown they were more advanced, for the profits on the industry of the scholars sufficed to pay for their food. Of 150 children who had passed through the school during four years, ninety-four were removed from school from satisfactory causes, forty from uncontrollable circumstances, and seventeen from unsatisfactory reasons.

The reader is here, in the concluding words, introduced to one of the chief difficulties the industria schools had to contend with, namely, the interference of parents. To this phase, however, and the development of industrial work it will be more convenient to refer after dealing with some of the towns.

In Dumfries the number of juvenile commitments in the year previous to the establishment of the school was forty. In 1848, the year of founding, it was twenty-four, and in 1851 twelve.

In connexion with the report upon the Dundee Industrial School in 1853, there is a letter from the superintendent of police of the town which says that

SHOEMAKERS' SHOP. BISLEY SCHOOLS OF THE NATIONAL REFUGES.

it is now " a rare thing to see a juvenile arraigned at the assize court," and that this fact, though not solely attributable to the work of the industrial school, other causes being also contributory, it is yet in a large measure due to it.

The other causes were probably economic changes. Apart from the influx of gold into the country there was a large increase in trade. The year before—1852— emigrants exceeding in number the excess of births over deaths went to the gold-fields, so that at home we had a stationary population to share an increase of employment and profit. The gold mine countries were also such good customers that the bad harvests of 1853–54 were more than compensated for. Flour was four times and meat five times its ordinary value. An egg or a pill cost a dollar each at the mines. In London wages rose from twenty to twenty-five per cent. Bricks increased fifty per cent. in value. The provincial towns benefited too by the scarcity of labour, and so many agricultural labourers took to other work that there was a suggestion that the Militia should do the harvesting.

In the Dundee school were eighty-five boys. Thirty-nine of these were fatherless, seventeen motherless, fourteen orphans and fifteen possessed both parents. Out of the thirty-nine children of widows, four of the mothers had been guilty of desertion, five more were drunkards, three more had been to prison, the majority of the remainder had seen drunken husbands consigned to early graves.

The seventeen motherless children were scarcely as fortunate. One father was a deserter, ten more were drunkards, three were gaolbirds, and the remaining three set a vicious example in other ways.

Of the fifteen who had both parents, nine would probably have been better off as orphans. The fifty-five girls in the school were in as bad case as the boys.

What happened at Dundee is indicative of what occurred in many towns. When institutions for taking extreme cases off the streets and placing them under industrial tuition were first started, it seemed to some that nothing more was wanted. Others held that the more valuable work was to influence and deal with the thousands of our growing population specially ham pered by their environment, but who had not as yet gone astray. These kept on with ragged school work. But the industrial school had the same glamour as the Board school over many minds. It was considered a complete solution of the slum-child problem. It is not surprising, therefore, to find that many northern towns put all their effort into the founding of an institution and considered then that the work was done. A small work at Dundee that began in 1846 with eighty-one boys and fifty-eight girls is now represented by two magnificent buildings, one at Balgay 164 ft. by 160 ft., built at a cost of £12,000, on the Firth of Tay, commanding a view of the Fifeshire hills. The other building, which cost £13,000, is at Baldovan and stands in its own grounds of thirteen and a half acres. They accommodate 200 boys and 119 girls. The juvenile convictions used to number 113 annually, now they have been reduced to two.

The Edinburgh work, founded by Dr. Guthrie, has taken the same form. The schools at Castle Hill and Ramsay Lane have become the institution for 100 girls at Lovers' Lane, Leith Walk, and the one for 200 boys at Liberton, standing in four and a half acres of ground. The report has illustrations of the boy gardeners, pipers, tailors, shoemakers and joiners trained in the home from the very poorest and roughest material.

August 17, 1851, was indeed a day of small things for the Gravesend Ragged School, as the attendance register shows three for the afternoon and seven in the evening. Yet it grew quickly, and in a year's time had 150 scholars. Now it has 320. For ten years it was in the main street, but afterwards moved to New Court. Very precious possessions of the school are the

Gordon flags—Chinese banners—that he took from the Taiping rebels.   These are lodged in the Gravesend Bank for safety.   The work is still growing, the latest addition being a crêche.

At Hertford a ragged school was built by a Quaker in 1859 to house a work that had been begun in a cottage in 1852.   A day school, with a fee of a penny a week, remitted to the poorest, was held until 1877.   It then became the Town Mission, but practically it is a continuation of the old work.   There are 200 scholars. A Band of Hope, Penny Bank, Bible classes, Mission services, lodging-house and open-air meetings all emanating from the old ragged school.

In 1853 the Norwich school had been four years in existence.   It originated in a resolution, " That there be a school formed free from all sectarianism, for the benefit of the lowest class of this city exclusively." The first workers ran the risk of broken heads and empty pockets, but at the time of reporting, all opposition had subsided.   There were then 220 children in attendance, and it was the opinion of the workers that another school might be opened in the Peafield with advantage.

The Nottingham ragged school had 144 scholars and thirteen teachers at the school in Sherwood Lane, and the committee were just about to launch out and secure a building in Glasshouse Street that would accommodate 300 and give rooms for dormitories and workshops.

Perth's girls' industrial school had thirty-six under its care.   Since 1843, when it was founded, seventy-three girls had passed through.   Of these twenty-one were orphans, twenty-eight were beggars, seventeen had both parents worthless, twenty-seven had one parent worthless, fourteen were fatherless, fifteen motherless, and six were deserted.

The boys' school had dealt with 135, of whom forty were orphans, forty-nine fatherless, fifteen motherless, and only thirty-one had both parents living.

A school at Ramsgate with fifty-one scholars is mentioned, and also a more important one with educational and industrial operations for upwards of 100 scholars at Woolwich. .

GARDENING. BISLEY HOMES OF THE NATIONAL REFUGES.

One of the Liverpool schools, the Soho Street Ragged Industrial School, is noticed, but no figures are given. Many instances of neglect, such as the Dundee particulars exhibit, are given, but need not be repeated here. At the conclusion it is pointed out that while the cost per child at a ragged school is between £5 and £6, the cost of a criminal is betweeen £60 and £200, apart from depredations.

An interesting account of a Liverpool Ragged School is given in Chambers' *Edinburgh Journal* for 1847, p. 93, vol. 7 :—

VISIT TO RAGGED SCHOOLS IN LIVERPOOL.

The establishment of what were called " Ragged Schools " in London, lately induced several benevolent and influential gentlemen of Liverpool to organize a few schools of the same kind in that town. Subscriptions were accordingly made, a managing committee appointed, rooms hired, and salaried professional teachers elected. The town of Liverpool contains large numbers of children who never attend dayschools, and who grow up with little or no school instruction. The field for such ragged schools is therefore very extensive. It was resolved by the committee that all children, from the ages of six to seventeen, should be allowed to attend the schools without any charge whatsoever. All who presented themselves were to be received ; but to prevent overcrowding, as well as to restrict the schools to that class for which they were more particularly intended, none were taken who were actually in attendance at a day-school, unless there was sufficient room in the ragged school for them. Operations were commenced in July, 1846. The schools for boys meet every evening (excepting Saturday and Sunday), from seven to nine o'clock ; and for girls on the same evenings, from half-past six to half-past eight o'clock. There are now in operation two schools for boys, containing 130, and two for girls, containing 140 pupils. A few notes of visits lately paid to these schools may perhaps be of interest to the readers of this journal.

It must be premised, that as yet the schools can only be considered in their infancy, and have been planted only in one quarter of the town. Their extension will, of course, depend upon the success of the plan, and the liberality of the public.

On one of the platform seats were about a dozen young boys learning to write on slates placed on their knees. Some could write their own names, but the majority were learning to form single letters. One little boy, about eleven years of age, was labouring anxiously to form the vowels on his slate. He was without stockings or shoes ; his clothes were ragged and worn, but there was an evident attempt to make them look as clean as could be. He said he had never attended a day-school in his life ; that his mother was a widow, probably living in one of the Liverpool cellars ; that she kept a mangle ; and that he, poor fellow, was required all day long, when he should have been at school, to attend and turn it. There he sat, his whole soul absorbed in the attempt to form the letters *a, e, i, o, u*. Beside him was a little rogue, younger even than himself, who had the good fortune to be attending a free day-school in connexion with a church, and who looked down on his less-favoured comrade as a peer would regard a commoner. Here, again, was another lad, about the same age, employed also in writing. This boy *had been* at a day-school. He was only twelve years old, and his school experience had already become a thing of the past. His father was a coal merchant in a small way, and this boy had, during the day, to go about with coals. A little farther on was another writing-class, which had advanced so far as to write in books with pen and ink, and at a regular desk. At another bench was an arithmetic class ; some learning to make figures, others working questions in proportion and simple interest. One rough, hardy, weather-beaten boy was as far as mensuration. He was an apprentice to a stonemason. Another boy, about fourteen, who attended a free school during the day, was working questions in simple interest with great quickness and accuracy. In another corner of the room were four or five young boys learning the names of the letters of the alphabet, and also receiving some knowledge of objects by means of a few coloured drawings. The master was assisted in his labours by a few young men, who gave their services out of pure love for the work. There was more order preserved than might have been expected ; and though the noise of so many classes proceeding at one time was considerable, still it was the noise of work, not of idleness.

The school closed at nine o'clock, and at half-past eight o'clock the books, slates, etc., were collected and put away. The boys all took their seats in front of the master, who read to them from the platform a portion of the life of Benjamin Franklin. It so happened that on this evening the teacher concluded the story of the life of Franklin, the same space on several previous evenings having been devoted to the rest of the life. The teacher took care to make the narrative as simple as possible, and made a practical application of the events in Franklin's life to the boys assembled, with the view of giving them encouragement not only in their studies, but likewise in their various occupations in life. It was really pleasant to notice the attention that prevailed among the boys, and the eagerness with which they drank in the narrative. Questions that were put to them elicited answers that showed they well remembered what had been told to them

be ore. The greater number of these boys were engaged
in labour of some kind during the day, and they were
asked, in connexion with Franklin's life, if they liked
to work ?   Only one boy, another apprentice in a
foundry, answered "No." But on being questioned, he
could give no reasons for his answer, and advantage
was taken of the circumstance to give a short and pointed
lecture to the school on the usefulness and honourable-
ness of labour.   A short hymn was then sung, in which
all the boys joined, and the school closed.

The room in which this school met was, shortly
after my visit, required as a soup-kitchen, and the boys
were removed to another room in the same quarter of
the town.   Later in December I happened to pay a
visit to it also.   The room was used during the day as
a girls' school, and was more convenient and comfortable, though not so large, as the first.   It could not
accommodate all the boys, and a desk and seats had to
be placed in a narrow lobby by which it was entered, to
receive an advanced writing-class.   On entering, two
boys whom I had seen in the school at its old room
sprang up, and asked me to decide which of their copy-
books was the better written, both being quite proud of
the progress they had made.   In the room itself there
was scarcely space to turn—boys reading, boys writing,
boys calculating on every side.   From this school I
passed to another containing about forty boys, all of
the same class as was found in that already described.
Here the teacher was engaged with a class which was
reading a poetical description of country life ; and so
completely town-bred and ignorant were nearly all the
boys, that the teacher required to give an explanation
of many of the unknown things alluded to in the lesson.
The boys were most attentive, and read the lesson over

and over again with great delight. In one corner I noticed three boys, the oldest about twelve, and the other two probably three years younger. Not one of the trio had either shoes or stockings ; their clothes were all most ragged and torn ; and they evidently belonged to the very lowest class of the population. ' The force of ' raggedness' could no farther go. "

The effort here described grew and multiplied so that at the present time there is a large union of schools at Liverpool with operations conducted upon a consider- able scale.

After 1853 individual notices of the work in the provinces appeared in the R.S.U. magazine at un- certain intervals. There has been no federation of towns, consequently it has been nobody's business to present the united work to the public. In some places the conditions have so altered that the ordinary agencies of Sunday and day school are now sufficient to meet the local need. In other cases the work has died out, though the need remains. In others again ragged schools still continue to work as vigorously as ever. Materials for a history of these are not forth- coming in sufficient amount to make anything like a complete account, but from such particulars as have come to hand, a suggestive survey has been attempted. The records will be given in alphabetical order.

Blackburn was a late beginner, opening in Lune Street in 1881. The schools afterwards moved to the old St. Peter's Day School, and ultimately had a building costing £4,000 in 1898. They have at present between 700 and 800 scholars, and a very flourishing work, in a very poor district, as may be gathered from the fact that the death rate among infants under two is 326 per 1,000 as compared with 45 per 1,000 in a neighbouring parish. Another sure sign is the number of beershops. Of these there are one to 118 as compared with one in 870 in the healthier parish. A

COOKERY LESSONS. GIRLS' HOMES OF THE NATIONAL REFUGES.

shoeblack brigade, a magnificent brass band, and an orphanage at Wilpshire are among the schools' possessions, as well as the usual operations. Free breakfasts, week-night suppers, sick-visiting, slum and lodging-house work, penny bank, clubs, and week-night services. 10,000 free meals were given last winter, and 1,200 children taken for a day to the seaside. In 1898 the workers found seventeen cripples, now they have 130 under visitation. The photos in the report show that the right kind of children are being dealt with.

The Coventry Ragged School opened on June 13, 1847. It began with 21 boys in the back room of a leather-seller. These were of a very rough order.

It was thought nothing but fun and frolic for the youths of Spon Street to come armed with sticks and staves to fight the boys of Gosford Street, and the beaten ones made good their escape down every court and alley in the neighbourhood. The teachers not only did the work, but subscribed the funds in the early days. Then for some eight years, from 1851 to 1859 there was a slackening of interest, after which there was a revival. Girls as well as boys were dealt with in 1862. Then in 1865, when there was distress in the town, a branch mission in Spon Street and in 1879 a school in Rood Lane were opened. For the past thirty years or more, the custom has obtained of raising a sixpenny levy throughout the town for the children's treats. For about the same period the school has had a splendid silver band, with instruments to the value of £60. There are between 500 and 600 scholars.

The story of the Ragged School cause in Ipswich is perhaps as instructive as anything to be found in the movement. The workers began in 1848 with a school confined apparently to Sunday work at first, and conducted upon a very small scale. The reason for uncertainty as to details is, that only the fifth report of the ragged schools is available, dated 1854. In that year they were dealing with rather more than 100 of the most unfortunate children of the town of both sexes. In the summer there were less. In the winter, more. By 1854 the social operations of the school were entirely confined to temperance and thrift. A dormitory and school of industry had been started in 1851, and the profit on the labour, it transferred to the school account in the school report of 1854 to the extent of £35. The entire cost of running the parent school was some £60.

In the first printed industrial school report (1852) occurs this paragraph—

" In connexion with the school there has been established a Temperance Band of Hope ; also a clothing club, to which every scholar who subscribes is allowed twopence bonus. During the past year five girls have left to go to service ; one put to shoe-binding ; fourteen of the elder boys have found employment ; two have set up for themselves, selling fruit, &c. ; fifteen boys and girls have been drafted to other schools, their parents being in a position to pay. The classes of industry formed from the most intelligent and best behaved of the scholars have been, for the boys, shoemaking, carpentering, tailoring and mat-making, occasionally under master workmen, partly paid for the purpose ; and for the girls, sewing, knitting, &c."

Those in charge of the dormitory had been the means of producing a change of character in some of the criminal class using it—and two lads, " most changed boys," had been emigrated to Australia at the sole expense of the President, the Recorder of Ipswich.

So the work went on. The industrial effort seems to have been as successful as anything that can be traced run upon voluntary lines. It was used mainly as a stepping-stone to other businesses, as the ragged school was used as a stepping-stone to the British and foundation schools of the town. In the 1869 report there is a reference to boys from the school being used as porters. Evidently a highly organized labour bureau for young people was in existence at this time. The year's income was £363. Changes brought about by the Education Act and other causes made the income drop by the year 1873 to £17. Yet the work has ever been kept healthy, and for over fifty years has concerned itself with assisting those children who have homes and parents, but yet need the help of friends.

In the fiftieth report the work is seen to have so far regained its position in popular favour that the officers were able in 1900 to launch out into the expense of rebuilding the girls' school in Woodhouse Street, and to renovate the boys' school in Waterworks Street at a cost of £2,000 ; while the annual income had risen to £70. It is to this school that we are indebted for the illustrations to the chapter on Industrialism.

A custom at one time existed of inviting a London deputation to attend the annual meeting, a practice pretty general in the provinces. More than one old friend's name appears in this connexion, notably those of Mr. J. G. Gent and Judge Payne. There was a fuller realization of the ground yet to be covered in the fifties than now, for we find that a magistrate who took the chair on one occasion said there was need for twenty such schools in the town.

Ipswich also set a good example in keeping the work unsectarian. At one annual meeting the chairman was a Quaker, while rallying to his support were the rector and another clergyman and the Congregationalist and Baptist ministers.

But it is time that Ipswich now gave place to Leicester. Here again there were small beginnings, for the first school consisted of five children in rags in a private house on December 6, 1866. In 1868 another room was taken at Belgrave Gate, and the numbers were greatly augmented, and by 1869 the workers had ventured to start a day-school. which within the year sprang from fourteen to 153 children. Three boys after being broken in and taught tidiness

DINNER TIME.   GIRLS' HOMES OF THE NATIONAL REFUGES.

had been passed on to other schools. A night school for lads and a sewing class for girls were in existence, and in the Sunday school there were over two hundred scholars. The sanitary inspectors having raised objections to the defects in the accommodation at Church Gate, the school was moved to Yeoman Lane, and from Yeoman Lane another move was made in 1872 to Gladstone Hall, Wharf Street, where its proximity to the brickyards and shoe factories brought the workers plenty of the right kind of material to work upon.   In 1874 Dr. Barnardo came down to plead the school's cause in the town, and place its support upon a better footing.   In 1879 the lease of Gladstone Hall having lapsed, a new home had to be found, and by 1881 the work which had been occupying temporary shelters had found the Primitive Methodist Chapel schools and cottage in George Street as its future home.   These buildings were bought for £1,700.   In 1885 part of these premises were rebuilt, and a London deputation travelled down to Leicester to take part in the proceedings.

After years of faith and struggle the teachers were now in possession of a handsome block of buildings, in which a grand evangelical work has been sustained to the present time.   Out of £3,000 there is still £1,000 to clear, but such work will never be forsaken by Him in whose Name it is done.   The special feature of the Leicester cause is its strength in work among adults, a feature that in the general movement has been allowed to lapse somewhat.   An aggregate attendance of upwards of seventeen thousand men and women at 328 meetings held last year is a record that prompts congratulations from fellow-workers in the field.

Among children the work is just as satisfactory, for at 215 meetings the attendance has been 42,343.

When we reach Manchester we encounter something on different lines, more of an institutional character, where the maintenance of children has been undertaken—a highly specialized work.   The Manchester and Salford Boys' and Girls' Refuges and Homes is a very important charity.   It has sixteen branches—

A Central Refuge and Home.

A Working Youths' Home and Institute.

A Boys' Emigration Training Home.
A Juvenile Street Boys' Home.
An Elder Girls' Training Home and Laundry.
An Orphan Home for Little Children.
A Home for Crippled and Incurable Children.
A Home for Motherless Little Girls.
An Open Day and Night Shelter.
Lytham Seaside Camp.
A Messenger and Shoeblack Brigade.
A Police-court Mission : Lads and Girls.
A Training Ship.
An Emigration Bureau.
A Prison-gate Mission.

As its annual turnover is somewhere about £16,000, the magnitude of the operations may be guessed. It is quite as important as the London R.S.U. In what esteem the work is held can be gathered from a few words emanating from the Bishop of Manchester—

" These homes are based upon Christian principles ; they are managed by practical methods, and are doing a great work for all the Churches. They are doing the work of ten Societies, and are in danger of receiving the support of one."

The tendency in any provincial city or town where the work has been advanced in this way has been usually to weaken that branch of the work with which we are more immediately concerned, but on the out-skirts of Manchester, at Pendleton, there is a ragged school that does not appear to be less heartily sup-ported than the refuges.

Of this important work we have no recent figures, but doubtless the work is still sustained with the old zeal. An aggregate attendance of 141,000 at the meetings of one school is a sign of very robust health

in any institution.   Open-air preaching to mill operatives in the dinner-hour is one of the agencies of John
Street Hall.   The distribution of pure literature is
another grand feature, so is the home visitation.
Under the first heading it appears that 181,903 tracts,
120,472 magazines, besides books and Testaments,
were distributed at the time this report was drawn
up, and 1,050 homes were systematically visited.   Upwards of 5,000 meals had been provided during the
winter, 3,000 children and adults had had an outing
in the summer, and forty a week at the seaside.   On
Sunday there was an average attendance of 1,077,
and between 230 and 300 were present at the Band
of Hope and recreative classes.   Altogether there is
every sign of blessing attending the labour of the
devoted staff.

For the past thirteen years a work has been carried
on in John Pounds' old workshop at Portsmouth,
similar to that which he began.   Like the original
work, it was for both sexes, but as the girls grew, it
was thought desirable to transfer them to a school
specially for them.   Accordingly, a home for a few,
and an institute open to outsiders, was started at 79
St. Thomas Street in 1898.   Eleven girls are resident,
and the institute has 58 members.   Forty-eight girls
altogether have been trained for domestic service.

A longer notice would probably have secured a
larger amount of material from our friends wherewith
to do justice to the work in the country towns.   Plymouth, for example, has a better story than it is at
present in our power to outline.   There was more
than one ragged school, but we have to hand only
the reminiscences of a lady who knew the Castle Street
school in 1853.   This was conducted at a house near

the fishmarket, in a very low neighbourhood. It had a boys', girls' and infants' departments, and had an industrial department as well. There were wood-chopping sheds and a shoeblack brigade attached. Like every true ragged school it had a Sunday night gathering and a week evening school as well. At this might often have been seen adults learning to write. It was a ragged crew indeed that went for the annual outing to the edge of Dartmoor or on the Down, but the old school trained some fine men, and not a few of these in His Majesty's warships all over the world bless the work that was carried on there.

It indicates how gradually the educational authority was able to take over its responsibilities that the school in Cannon Street, Jersey, in the old disused granary, was only closed in 1903, after an existence of forty-four years. The lady hon. secretary who sends this brief history says that during the entire existence of the school not more than half-a-dozen scholars have been before a magistrate, although the class from which they were recruited were the " half-clothed, ill-fed street arabs who went nowhere to school, begged of passers-by, or prowled about the piers, pilfering and stealing coals, apples or potatoes from carts carrying them to and from the vessels in the harbour."

" Merchants, captains, coachbuilders, an officer in the army, girls in high positions of trust, all gained their education in the ragged school."

The Newcastle and Gateshead Poor Children's Holiday Association and Rescue Agency is not unlike the Manchester work in some features, except that it seems to have a better grip of the town by means of its territorial committees. Its report for 1903 has the following summary of work done in the year : Newcastle children, 3,196 taken for seaside trips ; 244 sent for periods between three and six weeks to country homes ; 640 assisted with clothing and boots ; 2,500 entertained at Christmas ; 340 helped in various ways. Night shelter for 866, given 3,388 times ; 345 admitted to the boys' home ; 734 visited in their homes and on the streets ; 41 girls trained at the girls' home.

Gateshead Branch.—Shelter given to 254 boys and 12 girls 2,001 times, and afterwards dealt with as follows—Sent to institutions, 35 ; to situations and lodgings, 21 ; to Shotley Bridge Training Home for Girls, 6 ; restored to friends, 67 ; restored to institutions, 10 ; otherwise assisted, 98 ; dismissed, 2 ; sent to the workhouse, 17 ; boys in the home, 10 ; assisted with clothing, 198. A mission for poor children in connexion with this work held 200 meetings with an aggregate attendance of 20,000 children, and at a street vendors' club there was an attendance of 9,000.

At the Gateshead branch at similar gatherings, 19,840 were present. At the two places, 18,665 meals were given. All this work on account of the voluntary labour comes to less than £2,500.

At York the ragged school work was begun by Wesleyans in " The Bedern " on February 7, 1847, with twenty-five children. Mr. T. B. Smithies, the editor of the *British Workman and Band of Hope Review*, a friend of Lord Shaftesbury, was connected with it. " The Bedern " was classic ground, for here in Roman times Severus gave his dying charge to his two sons, and Papinian the jurist and Prætorian Præfect and the Emperor Constantine lived at the palace of Altera Roma. The spot gained its later name, " place of prayer," from the fact that it was given up in the Middle Ages to the vicars choral of the cathedral church of York. A branch school was also started upon historic ground at the Walmgate, once the home of the Percys. When, later on, the school made a shift again, it was to another hallowed spot. The day school then became part of St. William's College, built by Edward IV. for the chantry priests of the cathedral. It was here, also, that the Royalist Press during the Civil War was set up.

By 1847 the Bedern had become a slum, where the migrant population established their quarters, and where they stayed when tramping north from London. The children were summoned to school on Sunday by the ringing of a hand-bell. It surprised the workers not a little at first to find that though the numbers were kept up, it was with different children each week. They belonged to the families of hawkers, pedlars, and tramps. The school's first year's balance-sheet shows upon what a small scale the first efforts were. The rent was £3 7s. 6d., furniture, £2 11s. 2d., the caretaker's wages and firing came to £1 10s. 9d., leaving 3s. 1d. in the hands of the treasurer. Yet from such small beginnings grew a cause that three years later could use with advantage an empty workhouse.

Here there was every convenience and appliance for work. Wash-houses, mangle-house, pantries and workshops, dining-rooms, schoolrooms, bedrooms, baths, etc., etc. Very rapid development followed, refuge and industrial operations were added to the school programme. The entire enterprise was placed upon a broad unsectarian basis, and made more or less a municipal interest. The children were marched to church on one Sunday and to chapel the next. It was perhaps the earliest ragged school institution to crystallize into a State industrial school, receiving as it did its certificate in June, 1858. Since then, apparently, ragged school work proper has died out.

In studying the rise and progress of ragged schools in London and the provincial towns, the lines of growth are clearly observable. First, the Sunday ragged school, then the week-night class, ultimately bringing into being the day ragged school. The complete development of this with industrialism and emigration, constituted a Darkest England scheme for juveniles, in which every feature of the later work for adults is anticipated. The arrangements at the Newsboys' Home of the National Refuges are very interesting viewed from that standpoint.

In germ the industrial school was a ragged school, at which food was given, and where the time was divided between learning the three R's, and wood-chopping or other work that paid for the food. To attempt a little more than this, the managers found they must have the children on the premises to live and sleep. The industrial school accordingly became a more restricted institution, a few that were a certainty were less trouble than a crowd of migrants who spoiled material and often left the locality altogether leaving work unfinished. In teaching trades, this working loss always had to be faced—the child's meals, and the spoiled materials. If the school was on any considerable scale the loss might be heavy.

Thus, John Macgregor in an undated pamphlet, apparently issued in 1855, writes, " In fifty of our ragged schools of London, there are industrial classes. The number of children employed in these is about

2,000 ; but their example and influence is extended through five times that number of scholars, and generally they impart a healthy tone to the institutions themselves—not seldom to the neighbourhood around.

"Our industrial occupations are various, and dependent upon the choice of the committees, the money and premises at their disposal, and the demand for the products of labour. Boys are instructed by masters in tailoring and shoemaking, making and mending the clothes of their school, or the articles made are sometimes sold at low prices. Wood-chopping is another employment in which many are engaged, and the faggots thus prepared for firewood are bought by those interested in the school. Horse-hair picking, strange to say, is a remunerative employment. Others are engaged in carpentry, *which is expensive, and not advisable*. Mat-making is better, and the fabrication of fishermen's nets. In one of the Liverpool schools, about thirty boys are employed in making paper bags for shopkeepers, which are printed also in the school and find a ready sale. There is, in London, a small amount of ornamental work in leather pocket-books, paper cases, and other articles. For the girls, sewing and knitting of all kinds form, as may be supposed, their chief occupation in these classes. In Ireland, the highest style of embroidery has been introduced largely, and with great success ; more than £5,000 being paid annually in wages for this kind of work alone."

From this it will be seen how far things were carried in the ragged schools pure and simple and ragged schools with night shelters attached. The step towards a residential institution when a local committee came to the conclusion that "carpentry *was* advisable," was most obvious. But the distressing visits of drunken parents of waifs, apparently ownerless at the time they were picked up, children ready to perish, caused some re-consideration. The smashing of windows was not so serious as the fact that they could recover their children. It meant that these institutions must be made into orphanages, and if they were their usefulness would be curtailed. Here the law stepped in and deprived the worthless parents of rights for a period of years ; it also assumed control of children displaying criminal propensities where no apparent blame attached to parents. In both cases discretion as to committal to an industrial school was vested in the magistrates. No stigma of crime in the eye of the law rested upon the child, and the arrangement secured undisturbed possession during a period of training, and was so far satisfactory. It gave the magistrates, too, a welcome alternative to the painful duty of sending children to a reformatory just as that had been an improvement on sending them to prison. In spite of these advantages, the industrial schools lost much, when the basis was changed. The association with criminal jurisprudence was too close. The Government certificate to the Institution and capitation grant for each child, killed the last vestige of the old voluntaryism and the industrial school became part of Government machinery.

Dr. Barnardo's Homes, The National Refuges, and the Homes for Waifs and Strays, and others, still work on the old system with unsentenced children.

Robert Lowe used to say that the children must be taught " things," as well as " words," but in 1855 Macgregor wrote, " the hand and the eye must be taught to work. Our Poor-Law schools are here deficient, and many of our National schools, as well as nearly all the schools in our gaols." The Poor-Law schools were later on brought up to the right level by the labours of Miss Carpenter, Miss Cobbe, Miss Louisa Twining and others. We are not a little proud of the fact that the first two ladies were ragged school teachers, and the third, still living, is the sister of one.

The difficulty the managers of the industrial schools and homes now experience is that adjustment of such institutions to modern conditions is extemely difficult. It is, moreover, very costly. The trades on which the lads and girls used to be employed with profit to the schools between 1850 and 1860 are now dying industries, and no use as training for earning a livelihood.

But some of these homes have surmounted their difficulties and left the days of wood-chopping and kindred pursuits far behind. The National Refuges, Shaftesbury Avenue have an excellent technical school, and by the courtesy of the secretary in the illustrations to this chapter, we are able to show some phases of this work.

The difficulties of those who kept to the original work and catered for the recreation and industrial training of young people not resident in an institution, were fully considered by Dr. Leone Levi and others in 1881, but have never yet been quite overtaken.

Unless an interest in self-improvement can be aroused in the scholars, the club or lounging place cannot hold its own against cheap public amusements.

With that interest aroused the obstacles to giving efficient help are great. Each needs individual treatment, and irregularities in attendance frustrate all attempts at advanced class-work. To get efficiency the students have to be taken from a stable class who are sure of their time.

Even in 1904 we have to revert to the first principles of " expediency and love." We must do what we can if unable to do what we would, and we must ever remember that while the criminal is provided for by the State, and the waif by one or other of the Homes now in existence, " the thousands of boys whoare poor without being destitute, and tempted without having actually fallen, are left comparatively unnoticed and uncared for."[1]

[1] *The Boys' Club*, Newmann, p. 9.

CHAPTER XIV

Outgrowths and Offshoots

" The Ragged School Union is the mother of us all."—
J. W. C. FEGAN.

DR. BARNARDO, speaking of the R.S.U. in 1893 at Exeter Hall, said—

" It has been patronized, then ignored, then criticized, then tolerated, but now it is being imitated, and there are imitations in many ways, even in the statute-books of the nation. There are to-day a thousand activities, a crowd of philanthropic agencies in active operation, but if you ask where they all come from, you find it is not from the House of Lords, or the House of Commons ; not even from the palaces of wealth and fashion, but from the humble doors of some coach-house or stable, where began the ragged schools, which have grown and spread out in so marvellous a manner. I say, then, that in the consecrated thought of the ragged school pioneers there is the whole potency and promise of helpfulness and blessing which are now leavening the world in which we live.

" The R.S.U. has contained within it the germ which has led to the establishment of most of these useful and beneficial agencies now labouring on behalf of neglected children and of which we are so justly proud. Where shall I begin ? for I cannot cover the whole ground. Shall I speak of education ? Then I say that the Education Act of 1870, which has been extended into the great boon of free education, is due to the ragged schools, and is indeed but an extension of the ragged day schools—carried on by this Union for so many years. Now free education lies at the door of every child but *you* first pointed the way and carried it out into the slums and back courts. You showed what loving, wise teaching could do. The tender teaching on week days and on Sundays of your devoted teachers showed how it could be done and what would be the results.

" But to go a step further, there is a Society which has of late deservedly become very popular—the National Society for the Prevention of Cruelty to Children. Well, I say that that Society owes its origin to your movement, and for this reason, that every ragged school carried on with energy and success was really as a matter of fact a society for the prevention of cruelty to children. We all know that down deep in the heart of the very poorest there is a great compassionate love of their children. I am here to testify to that fact, which is not sufficiently understood in some quarters. I have had much experience—ofttimes very sad experience—but I have seen as deep, true, warm love in the hearts of the poorest as in the hearts of the wealthiest of this country. Yet it is the fact that at times we have been startled by terrible revelations of cruelty and the wrongs of childhood. Why is this ? I have no hesitation in affirming that a large number of such cases are due to that curse of the land which this Union is endeavouring

to stamp out and remove—I mean to intemperance.
Now what agency has been most active in promoting
temperance principles in the homes of the poor, and
of inculcating kind and gentle and considerate treatment of the children ? I do not hesitate to say that
wherever this Society has established a hold it has
become a vigorous and successful Temperance Society
on Christian and humanitarian principles. Moreover it begins at the right end, it begins with the
children. It is a sad outlook to view what are called
the lapsed masses, to see their sunken and well-nigh
hopeless condition in our great cities. I doubt if any
observant man can really have to do with these without
becoming conscious of an intense sadness of heart.
One looks at the intolerable conditions under which
vast numbers are born, and live and die, and one asks,
What can be done for these people ? Is there no
hope ? Yes, there is ; if you go the right way about
it. This R.S.U. begins right by going down to the
children, implanting true ideas, giving the warmth
of human sympathy, teaching them to love each
other, and best of all, teaching them the love of
Christ, gilding their lives with the rainbow hues of
hope, which shall never fade away.

" Then I think of the many homes and institutions
now established for the rescue and training of the waifs
and strays of society. These are now, I am thankful
to say, numerous ; and I think it may be truly said
that in most cases they found origin and inspiration
in the ragged schools, and that directly or indirectly
they sprang out of the ragged school movement. To
take but two examples. I believe I am right
in saying that the National Refuges for Destitute
Children, founded by the late William Williams, had

its origin in the efforts of a few humble, earnest men in St. Giles' to gather the children into the ragged

THE TRAINING SHIP "ARETHUSA" FOR POOR BOYS OF GOOD CHARACTER BELONGING TO THE NATIONAL REFUGES FOR DESTITUTE CHILDREN.

school. These National Refuges now include many and excellent homes, as well as the training ships

Chichester and *Arethusa*, all of which may be said to have sprung out of the R.S.U.[1]

"But to come nearer home. My own rescue work, the work with which I am personally connected, sprang out of the ragged school. I am an old ragged school teacher. I am not ashamed of it—I rejoice in it, and I may say that I learned much in those experiences in the ragged school which I would not be without for anything. I ask then, as we look around us and view with alarm, it may be, the existing state of things, Where can we find a new aspiration, a new hope? I find it in the ragged schools and kindred movements on behalf of the children of the poorest. Are there any here who are looking for a useful sphere in life, who wish to become of service to their fellows, to make their mark on humanity? If there be such, they can find no nobler and no better sphere than in the ragged schools. Thousands of young men, and women, too, seeking some noble purpose in life, may begin to feel their way and gain experience by joining in ragged school work. Serving there, they will learn the longing of the poor children's hearts, they will discover the condition of their lives: and they will gain a singularly useful experience in learning how to bring a great noisy school of restless boys and girls into something like order and discipline. But they will learn more. They will discover that the old, old story of Jesus and His love, told in a childlike but not childish way and spirit, has more charm for the wayward street arabs than any fairy tale you can devise."

[1] The ragged school from which the National Refuges sprang started before the R.S.U. in 1842.

Dr. Barnardo disclaimed the intention of covering the whole ground, so the story of R.S.U. developments must be taken up from this point.

Sixteen years ago the Conservative Government of the day placed before Parliament a temperance measure. " Part of the purpose of that measure was the extinction of certain public-house licenses. By way of compensation for this prospective scheme the sum of about three-quarters of a million was put into the Budget. This sum was voted, but the Temperance Bill afterwards broke down. What about the money ? If it was not promptly diverted it would drift silently and mysteriously into that bottomless pit known as the Sinking Fund. Just then our ears were very full of the wonderful things the Germans were doing in the way of promoting technical education. So, Liberals joining with Tories, it was decided to send the money down to the localities nominally in relief of local taxation, but with a very plain hint that if it were to be continued year by year the best thing to do with it was to apply it to purposes of technical education ! Excellent ! But to what local authority could it be sent ? The School Boards were the only public local authorities for education. But they only covered about two-thirds of the country, and where they did exist they were not always everything that could be desired. The Government, however, had just passed the Local Government Act of 1888. Why not therefore send it to the newly created County and County Borough Councils ? This was done ; and from that day forward these universally existent municipal bodies became more and more concerned in the work of technical and modern secondary education." [1]

[1] Dr. Macnamara. *Burning Problems—Education.*

HOME FOR NEWSBOYS NATIONAL REFUGES.

BUYING CLOTHES.

ARRIVAL OF A NEWSBOY.

SOME OF THE LODGERS.

THE ORDER OF THE BATH.

THE GYMNASIUM.

The spread of the polytechnic system was one result of this.

The work of a polytechnic is of an extremely varied character. Within the walls of a single institution, theoretical and practical instruction is given in all branches of chemistry and physics, from the elementary to the most advanced stages, the laboratories being equipped with apparatus suitable for both general work and research work ; biology, botany, physiology, zoology, and other branches of natural science are taught on practical lines ; thorough courses of training are provided for mechanical and electrical engineers in laboratories and workshops of the newest type ; on the art side not only is teaching given in the ordinary branches of drawing, painting and modelling, but the students are specially trained in the application of design to existing industries ; instruction is provided in foreign languages, literature, and commercial subjects, and at most polytechnics there is a special department for the teaching of various branches of domestic economy to girls and women.

These institutions that have various origins and various sources of revenue have been only slowly extended. As late as 1893 there were but six in existence. But the original polytechnic, upon which all have been modelled, is the Regent Street one founded by the late Mr. Quintin Hogg, and that was a development of his ragged school. The polytechnic was a ragged school youths' institute magnified and glorified.

Before being used for its present purpose the Regent Street Polytechnic was a place of entertainment where science and mild amusement were blended.

At the present time when our trade and manufactures and world markets are being made a subject of special study, when the importance of technical education is being urged by prominent men, and just as we are put in possession of the report of the Mosely commission upon the education of our American rivals, the history of the growth of our first important technical institute has a special interest. Mr. Hogg has told the story of its evolution, and as it reveals incidentally the spirit, genius and fire of the pioneers it may without apology be given almost in full.

He says, " My first effort was to get a couple of crossing sweepers, whom I picked up near Trafalgar Square, and offer to teach them to read. In those days the Thames Embankment did not exist, and the Adelphi Arches were open both to the tide and the street. With an empty beer bottle for a candlestick, and a tallow candle for illumination, two crossing sweepers as pupils, your humble servant as teacher, and a couple of Bibles as reading books, what grew into the Polytechnic was practically started. We had not been engaged in our reading very long when, at the far end of the arch, I noticed a twinkling light. ' Kool esclop ! ' shouted one of the boys, at the same time doucing the glim and bolting with his companion, leaving me in the dark with my upset beer bottle and my douced candle, forming a spectacle which seemed to arouse suspicion on the part of our friend the policeman, whose light it was that had appeared in the distance. However, after scrutinising me for some time by the light of his bull's-eye he moved on, leaving me in a state of mental perturbation as to what the mystic words I had heard halloed out meant. Afterwards, when I became proficient in slang, I knew that ' kool esclop ' was ' look (out for the) police,' spelt backwards, the last word being evidently the original

for the contraction ' slop,' the word generally applied
to the police in London to-day. Altogether I did not
think my first essay a very successful one, and I cast
about to know how in the world I could learn the
language of these boys, and ascertain their real wants
and their ways of life. I went down to the New Cut,
on the south side of the river, and bought a second-
hand shoeblack's suit, also a box with a strap to go
over the shoulder, brushes and all the necessary
fittings. With this I used to go out two or three
nights a week for about six months, blacking boots
and sleeping out with the boys, on barges, under
tarpaulins, or in the so-called ' Punches Hole,' on a
ledge in the Adelphi Arches, and elsewhere. Of course,
my father knew nothing at all about it, and sometimes,
if I found my companions in these holes particularly
full of vermin, I would go and roll myself up in a
blanket on the table in our Mission Room and sleep
there. My real object, of course, was to learn how the
boys lived, what they fed on, what it cost them to live,
and how they could be best reached. Of course, I
was not bootblacking all the time ; sometimes I would
go out about Covent Garden Market, or hold horses,
or do any odd jobs which I saw boys doing. The
following winter the ragged school began in real
earnest, at first only as a day school. The room—
the rental of which was £12 a year—was situated in
Of Alley (now York Place, a name which it was just
beginning to bear), off the Strand. It was a part of
the Buckingham Estate, on the site of the old palace
of George Villiers, Duke of Buckingham, whence the
names of George Court, Villiers Street, Duke Street,
Of Alley, and Buckingham Street.

" I had a very earnest female teacher in charge of

the ragged school, and she used to beg me to open the room in the evenings, when it was not required for mission purposes, for the purpose of teaching the elder lads. I did not feel myself in the least called upon for this kind of work, but I told the good woman that I would let her have the use of the gas and of the room, but that she must undertake to keep the boys in order for herself, as I could not promise to help her. On the following Monday the experiment was to be commenced, and I was in bed with a heavy feverish cold. Suddenly, about eight o'clock in the evening, one of the elder boys living in Bedfordbury came racing up to my father's house in Carlton Gardens (the same house which Mr. Arthur Balfour now occupies), where I lived, to beg me to come down at once, that there was a row in the school with the boys, who were fighting the police, and pelting them with slates. In about three minutes I had huddled on just sufficient clothes to suffice me, and, slipping on an overcoat as I ran through the hall, I made for the ragged school as hard as my legs could carry me. On arriving, I found the whole school in an uproar, the gas-fittings had been wrenched off and used as batons by the boys for striking the police, while the rest of the boys were pelting them with slates, and a considerable concourse of people standing round in a more or less threatening way, either to see the fun, or to help in going against the police. I felt rather alarmed for the teacher, and rushing into the darkened room called out for the boys to instantly stop, and be quiet. To my amazement the riot was stopped immediately. In two minutes the police were able to go quietly away, and for the first time in my life I learned I had some kind of instinct or capacity for the management of elder boys. From that day to 1868, when I had to go abroad for the first time, I scarcely missed the ragged school for a single night. The class prospered amazingly, our little room, which was only 30 feet long by 12 feet wide, got so crammed that I used to divide the school into two sections of sixty each, the first lot coming from 7 to 8.30 and the second lot from 8.30 to 10. There I used to sit between the two classes, perched on the back of a form, dining on my ' pint of thick and two doorsteps,' as the boys used to call coffee and bread and treacle, taking one class at reading and the other at writing or arithmetic. Each section closed with a ten minutes' service and prayer.

" During all this time the boys had been getting of a very different character and appearance to those who first came. When we first opened the school, no less than five boys came absolutely naked, except for their mothers' shawls, which were pinned round them, and one of the boys, named Flannigan, never could be persuaded to come in any other dress. There were five separate gangs of thieves who attended the ragged school, all of whom, within six months, were earning their livelihood more or less respectably. Those who showed any desire to get on were passed through the Shoeblack Society and apprenticed to various trades. The young mechanics began to bring their fellow apprentices and other mechanics to the school, so that the truly ragged, unkempt boys of 1864 had been succeeded by the orderly and fairly dressed lads of 1868. In the meantime, we had also increased our premises. In 1865, we added a second room to our first ; in 1866 we took the next house, at a rental of £30, and turned it into what our boys called a ' Twopenny doss house.' The intention was that boys who had been picked up

THE NEWSBOYS
HOME,
No. 80, GRAY'S INN ROAD,
HOLBORN.

The NEWSBOYS' HOME is not a School, but a Lodging-House for Boys under sixteen years of age who are occupied in selling Newspapers, Lights, &c., and have no home of their own.

Breakfast and Supper will be provided as cheaply as possible, Dinner if necessary. Cooking done for the Lodgers gratis. A Meat Dinner will be given every Sunday, at 1 p.m., to Boys who are in the Home on that day.

CHARGES:

Bed, Twopence per Night, or One Shilling per Week.

Pint of Coffee or Tea - - -	One Penny.
6 oz. Loaf of Bread - - -	One Penny.
Butter - - - - - -	One Penny.
Soup - - - - - - -	One Penny.
¼ lb. Cold Meat - - - -	Three Halfpence.

The House will be opened at 6 o'clock in the morning, and closed at 9 p.m. in the Winter, and 10 p.m. in the Summer. Lodgers are required to go to Bed when the House is closed for the night.

There is a Bath and Washhouse; every Boy on first coming in is required to wash himself thoroughly, and every Lodger must use the Bath once a week. Hot and Cold Water, Looking-glasses, Towels, and Combs provided.

A Gymnasium will be opened, and games of Draughts, Dominoes, &c., provided for the amusement of the Lodgers. A Savings Bank will be opened; and all Boys who wish to learn to Read and Write can do so.

The Rules of the House are three:—

BE ORDERLY.   USE THE BATH.
DON'T USE BAD LANGUAGE.

No Boy will be interfered with as long as he behaves himself well; but if any Boy refuses to obey the Rules, or causes trouble among the other Lodgers, Mr. ROSKILLY, the Superintendent, is empowered to turn him out, and will give him back his lodging money.

W. E. HUBBARD, JUN., *Treasurer.*
W. WILLIAMS, *Secretary.*

CLAYTON & Co., Temple Printing Works, Bouverie Street, Whitefriars, E.C.

"ATTRACTIVE BAIT."

in the street and started at the school, and who had no homes, could be kept from bad surroundings such as thieves' kitchens and low lodging houses, and housed under respectable and improving influences. The house was in a state of utter dilapidation when we took it over, but the boys and myself set to work as amateur painters, carpenters and whitewashers, and we were very well pleased at the result, though even to this day I cannot think of the job we made of the doors, and indeed of our whole carpentering, without laughing. I had a little room in the attic, which had been inhabited by a man who used it for the double purpose of a habitation and a place in which to dry fish. The smell of the latter clung about the walls, in spite of all we could do, and the boys declared that to come into my room made them hungry for supper."

In 1869 a move was made to Castle Street and the work was christened as the Hanover Institute, from the name of a portion of Endell Street then called Hanover Street.

In 1871 the lads attending the night school were so respectable that the word ragged school was a misnomer, so their portion was called the Institute, and the ragged school was severed from it and conducted in Castle Street. In 1878 the numbers had so increased that a further move was necessary ; there were now 500 members, so premises were taken in Long Acre. By this time the Institute was so valued that an applicant for admission had often to wait twelve months before there was a vacancy. The work then got into connexion with the Science and Art Department.

"By this time," continues Mr. Hogg, "I had got pretty well into my mind what it was I wanted in the

way of an Institute, the idea in my mind being that
no Institute then existing was sufficiently catholic in
its tastes and aims.   There were purely religious associations like the Y.M.C.A., most of whom had neither
athletics nor even sufficient educational attractions.

" There were educational institutions, of which the
Birkbeck may be taken as a notable example, which
made no effort at all, either on the spiritual or physical
side ; there were athletic clubs, but these too confined
themselves solely to athletics.   What we wanted to
develop our institute into was a place which should
recognize that God had given man more than one
side to his character, and where we could gratify any
reasonable taste, whether athletic, intellectual, spiritual
or   social.   At the end of 1881 the Polytechnic came
into the market.   In those days I used personally to
see every member who joined the Institute."

On the opening night he was engaged from a quarter
past five till a quarter past one the next morning
booking new members.   Mr. Hogg had in his mind to
make provision for 2,000 members, but in the first
season it reached 6,800, and at the time when the
pamphlet from which this account is taken (about
three years ago) it had reached 15,000.

To dogmatize upon the origins of the more obvious
forms of social service is to be inexcusably narrow.   A
man who was a dried mummy millenniums before the
Christian era, has these words upon his funerary
papyrus—" Doing that which is Right and hating that
which is Wrong, I was *bread* to the hungry, *water* to
the thirsty, *clothes* to the naked, a *refuge* to him that
was in want, that which I did to him the great God
hath done to me." [1]

[1] *Rénouf*, pp. 74, 75.

Who is to say that he was not a ragged school man ?
Similarly a scribe who wrote—" Do not be engrossed
in the house where beer is drunk " may have held a
Band of Hope.   It will be safe likewise to challenge
contradiction that the good Egyptian lady, charitable
to all of her sex, whether " girls, wives or widows,"
whose inscription is at Miramur did not hold a mothers'
meeting.   It says—" My heart inclined me to the
Right when I was yet a child, not yet instructed as to
the Right and Good.   And what my heart dictated
I failed not to perform.   And God rewarded me for
this, rejoicing me with the happiness that He has
granted me for walking after His way." [1]

We had been accustomed to regard Mrs. Bayly,
of Notting Hill, as the originator of mothers' meetings,
but it appears that these meetings, now a national
institution adopted by all religious communities, were
already in a certain stage of development in ragged
schools before she took up one in a ragged school, at
the instance of a City missionary.   She popularized
by means of her pen this means of helping the poor,
and made it the boon it has become.   The actual
origin as far as can be ascertained lies to the credit
of Miss Elizabeth Twining at a ragged school in
Clare Market.   Miss Louisa Twining, her sister, well
known in Church circles, one of the veteran social
workers spared to this generation, has furnished us with
the fact that this school existed in the late thirties. [2]

It is a very precious link, because it establishes
contact with one who has given her life to the better-

---

[1] Hibbert Lectures, 1879.

[2] *Thoughts on Social Questions*, Louisa Twining.   Elliott
Stock, 1903.

ment of the condition of the pauper and the workhouse child.

In this connexion it is fitting that a passing tribute should be paid to Miss Cobbe, who has just gone to her rest. She was engaged in a similar work and was a ragged school worker with Miss Carpenter in Bristol.

JOHN MACGREGOR, M.A., FOUNDER OF THE SHOE-BLACK BRIGADE AND OPEN-AIR MISSION.

Any one who has read Mrs. Bayly's *Ragged Homes and How to Mend Them* can understand why it was that her experiences when printed were so stimulating. Her power in her meeting had the same origin as her literary power. It arose from a deep piety, long and careful pondering upon the problems of life, exceptional sympathy and imagination, a healthy sense of justice and an abundant sense of humour.

Accordingly she was able to write a very human book that profoundly stirred the public and from that time the universalism of the mothers' meeting dates. One or two quotations will indicate the spirit of the book.

" It is the realization of this great thought of being one with them (the mothers) which is the true qualification.

" It has been quaintly said, that ' there are more points in which a queen resembles her washerwoman than in which she does not.' Without dwelling upon these extremes, nothing is more certain than that wherever a lady goes amongst the poor, hoping to benefit them by her influence, she must be impressed much more by the points of resemblance that exist between them, than by the points of difference."

The book is very much more than good advice. The insight shown in the character sketches betrays a proficient in the lore of life's school—the earnest, kindly observer genially interpreting human nature by the aid of a shrewd head and an unselfish heart.

The argument for mothers' meetings is put very cogently.

" I have known many women, under thirty years of age, with six or eight children, so totally unqualified for almost everything which they had to do that I have wondered how they managed to exist at all. I am now, of course, speaking of those below the class from which we usually obtain our domestic servants ; and amongst this class, more unfit for life's solemn duties, the earliest marriages are contracted, apparently without any idea that at least as much preparation is needed as is deemed necessary for breaking stones on the road.

" If a mother cannot train her children during the first years of infancy, they remain untrained ; and not only are the wise man's words proved true that ' a child left to itself bringeth its mother to shame,' but it is found that the multiplication of these families left to themselves, bringeth a nation to shame.

" It is to the poor man's wife that we must chiefly look when we indulge the hope of reducing that frightful amount of crime which, with all our inventions, discoveries, and improvements, sometimes awakens a fear that we may not really be in so prosperous a condition, socially and nationally, as our rapid progress in what is called civilization would lead a superficial observer to suppose.

" The question then arises, considering that nineteen girls out of twenty do not receive a proper home-training, what is the best substitute for it ?

" If we were to see seven people struggling in the water and could only save one from drowning, we could not plead as an excuse for neglecting to help that one our inability to rescue the six. In like manner, we must use the little light that is given to us, trusting that, as we advance, more light will be granted.

" I have never yet been able to see how schools, or any system of national education could meet this difficulty.

" Much has been said and written about ladies devoting their leisure to the poor, and there is no doubt that much more good might be done by them in this way than is done ; but the work we refer to demands something far beyond the occasional call, the book lent, and the garment cut out."

The value of this one operation to our own movement and to the entire nation is incalculable.

The R.S.U. can scarcely claim to have been the very first with the " pence bank." But in this, as in other operations, it has been receptive of ideas, and by the multiplication of a simple notion has gained for it an acceptance it did not have previously. Miss Twining had a pence bank at the same time as her " Mothers' Meeting," and we know of nothing antecedent to the Clare Market Ragged School. Mrs. Bayly gives an amusing account of one of her first depositors.

A ragged urchin came one day to the schoolroom where the bank was held and wanted a penny minded. He also said he would bring another that night and every evening if she would come for it. She said she was unable to do that but would be glad to receive sevenpence from him every Monday evening. The boy was afraid he would lose it at pitch and toss. An arrangement was, however, made by which he could leave it in the dinner hour.

Then he wanted to know what Mrs. Bayly would do with the money he intended to bring.

Satisfied on that point he wanted to know what would happen if he died. The lady said she had not thought of that : perhaps he had better make a will.

" But I can't write, and I've heard as how wills is ' allus writed.' "

" Then you had better come to the Ragged School and learn."

" Well, I think I will. I have heard it takes a sight o' money to bury anybody. If I should die afore I can write, you can spend the money for that."

In 1859 the reformatories and refuges, till that time

under the wing of the Union, were united for convenience into a distinct society called The Reformatory and Refuge Union. The R.S.U. was at that time disbursing funds to the extent of £550 a year in capitation grants at the rate of £3 a year per head for destitute scholars, besides giving grants to the refuges themselves. There were then some 500 institutions providing food and shelter.

Government aid and supervision was brought in at this time, so this pairing off was thought desirable. The growth of the shoeblack brigades has been already referred to. Another offshoot was the Open-Air Mission that had its origin in a suggestion contained in the R.S.U. Magazine.

The process is continuous; the R.S.U. while it remains healthy will have no final and rigid form. Changing conditions bring new expedients. Out of these may arise at any time a specialized form of service sufficiently important to be regarded as an off-shoot. The voluntary workers are in relation to the solid structure of the movement, to the fixed core of achievement, just what the living velvet is to a stag's antler. So long as it lives and is full of pulsing arterial blood, the ramifying goes on. While our staff is thousands strong there are likely to be new developments.

CHAPTER XV

Growth and Progress

PERIOD 2. FROM THE GREAT EXHIBITION OF 1851
TO THE EDUCATION COMMISSION, 1862.

" Some years ago, Ragged Schools were an untried experiment ; and it is not to be wondered at that some persons then considered both the practicability and the expediency of such an attempt very doubtful ; but when we see what that system has now become, I think it must be admitted, that it was a grain of mustard seed, planted by faith, which has been watered by the dew of God's Holy Spirit, and which has now increased to a large and umbrageous forest tree."—LORD ROBERT GROSVENOR, *Annual Meeting*, 1851.

THE year 1851 marks a fresh start in several directions. The country entered upon a period of unexampled business prosperity. There was also a rapid practical application of recent inventions and discoveries. Since the Queen's Speech was sent by telegraph in 1847, wires were put up in all directions.

In our own movement the all-round tutelage of the poor child had been completed. The structure was finished in a measure, and for two years it had in public estimation been removed from the position of being a questionable fad of fanatic evangelicals to that of a useful institution upon which Royal and Governmental approval could be put.

Lord Shaftesbury's career was a great factor in public life as well as in the Ragged School Union. He also had reached a point of departure. In that year he left the Commons for the Lords. Although he missed the life and stir of the lower chamber there can be no doubt the change was good for his health, and the whole atmosphere after he had made a speech or two was more congenial to him than that of the other house. By destiny a fighter, he was yet a sensitive, shrinking man by nature, " too bilious for public life." Henceforth " the brazen faces," " low insults," as well as " the accursed effrontery " of the Radicals would make him suffer no more.

But we must not be unfair to these Radicals, who often voted in the same lobby with him. To them, no doubt, he seemed a friend of the down-trodden, if family interests were not touched. They knew the condition of the tenantry on the Shaftesbury estates. They saw the display and the " incredible waste " of the establishment while the father still lived, and knew not of the entry in Lord Shaftesbury's diary after one of his father's banquets, " The few pounds which I want for Ragged Schools seem wasted in every dish." Bright would have been a friend, though an opponent, had he known the man. Cobden had a flash of insight during the delivery of the famous speech of 1843, and ever after treated him with respect. But there were other men, of lower moral tone, who, nevertheless, did good work for England, who would possess no key of interpretation of his nature at all. To them he was a solemn fraud who *could* be exasperatingly haughty.

One figure stands out prominently as typical of the group. Dashing Tom Duncombe, dandy, sportsman, man of the world, *cher ami* of Vestris the dancer, had a real interest in the people. To run risks on their behalf rather than curtail pleasures was his way of showing it. It is due to him that a very pretty conspiracy against the working-man was defeated in 1844.

A Mr. Miles brought in a Bill in which the Government took enough interest to refer it to a committee.

It contained a provision that an employer could bring his man before a justice, upon a *verbal* or written contract, in case of refusal to work or *other misbehaviour*, and get him two months' hard labour upon his own unsupported statement or that of *his agent* or *manager*.

One would think that any legislator would see what a tool of oppression this could be. A man with an attractive wife or daughter could be made a jail-bird at any time by an intriguing foreman. Yet, incredible as it seems, Duncombe and Ferrand had a hard fight of it before they brought the House to see it.

Men of this stamp were supporting the efforts of the noble Chartist lawyer, W. P. Roberts. This man, by his magnificent energy, was able to prove to the country that there was law enough in England to defeat the great labour captains in their astounding and cynical campaign upon liberty.

Upon the most flimsy charges, the Justices, of the Peace of the mining districts who were mine-owners, were casting men into prison wholesale. Roberts seemed to be for ever on the top of a mail-coach. On January 13 he obtained, through Judge Williams of the Queen's Bench in London, the acquittal of three miners condemned by the Justices of the Peace of Bilston, and before this he had got six set free by Judge Patteson. In Preston there were four, and in Manchester seven for whom he obtained a writ of habeas corpus and acquittal from Judge Wightman. He seemed to fly over the land. In Prescott there were nine in jail, but when news of the coming of Roberts arrived, they were set at liberty. After this, prison doors seemed to fly open at the very mention of his dreaded name. In April there was one man condemned in Derby, four in Wakefield and four in Leicester, but he had them all released. He brought mine-owners before the courts until they cordially feared and hated him.

If Lord Shaftesbury took any part at all in these events it would be similar to his attitude towards the measure for corn-law repeal. He may have given a laggard sanction to them. Probably he outgrew more prejudices than any man of his time, but he did so slowly. This is the reason that the upholders of the " rights of man " and the man who righted " the wrongs of the child " had so little in common, and the reason that made Lord Shaftesbury glad to turn his back upon those who, from his point of view, had nothing but " sneers for every sentiment of a gentle-man."

The reader may here think that an apology is due. Up till this time Lord Shaftesbury was known as Lord Ashley, and it is, from a strict College-of-Arms stand-point, an error to give him the title before the time. But he has passed into history as Lord Shaftesbury, and two names to one man have before now confused the unwary. An amusing instance of this happened at the time that Lord Shaftesbury gave his support to the emancipation movement in America.

An American paper had the following paragraph :—

" Who, then, is this Lord Shaftesbury ? An unknown lordling—one of your modern philanthropists, who has suddenly started up to take part in a passing agitation.

It is a pity he does not look at home. Where was he when Lord Ashley was so nobly fighting the Factory Bill and pleading the cause of the English slave? We never even heard of the name of this Lord Shaftesbury then."

It must have been a great pleasure to him to bring to an end such stinging taunts as that from Harriet Martineau and others, " Physician, heal thyself."

Not only were the cottagers on his estate re-housed at no advance in rent, but a crusade was begun against the farmers who oppressed the labourers under the truck system. As Engels very truly says, in this respect economics and not morals are to be credited with a beneficent change. Before Free Trade came in, employers of all kinds were accustomed, by every sort of petty exaction, fines and frauds as general dealers and house providers to their helpless workpeople, to squeeze secondary profit out of their earnings. Afterwards it was not worth while. Time was worth more money. One of the Assistant Poor Law Commissioners on the 1843 Commission was fortunate enough to get a labourer's housekeeping book for a year. In that the prices paid for groceries and other things at the one shop of the village are very high.

Lord Shaftesbury set his face against all such practices and lost many tenants. The system was very profitable, and without it the farms were not worth so much. The expenses of his repairs and rebuilding were very heavy ; then he had the empty farms, as well as the surprising discovery of the serious embarrassment of the family estates. Yet he never flinched, but paid the penalty by being a harassed man for the rest of his days. Lord Shaftesbury had many people disliking him who were good men and women, and these changed toward him when they realized how much more and how much different he was than they had thought. The frigid aristocrat posing as a philanthropist at other people's expense was found at the near view to be one of the Greathearts of all time.

The inquiry into the condition of the women and children in agricultural England in 1843 seems to have been directed against him. The haste (for a State inquiry) with which the inquiry was conducted and the report printed and issued, gives one the suspicion that an enemy, or many enemies, had done this. One of the Commissioners complains that he only had thirty days altogether, and two of these were spent in coach rides. What seems probable is that some one was interested that the report should appear at the same time as the report of the Small Trades Commission, the report on children engaged in trades not included under the Factory Act. There is no denying that the state of things in the south-west corner of England was terribly bad. " Physician, heal thyself," was not in the least out of place addressed to the man who had the power to do it.

Turning now from the leader to the movement, it should be said that the opinion began to grow that perhaps after all these rough children were not irreclaimable. Lord Shaftesbury, in 1843, in his famous speech in the House, had spoken of the lad of fourteen as almost beyond help. That reference, and a sentence from an annual meeting speech by the Rev. William Arthur, are very illuminating as to general opinion. His words were: " It appears to be ceded that the recovery of these hapless ones is not beyond hope." It may be thought that all the schools in the movement now moved forward at the same rate of speed, but it was not so. Right through the sixty years, schools were born and schools died. In some there was arrested development, in others a rapid material progress culminating in a quite exceptional position among the sister schools. Where this was not accompanied by a selfishly isolated pursuit of local interests, cramping and limiting a grand conception of citizen service, they were the pace-makers of the association. They carried to successful completion the experiments in new devisings. The smaller, poorer, schools kept closer to the lowest class of child for a longer time than the larger and most business-like schools, partly because the urchin feels at home in a shanty, and partly because, where the numbers are few, the fisher for souls can ply his fish with a slack line.

In a few weeks a disorderly, dirty set of children in a well-conducted school alter entirely in appearance and obedience to regulations. When they reach that point the attempt to pass them on to another agency usually means a dropping out altogether. This process of betterment in externals began early, but the scholars were immovable for the most part; they introduced companions and thus interfered with that ideal of a continuous current of rough material coming into an institution, passing through, being improved, and then transferred to higher-grade agencies. That, on general principles, seems the proper thing. But a little reflection convinces the reader that human nature would never work that way. An attachment between himself and a scholar is the teacher's lever of influence for doing his work, and at the same time his own comfort when wearied with the difficulties.

In spite of this it is surprising how faithful the work was kept to its objects and origin. " Stick to the

gutter " was an admonition always being heard. In
1852 we get the first mention of a crêche and references
to mothers' meetings. The broomers, steppers and
messengers are referred to in the report.

In this year a Select Committee of the House of
Commons was appointed to consider the question of
juvenile crime. The Ragged School Union was approached as being a preventive agency. It was suggested that it should come under Government. A
conference was held at which forty delegates, representing thirty-two schools, were present. To Lord
Shaftesbury's great relief the majority were against
Government aid. The figures were; five for Government
aid on any terms, six for Government aid without
interference, twenty-one against the proposal altogether.
Nothing has been said hitherto about the schools outside the Union. It should be remembered that there
were a good many of these. The recollection of this
fact makes the President's claim for the effects of
ragged schools upon the Chartist riots as more feasible.
The only other Ragged School Union event of importance was the appointment of an inspector. About this
time, or a little before, the emigration of Germans to the
United States became brisk, and about three years
previously, Irish immigration to this country. The
Irishman, famine-expelled from his country and without
resources, was the prey of the capitalist and was looked
upon as a blackleg by the English labourer. Like the
pauper alien or the Chinese coolie to-day, he had no
friends. On his part, he brought with him black hate
towards the English in his soul, as was natural. Thousands of his countrymen had crossed the Atlantic in
1848. In America they prospered, and became the
parents of England's bitterest and most powerful foes,

the prosperous Irish-Americans. But the Irishman of
the London courts did not prosper; he usually de-
teriorated. The English labourer, himself oppressed,
could not make allowance for the Irishman who,
hunger-driven, took the bread from English children's
mouths. The brave struggle of the miners against
Lord Londonderry was defeated by Irish labour.

But the Irishman had children too ; and, being a born
fighter, and being unable to see that Society did not owe
him a maintenance, there was trouble in the courts and
alleys and lanes of our city. In those " good old days "
of " thin arms and thick sticks " there were often most
murderous affrays. In the earlier pre-police days,
luckless Bow Street runners, with a few special constables hastily sworn in, would often have to take their
lives in their hands to quell a riot in an Irish colony,
such as Saffron Hill. These thief-takers were a motley
crew, frequently ex-convicts. When they went on
such expeditions, never relished, they were armed to
the teeth with cutlasses, pistols and batons. Inter-
cepted in Clerkenwell on their way, they might have
been mistaken for a shipwrecked pirate crew.

The experiences of one in this district may here be
given. In the story, told by himself, he relates how
he and his fellows, reluctantly and under pressure from
the chief, went down. He had a look at the crowd and
did not like its appearance, so, like the Irishman at the
Parnell Commission, who thought it wiser to be a
coward for five minutes than be dead all his lifetime,
he slipped away. All the shops were closed, and blanched
faces peered over the house-copings. At the door of
one of these shops he hammered with his fists. Getting
no response, in a raucous voice he summoned the ter-
rified proprietor to open in the king's name.

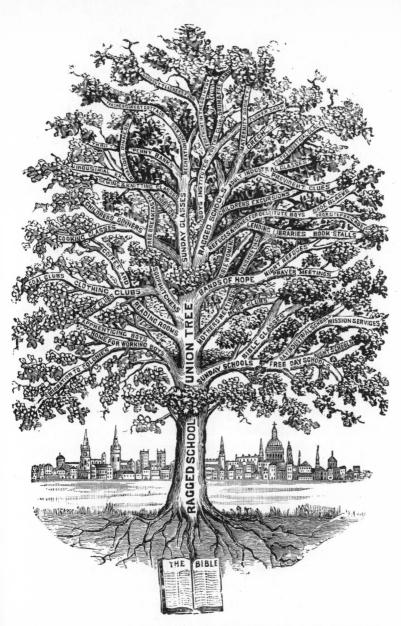

RAGGED SCHOOL TREE DRAWN BY THE LATE MR. S. E. HAYWARD.

When he was inside and the door was bolted he drew out a horse-pistol, to the shopkeeper's great dismay, and began to load it. First there was the powder-charge; then came a wad. "Look sharp—some red paint; now some paper. Thanks!" There was a grin on the shop-keeper's face as he put the chain on behind the officer. That sagacious man had an inspiration. It is an instance verifying the truism that great minds think alike. Napoleon at Marseilles put an end to a riot by using grape-shot in the first charge of his guns and blank powder afterwards. This man did better: he dispersed a crowd with red paint.

Advancing boldly in the middle of the road he awaited the oncoming of a wild Irishman in front of the rest. When he was quite close he fired. Down went the man from the combined effects of the powder-charge and his own fright; the wad also came with some force. Had he been rent to rags by a shell he could not have looked worse. The horror-stricken crowd melted away, and the victim was taken to the nearest hospital. For a moment he puzzled the surgeons, and then he had to wait to be wiped down, till the laugh was finished.

In the district where this happened, and while such wild scenes were constantly being enacted, a small ragged school was being carried on by a delicate, frail little woman, who was accustomed to say that "if one of those big roughs were to take her by the arm she was sure it would cause her death." A lady, now aged, sends this testimony of her: "She was of such sweet moral suasion and strong Christian character that she was able to maintain order amongst the roughest lads as well as children." The lady who volunteers this information also helped, and found she could keep the interest of rough young thieves in Bible stories because

of the illustrations she could give as the result of travelling in the Holy Land when she and her husband were
on their honeymoon. She lived at Clapham.

But returning to our Irish. They played a large part
in ragged school history. Among the many personal
reminiscences that have been sent us, there are repeated
references to the Irish; and even when they are not
specifically mentioned, wherever there is a notice of
trouble they were certainly there. This does not mean
that the Irish were ill-disposed towards a ragged school.
Quite the contrary. Upon occasion they would even
patronize it. If not quite able to make the best of
both worlds, they knew how to exploit two Churches.
When a baby was safely baptized by a Roman priest,
what was to prevent a second christening by the curate
fresh from the country, especially if nice little frocks
were given away. Then, too, those half-crowns from
the same source, after a sham illness, were very convenient. It was a little chat with the priest and a
local chemist that spoilt all that. There was a good-
humoured tolerance of the ragged school till the priest
sowed discord. Irish children *would* come into the
schools for shelter and warmth and any little benefits
that might be going. The parents as often as not did
not know and did not care where they were. But the
priests knew, because they watched and they cared very
much. That was the beginning of all the unpleasant-
ness. Irksome penances and even excommunication
were used to quicken a sense of parental responsibility.
The means were effectual, and teachers were pelted
with refuse and stones. A letter of recollections from
another old friend refers to this kind of thing, and
calmly says: " I believe that rotten eggs were used, but
I was not there at the time." Others were not so
fortunate in a well-timed absence.

The curate who christened the babies and gave the half-crowns had a taste of the quality of the Irish of Islington.

St. Mary's wished to start a ragged school, and Mr. Locke was asked to advise. No doubt he had a good deal of this to do at that time, and was as non-plussed as Opie when asked to explain the mixing of his colours, or Matthew Arnold challenged to explain the mysteries of literary style.

Whatever Mr. Locke advised, this placid clergyman never expected what he got.

There were six adults in charge of forty children. A simple chorus was given out. In a little while the youngsters caught the tune and the words. After that there was no stopping them. The workers looked across the room into each other's faces in the vain hope of receiving suggestions. But the climax came when an Irish mob broke every pane of glass in the place, and there was no Mr. Locke present to advise.

Idealize these Irish as one may, they were certainly undesirables. If, in the opinion of lodging-house tramps, they were not cleanly in their ways, they must have been very bad indeed. We know for certain that they would not forego the holding of wakes around the corpses of victims of cholera, if they could get their own way. The end of the conflict was that the priests themselves started ragged schools. Rome usually does know a good thing when she sees it. Our shoe-blacks were persecuted by Irish boys, and often one might be seen overpowered by a crowd of desperate little urchins. Set upon in that way, like a canary among sparrows, he was helpless. The police and magistrates had to interfere. What the public saw was only half this quarrel, and thought it was a struggle for monopoly

by the Shoe-black Society.   Then the Roman Catholics
had their own brigade, and after a time there was peace.

The support the Society received was not commen-
surate with its deserts, nor the increasing wealth of the
country.   Those two things that under our present
economic arrangements must go together, increase of
real wealth and increase in amount of the medium of
exchange, were leaping up between the years 1847 and
1853.   In nine years the gold in currency increased
throughout the world by one-third.   It came into
England at the rate of £25,000,000 a year.   The increase in trade was larger.   Had it not been for the large
amount of gold available, the Bank would have had to
suspend specie payments.   There was an unprecedented demand for English goods, both from America
and Australia.   The new supply of gold had its snares,
and this country made mistakes for which it paid in
1857.

But for the moment the bad harvest of 1853 and the
Crimean war did not affect the country's finances
seriously.   From this time the scale of living and the
scale of business altered.   Just about this period grain
began to come from the United States in large quantities.

Yet in the Ragged School Union there was no phe-
nomenal increase in funds.   Perhaps an overruling
Providence ordained that it should depend upon enthusiasm rather than money.   It has always been a starved
cause.

There were legacies, and the money available served
to disguise the fact that the Society was not keeping
pace with the national growth in its finances.

It may be only a tale, on the other hand it may be
true, that General Gordon and Cecil Rhodes discussed
the roomful of gold offered to Gordon by the Chinese

at the close of the Taiping rebellion. " What would you have done ? " Gordon is said to have asked. " Taken the gold," said Cecil Rhodes.

In the case of a society a blend of the two seems needed. Spirituality and Materialism give the embodiment of an ideal.

In 1854 the Society made a good use of its windfalls. They paid half the debts for current expenses of all the local schools; appointed two agents to supervise and report upon what was being done. A £50 prize was also offered for the best essay on ragged schools, and £600 set aside for a grant for a fund for refuges. In the same year it began its faithful service prizes. Money was also voted for the training of school teachers.

The report for 1855 refers briefly to the Sanitary Commission.

What a humiliating disclosure was that speech of Sir Benjamin Hall, in 1855. Remembering that this is but fifty years ago, and our fathers, for our sakes, thought England worth saving, should we not look leniently upon the Russians in their trouble, even if some officials have been corrupt ?

It would be difficult for Russia to beat the English record. It cost the ratepayers of Ely Place, Holborn, a sum that amounted to £842 15s. per mile for just *supervising* the paving. The paving itself was another matter.

St. George's-in-the-East was under five separate boards. Somebody must have made some money when it cost 16s. 7½d. each per lamp for 363 lamps just to keep an eye on them. It is a most loathsome account—this story of the vestries brought to judgment.

One charitably hopes that the first R.S.U. secretary

never read this. Had he done so, he must have instantly returned the cheque that St. Pancras sent to the Ragged School Union in 1856. It was a grant to the Society as an agency for reducing pauperism.

At this time Marylebone had its faults, but compared with St. Pancras it was purity itself. There was a difference of 10,000 inhabitants between them and 1,400 acres of surface; yet the wages at St. Pancras vestry were £4,000 as compared with £657 in Marylebone. Marylebone had a debt of £16,000 and St. Pancras £135,000 for paving alone, and it should be stated that the debt of Marylebone was mainly produced by St. Pancras before the two parishes were separated for purposes of administration.

What awful contrasts we have in the social history of the middle of the nineteenth century. A sickening story of parish after parish, where sordid scoundrels feathered their nests at the public expense, and escaped unpunished, is contrasted with that of a poor child compelled by hunger to an act of petty larceny and henceforth launched into a career of crime.

But God did not leave Himself without witness, even in the law courts. A delightful story is told by Guthrie of a Scotch advocate, in fighting mood, defying all law to preserve the spirit of law—the spirit of equity.

Tracing the child's antecedents, denouncing the villainy of the statutes, he lifted the prisoner, whose head did not reach the top of the dock, to a position where the jury could see him. Then he defied the jury, as family men, to bring his client in guilty, and won his case while the judge smiled over his notes.

It was a happy thought to put by a reserve for a refuge fund in 1854. Many a boy just about to enter upon a career of wrong-doing could be taken in hand by a refuge. Ned Wright, the preacher, was such a boy when, afraid to go home because of wrong doing, he determined to trust to luck and be a vagabond. What he did, shows how some of these poor waifs lived.

Raking among the shingle of the Thames shore at low tide, he found enough rusty nails out of the barges to sell for a halfpenny. The halfpenny was taken to a baker, who gave him a hatful of crusts. Where the night would be spent for such a lad might be the turning-point of a lifetime.

All through the fifties there are cheering stories in the reports about the young emigrants. In 1854 it was reported that one scholar, who was earning £150 a year at Melbourne, had saved £250, and was sending £100 to England for the old folks at home. In 1855, poor lads who had become shoe-blacks had paid their own emigration expenses out of their earnings.

The difficulty that a Society experiences, is to know how far it is safe to assume recurring financial responsibility. Subscriptions *must* be the backbone of finance. Donations are liable to fluctuate. The arrangements of many of the local schools were dependent upon the Ragged School Union grant, and the absence of certainty was embarrassing all round.

The subscribers, in 1856, were asked to double their subscriptions. Of the £1,600 aimed at £1,400 was raised. Lord Shaftesbury made one of those stirring appeals for teachers at the annual meeting in 1857 which never went unheeded, the result being that in 1856 the staff was increased by one-third.

The great financial crisis of 1857 does not appear to have affected the Ragged School Union, and considering its serious nature this is rather surprising. The failures in America; expenses of home railways; an over-confidence created by a plentiful gold supply from California and Australia; the sudden stoppage of war-created trade when peace was signed after the Crimean War, were all factors in the trouble. The disturbance of trade due to the China War and Indian Mutiny was another cause. The Western Bank of Scotland, with ninety-eight branch banks, fell in November of that year. The Bank rate rose to 12 per cent.; but an over-issue of a million in bank-notes saved matters from being as bad as they might have been, but still they were bad enough as it was. In Staffordshire 30,000 potters were thrown out of work; sixty-nine blast furnaces were extinguished in England, rendering 28,000 people workless, besides another 16,000 in Scotland. In South Wales, wages were reduced 20 per cent.; and in Yorkshire and Durham wages dropped by £5,000 a week. By the operation of some inscrutable law we appeared at that time to have a financial crisis, roughly speaking, about every ten years. 1837, 1847 and 1857 were all bad years. From this last one it took this country and the Continent a long time to recover. So far from feeling the strain, the Society was able to devote money to the payment of debts of some of the local schools.

In 1859 there was another drop in the numbers of voluntary teachers. The entire history in this matter appears to have been a series of slippings and grippings. Lord Shaftesbury was sterner than usual, and the result was that another 190 joined. A further appeal next year, brought an addition of 300 teachers. Then, in 1862, there was another drop, this time of 170. 1861 saw the earl expending the lightnings of his wrath and the thunders of his invective upon the Educational

Commissioners. In their report they had given but a slighting notice to ragged schools, were outrageously in error with their statistics, and had evidently made only the most superficial inquiries. Just as a traveller in India will learn nothing at the ports, of the schools in the jungle, where they may be less known perhaps than in London, so did these gentlemen manage to miss the ragged schools.

But the friends of these institutions did not allow matters to rest. Sir Stafford Northcote introduced the matter to the attention of the House of Commons by a motion " To inquire how the education of destitute and neglected children may be most efficiently and economically assisted by any public funds." Lord Shaftesbury in the Lords, and the Hon. Arthur Kinnaird in the Commons, moved for a Supplementary Commission to inquire into the working of ragged schools.

The report of this body was inferentially a severe censure upon the Commissioners. A few sentences may be quoted : " It is established by the evidence that there does exist, in many of our large cities and towns, a class of children whom the national system of education does not reach, and who are excluded, in consequence either of the faults or misfortunes of their parents, from any participation in its benefits."

The only thing to be said by way of criticism to this is, that there was no national system beyond the granting of subsidies to the National and British schools which were in private hands. The paragraph expresses a wish for a State-controlled elementary system a device that had been in the minds of the most enlightened men throughout the century.

Returning to the findings of the new Commission. It

was declared "That ragged schools appear by the evidence to be well organized, and to be carried on with much zeal and discretion, and to be calculated to effect a great deal of good." Also that these schools, " when properly managed, are beneficial and not injurious to the day schools, and that a considerable number of children, through their instrumentality, are brought into the National schools, while they provide an education for many that could not otherwise be educated at all."

The final recommendation was, " That ragged schools should be left to the missionary exertions of the ragged school managers, without any interference by the Government further than had already existed."

CHAPTER XVI

Further Development

Period 3. From the Education Commission, 1862, to the Passing of the Education Act.

" I do not wish to disparage or deny kindred efforts. All have worked together in accomplishing this great result ; but without such efforts as these, what could have been expected to result when we presented to the civilised world the spectacle of four millions of human beings, living together within a ring-fence, with a police not equal to that of a third-rate capital in Germany, and with an army hardly sufficient to form the bodyguard for her Majesty."—Lord Shaftesbury, 1870.

ANY one acquainted with the two movements must be struck with the striking resemblance between some of the early work of the Ragged School Union and some of the social and evangelical work of the Salvation Army.

The furnishing and equipment of the Refuges is one point of resemblance. The rag-collecting brigade is another. The " open-airs " in the courts and alleys that preceded the formation of " The Open-Air Mission " is a third. But the feature that prompts this remark is the serious lack of a suitable hymnology that the teachers experienced when beginning their work. The beautiful and sonorous psalmody of the churches was made up of theological tabloids not meet for babes ; accordingly, many of the teachers had to be their own hymn and tune writers, though no doubt they took their own, wherever they found it, from among the choruses of the Primitives or anywhere else.

The one taught to the children of the Islington school already referred to, and with such ultra success, was—

> Come to Jesus just now,
> He will save you—
> I believe it. Hallelujah.

But the teachers were not only hymn writers, but song writers, too. Like " the Army," but before the time when " the Army " was being represented by General Booth alone, a preacher on Mile End Waste, the teachers had their " free-and-easys " for the roughs.

With very little equipment, it was difficult to keep a sustained interest all the year round, week in and week out. Yet the scholars had to be kept off the streets even when nothing was being done with them. Sometimes the teachers were quite at their wits' end. One man bought a spider-monkey. On certain nights Jacko was allowed to perform among the beams and rafters. To this exhibition only those were allowed to come who by attendance and behaviour at the other meetings had qualified themselves for the treat of a good laugh. For these a cup of cocoa each was provided.

But the resemblance to Salvation Army work is closest in this matter of songs. Any one who has seen a Salvation Army captain deal with some half-fuddled and quarrelsome bricklayers by vamping on a banjo and improvising lines to a popular tune would realize it. He is discursive and general till they are in a good humour and take a liking to him; then, the opportunity offering, he strikes right home with a verse about drink and the children's shoe leather.

All this had its counterpart forty years ago in such songs as "Paddy O'Shea," sung to young thieves, and recommending the ragged school, the industrial class, and the young emigrant's life. One teacher alone wrote a hundred hymns and fifty songs. Hymn writers whose compositions are permanent contributions to hymnology have not been lacking amongst us, though we cannot advance an exclusive claim. "God who has made the daisies" was written by Paxton Hood, a very earnest ragged school friend.

Right from 1840 to 1870 we find cholera rampant. A blood tax as well as a money tax was levied by the old vestries. Anybody anxious to study the whole subject may read with advantage Creighton's *History of Epidemics in Great Britain* (1894).

Cholera is responsible for a drop in the numbers of children during the sixties, and perhaps for some teachers. Ageing parents would, as now, overrule the will of a daughter teaching in a plague-stricken district. Only think of one school giving a return of 340 cases of cholera in a week, fifty-three of which, including six in one house, proved fatal. Many schools in the afflicted areas closed for a time. 1866 was a specially bad year. One school has an anniversary called "Black Sunday." It was the first day of opening after a vacation thought prudent when the disease was at its height. On that day the teachers were surrounded by weeping children who had lost relatives.

But though some schools were closed, few of the teachers in them had a holiday. In the one referred to, several of them combined and took a house upon the spot, and worked as a relief agency, caring for the sick, sending some to hospitals, and distributing necessaries to those needing them. In this instance, 1,449 lbs. of meat, 693 lbs. of rice, 414 loaves, 23 gallons of beef tea, 21 gallons of port wine, 7½ gallons of brandy, 56 lbs. of arrowroot, 575 yards of flannel and calico, and other things, were given away. Such activity was exceptional in degree but not in kind. In addition to cholera, there were periods of epidemic of other diseases. Small-pox, scarlet fever, and measles, accompanied by typhus, were prevalent in Ragged School Union history from 1847 to 1848, inclusive, 1862–1864, and 1869–1872. Scarlet fever was also raging in 1869–1870.

Desiring to dispose of this unsavoury subject at once, without referring to it again, we may here say that diphtheria was an epidemic in 1889. As compared with the whole population, the percentage of victims is small; but in the affected districts the concentrated effects on a small scale were not unlike those of the plague of London. Splashes of sombre colour occur throughout the reminiscences of veterans, like vignettes from the brush of Verestchagin (who has just met his death on the Petropavlovsk), as, for example, three cabs with the numbers taken off, in a liveryman's yard, each containing a coffin and a corpse, the head and foot in each instance protruding from the doors.

It is but poetic justice that the Houses of Parliament [1] should probably now be the most insanitary

1 *The Sanitation of London.* By R. Harris Reeves, C.E. (p. 29). Hodgett's Limited, 1902.

spot in London. As we are still only experimenting in drains, the hope of the future lies in this fact.

Another cause of shrinkage in numbers in 1862 is the commencement of the Thames Embankment. Numbers of rookeries were swept away, and schools with them. In 1860 there also began an economic change in the trade of the Port of London, and therefore the maintenance of the riverside population, apart from the thieves and pilferers. In thirty years —that is, up to 1890—its foreign trade had made no proportional increase, but had actually receded one per cent. Other ports absorbed the increase. The thieves had to a large extent been circumvented by the building of docks and the vigilance of the river police. These docks had been built in the following order : West India, 1800 ; East India, 1803 ; London, 1805 ; Commercial, 1810 ; Surrey, 1811 ; St. Catherine's, 1823. These were already in existence when the Ragged School Union started, and were checking the alarming increase of human water-rats. But to these were added the Victoria docks, 1850, Millwall docks, 1868, followed by the extensions of the West India docks in 1870, and the Albert docks in 1888—all within our period. Robbery from the ships brought them all into existence. A check upon this, an inexpansiveness in trade, and structural changes have left the river banks the poorest parts of London. Another thing must not be lost sight of : the watermen have been interfered with by the railways and bridges, and as for the thieves, the change from small sailing craft to large steam vessels increases the difficulties of those upon larceny intent. Probably the Southern Embankment and St. Thomas' Hospital displaced few homes and schools. The

Albert Embankment was completed in 1869. The City improvement—Queen Victoria Street, connecting

MR. JOSEPH G. GENT, FIRST SECRETARY OF THE RAGGED SCHOOL UNION.

the Mansion House with Blackfriars—may have caused the destruction of some dwelling-houses, as also the clearances around Tower Hill. The destruction of

Middle Row, Holborn, and the preparations for the Holborn Viaduct may have slightly affected ragged school interests.

It will be a convenience to dispose of all the street improvements affecting ragged schools at once, although they are subsequent to the dates at the head of the chapter. By the reader's indulgence it is submitted that the widening of parts of Tottenham Court Road in 1877, the widening of Garrick Street, 1861, Coventry Street in 1881, and the making of Charing Cross Road and Shaftesbury Avenue in 1886 and 1887 would affect some families for which ragged schools cater. Other improvements having the same effects took place in Marylebone in 1872, and in the Edgware Road in 1877. In 1888 parts of Hammersmith Road were widened, and small improvements in Fulham in 1891 and Hammersmith in 1897.

Coldharbour Lane, Brixton, was widened in 1890, and South Lambeth Road in 1896. The widening of a part of Newington Butts began in 1877, and a portion of Walworth Road in 1888. An avenue to the New Kent Road at Victory Place, Walworth, was completed in 1887. High Street, Camberwell, and High Street, Peckham, had more breathing space in 1882. From 1884 to 1887 there were demolitions in Bermondsey. In East London, Commercial Street in 1876, and the widening of Shoreditch in 1877, made great changes, as well as the new road leading to Oxford Street, completed in 1879. Bethnal Green Road was also widened in the same year.

Goswell Road, opposite *The Angel*, Islington, came under treatment in 1879, and Upper Street in 1888. The cost of these changes up to the date of the Queen's

Jubilee was about 11½ millions. Now we have the district between Holborn and the Strand broken through with a new thoroughfare, destroying the old Clare Market area and part of St. Giles'. Where are the displaced people? They have not perished; they have not all reformed. Large families are still usual among them as well. They are in new districts. In the police court items of local newspapers some of their doings are recorded, and any one who collects them for one district only, will be surprised at what is going on. If men were not so busy, more notice would be taken of the mischief that is being done in many directions.

Lord Shaftesbury always maintained that arrangements for the accommodation of the unhoused poor should always accompany these changes. " Whither can the poor go? They have no means of living away from their work when they have it," was one of the points he was continually raising. In 1851 he said, " A number of dwellings was cleared away, and no provision made for the accommodation of those who were displaced, so that, while the new street added to the beauty of the town, it had the effect of exaggerating the evil that pressed upon the humbler classes."

By 1863 the Ragged School Union found that playing the part of the fabled pelican towards its young involved serious blood-letting. With its legacies it had been paying local debts. Now that this money was swallowed up, they wished to have a year's grants in hand. In possession of that, they would be able to give local schools sufficient notice if support would be withdrawn or lessened.

The President again appealed for teachers, and in the next year there was a rise of 140. Lady readers will be interested to learn that the London ragged schools in 1864 supplied 1,920 domestic servants. It is to be feared this is one of the lost arts. Another grumble about insufficiency of teachers produced an additional four hundred in 1865. The first President seems to have kept his finger upon this, the position of voluntary labour, as the pulse of the movement. He was in a unique position for drawing workers, because he had some sort of connexion with nearly all the available people in the metropolis. He was not sparing in criticism of any association that he thought was becoming narrowed in its objects, that should, in his opinion, supply teachers. It certainly was a great need, and is so still, for no unsectarian body is automatically fed.

His appeals were always directed to the highest motives in human nature, and calculated to attract those who would give whole-hearted service. A passage from the personal pleadings of 1865, from Exeter Hall platform, may be given here, because the pleas advanced hold good at the present time:—

"You must have in mind that the whole system of Ragged Schools turns upon voluntary teaching.

"We have a number of paid teachers, among the very best to be found in the whole world—zealous, true, diligent—I will say, unparalleled teachers. But the system cannot rest upon paid services. We have not the funds to meet the demand, and if we had them, the system is of such a peculiar nature that it must be governed, it must be bound, it must be imbued, it must be inspired altogether by the voluntary principle. There are many forms of things to which the established principle is applicable ; this is one of those to which it is altogether inapplicable. If you adopt it to any great extent, you will go on till you are brought under that which of all things I should most deprecate—Government influence. The voluntary principle is essential to this movement ; it requires so much self-devotion, so much zeal, so much taste for the work. There must be more than an ordinary sense of duty ; there must be affection ; there must be love ; there must be a burning desire to save the souls of these poor children ; there must, in fact, be an ungovernable impulse to go among them and bring them out of vice and institute them in the ways of truth and holiness ; and this cannot be done by the established principle ; it must be done by the voluntary principle, and the voluntary principle alone. I must entreat again and again that more teachers would offer themselves for the work. We have at present barely enough to keep up the state of things that exists ; but our desire is to increase the Ragged Schools and to spread them over the whole metropolis."

In 1866, a year before the usual decade year of disaster, came the failure of the banking firm, Gurney, Overend & Co., which caused the winding up of 180 companies in a few months. The result was sufficiently serious to induce the Foreign Secretary of this country to send a circular letter to our ambassadors in foreign countries abroad, advising them " to assure foreigners that the bottom had not fallen out of our island." [1]   Again the same remarkable phenomenon

---

[1] *Commercial Crises of the Nineteenth Century*, p. 96. Hyndman.

was witnessed as in the last crash : that a movement having several hundred weak spots, financially, drawing money from all kinds of sources, was but very slightly affected by a disaster that shook the nation. The Ragged School Union made no headway financially in this year ; at the same time, it lost no ground. For a little while it seemed as if headquarters would lose its little all, for the Bank of London, the Consolidated Bank, and the Agra and Masterman's Bank, at which they banked, all suspended and closed their doors. But the clouds cleared, and the Society actually gained by the temporary suspension.

After Lord Shaftesbury's appeal for teachers in 1865, there was no further difficulty till after the Education Act was passed.

Nothing calling for special remark occurred during the few years preceding that great event, except a general gratifying development.

The two pioneers whose names have been associated with that of Mr. Starey and Lord Shaftesbury in the founding of the Society are Mr. William Locke and Mr. Joseph G. Gent.

Mr. Locke succeeded Mr. Starey as honorary secretary in 1846, and from that date till 1864 always read the report at the annual meeting. There is but a meagre record, in the sketch that appeared at his death in the Ragged School Union Magazine, but the internal evidence of the early history exhibits him as a thinker and a self-effacing man. Associated with Mr. Starey from the commencement, he was thirty-nine years of age when he took his place, and fifty-seven when ill-health compelled him, in 1863, to relinquish the position and retire to Margate. His early reports show a patriotic · and statesmanlike view of the position of the ragged schools in national education. He never made a claim for the day-schools that by its extravagance would hide from the view of the average Englishman the real significance of the all-round work.

For himself he made no claim, and thus deepened it; but he was extremely anxious that his friend Starey should have the credit that belonged to him. Imperfect versions of the origin of the Society had currency given them before all the records now to hand were available. These made him very indignant, and his letters show his chivalrous jealousy on his friend's behalf. In one of them to Mr. Starey he says, " You were the mainspring of the whole thing, and dragged me into it by degrees. You suggested Bevan's name, and I think Lord Ashley's."

Mr. Joseph George Gent had been a schoolmaster at Stone, in Staffordshire, before he came to London to take charge of a British School near King's Cross. While occupying this position, he became secretary of the Local Auxiliary of the Sunday School Union and visitor of Sunday Schools. This brought him into contact with Mr. Locke. He became assistant secretary to him; and in 1849 the secretary of the Society. In 1866, a telescope and microscope were presented to him by Lord Shaftesbury, on behalf of the teachers. The earl's testimony of him was, " I know he is a deep and sincere friend of the cause of God and suffering humanity." In 1880, upon his retirement, he received an illuminated address also. All the officers and teachers in the affiliated schools held him in the highest esteem, and he enjoyed the complete confidence of the Committee and President during the whole of his long term of office.

From this date a new period is entered upon, characterized by new conditions; but the work in essence was the same, as in the nature of things it must ever be. An adjustment, however, was not quickly attained, and much mischief was done to the cause by some of its best friends. How this arose it will now be necessary to describe.

CHAPTER XVII

The R.S.U. and Diminution of Crime

"We have stood between the living and the dead and the plague."—GUTHRIE.

IT will be scarcely convenient to deal with this matter in a piecemeal fashion in connexion with the general history, so a brief survey of the whole field as far as it concerns the work may as well be taken now. In the early reports and appeals the subject had a very great prominence. The visitors' book of the R.S.U. School of Industry at Westminster, had some much-prized entries such as those of: The Rev. H. Smith, Chaplain, Parkhurst Prison:—"This plan, by God's blessing, must do good, and is the thing that is so much wanted."

Rev. W. C. Osborn, Bath, Chaplain of the jail:— "I am much pleased with the arrangements in this school, because they are in keeping with the nature of the institution. There is no lavish expenditure, and everything is done that the situation admits of."

The alarming increase in the cost of maintaining criminals drew attention to any proposal for the prevention of crime, and the fact that one-fourth of the offences were committed by lads and girls was not lost upon the public. "Millions of pounds are spent

in punishing crime, thousands are grudged for preventing it," was the argument in 1847.

There was point in this, as also in the following—

" The total cost of punitive machinery is two millions
of money annually, and the cost of a convict is from
£100 to £150. When he has graduated he is not only
a non-producer, but till he ends his career he will exist
by rapine and produce his own kind in a multiplied
form.

"On the other hand, give a child who, left to itself,
must before long be a convicted or unconvicted thief
five years' industrial training, it costs £50 all told, and
the chances are you get a wage-earner who becomes a
national asset."

A choice of lower ground than an appeal to conscience and enthusiasm this might be, but it reached
a large circle upon whom sentiment would be wasted.
The " Stitch in Time " appeal was used for all it was
worth, and fear of revolution and anxiety as to taxation
made it worth while. There was wind in the sails of
the mill of reform, and the millers were hungry for
grist. They obtained it from the prudent, as well as
the warm-hearted and the devout.

The committee got into touch with the chaplains of
the jails—working with them. Any hopeful sign was
looked for and made known, as when in 1850 the
Governor of Coldbath Fields in his report, said that if
the figures relating to crime were understood it would
be seen that crime was decreasing. The workers were
encouraged in their efforts, and the committee fortified
in their position by a passage in the report by the
chaplains of the same prison.

" Much might doubtless be effected if the benevolent
scheme for some time past in agitation could be brought

to bear, and prisoners of tender years be subjected, not to the discipline of criminals, but to religious and industrial training, apart from the hardening associations of the felons' prison."

Lieutenant Tracy, Governor of Tothill Fields, went out of his way to mention the ragged school held in the thieves' public-house, Duck Lane, Westminster, as doing a good work for 200 outcasts.

A CHRISTMAS DINNER TO TRAINING SHIP BOYS.—NATIONAL REFUGES.

On the R.S.U. Visiting Committee were : The Chaplain of the Giltspur Street Compter, the Ordinary of Newgate, the Assistant-Chaplain of the House of Correction, and the Chaplain of the Reform School, Red Hill, Reigate, the Chaplain of Holloway and the Inspector of Prisons and Reformatories.

Reformatories, refuges, and industrial schools are now united under a separate Union, but a very large

proportion of them had their origin in ragged school
voluntary effort.   From the reformatories and industrial schools the usual outlet was emigration.

A list of ships and the number each took is given in
the 1849 report, and is very interesting.   The destina-
tions were Port Philip and Adelaide.

The *Labuan*	took out	. . .	14
,, *Marian*	,,	. . .	13
,, *Osprey*	,,	. . .	16
,, *Ramillies*	,,	. . .	13
,, *George Palmer*	,,	. . .	8
,, *Lord George Bentinck*	,,	. . .	14
,, *Mary Shepherd*	,,	. . .	19
,, *Caroline Agnes*	,,	. . .	11
,, *Sir Ed. Parry*	,,	. . .	16
,, *Saxon*	,,	. . .	16
,, *Eliza*	,,	. . .	3
Waiting for a ship , ...		. . .	7

150

There were sixteen refuges to which subsidies and
capitation grants were paid for scholars introduced by
the Society.   Undoubtedly refuges, apart from a
work of mercy, did much to diminish youthful crime.
A common lodging-house is no place for a child now,
but what such places were like in pre-registration days
is too horrible a tale to tell, but one suggestive fact
will explain the need for refuges.   Lads and girls
were herded together in the same rooms, and sometimes in the same beds.

In the idea of a shelter there was no monopoly, so
it was copied until at the founding of the Reformatory
and Refuge Union there were 150 of them.

Of the thieves in the schools something has been said
already, but we can form but a small idea of their
number and their tricks.   A friend who was a curate

in Islington in 1845, and was engaged with others in conducting a ragged school, sends a manuscript that gives an amusing account of the way the Bible was introduced into some Irish Catholic homes. The Bibles in use at the school were in superior bindings, and the boys having concluded they were worth having to keep, laid a plan. In the middle of the evening the lights were put out and all stampeded away with the books. Into the homes where the Bibles went visitors had not been allowed an entrance. The expertness of the pickpocket of that time is almost past belief. Ned Wright, the evangelist, in his life mentions an incident that happened when he was at Brixton Prison. He, with some others, was at the treadmill. Among the gang of thirty were several noted pickpockets. One of them, more daring than the rest, laid a wager with another during the morning task that he would get a piece of hard tobacco from the turnkey's vest pocket. About three in the afternoon the turnkey dozed on his seat. The convict had to pass him on his way from the seat to the wheel, and in a twinkling he had the tobacco. Needless to say there were smiles among the men at the wheel. The turnkey never referred to it afterwards.

A former Recorder of London once said that juvenile crime had been reduced 75 per cent. mainly by the ragged schools. Without arrogating to the Society, or the movement, any such claim, which must leave out of view a mass of work done by others, and the play of subtle influences and forces economic, legal and administrative, as well as moral, that make such a broad generalization impossible, it may be fairly said that the share of the R.S.U. in the diminution of crime is not small.

Upon one occasion (1862) the head of the police of London (Sir Richard Mayne) called attention to the fact that from a ragged school, at its foundation attended mainly by thieves, through which in five years 12,000 children had passed, there had not been a single police-court case. This was in the district where Fagin, the Dodger, Charley Bates, and Noah Claypole were drawn from the life.

But criminal law and administration have also been greatly changed, and by those changes a large number of criminals have ceased to be made. The silent and cell systems have prevented the contamination of the young offender by the hardened scoundrel, as used to be the case. Even with adults a more humane treatment has increased the chances of reform of life. The bulk of these improvements took place in the reign of Queen Victoria. Before that time, law and practice were very barbarous. In 1833 a child of nine standing in the dock, saw the judge put on the black cap and then heard himself condemned to be hanged. His offence was poking a stick through a window and stealing paint value $2\frac{1}{2}d$. He was reprieved. Taking the period embraced between the accession and jubilee of the late sovereign is sufficient for our purpose to indicate the interaction of ragged schools and treatment of offenders upon each other.

The calendar is prepared from that in the Rev. J. W. Horsley's *Jottings from Jail*, but is confined to facts having a more or less direct bearing on child-life. Much, therefore, that is in that interesting calendar is omitted—

Prison Calendar from 1837 to 1887.

1837. Pillory abolished. Parkhurst opened as a Reformatory for boys. 256 prisons in England and Wales. 14,068 transported to Australia. Convicts at Norfolk Island have a Chaplain (settlement established in 1826).

1838. House of Commons Committee reports against transportation. Assignment system abolished in Australia. Total Assignment while system lasted, 134,308. 158,000 lashes inflicted in one year in New South Wales and Van Diemen's Land.

A DISTRIBUTION OF PRIZES BY THE LORD MAYOR.—NATIONAL
REFUGES.

1839. Designs for new prisons and plans for alterations of old ones to be submitted to Home Secretary.

1840. Pentonville prison begun. Admission of public to hear " the condemned sermon " at Newgate abolished.

1841. First Industrial School opened (Sheriff Watson's at Aberdeen).

1842. Separate system introduced at Pentonville. 124,822 in English and Welsh prisons in the year.

1843. Sarah Martin, the prison visitor, died.

1845. Surveyor-General of Prisons appointed.

1846. Clerkenwell House of Detention commenced.

1847. Committee of Parliament on Prisons and Punishments. Juvenile Offenders Act.
1848. 296 transported to Bermuda.
1849. Elizabeth Fry Refuge founded. Holloway prison commenced. 7,000 young persons at Parkhurst.
1850. Board of directors of convict prisons constituted.
1851. Mark system in prisons commenced. Wandsworth Prison opened. Reformatory Conference at Birmingham.
1852. 2,541 transported to Australia.
1853. Ticket-of-leave system commenced. 14,507 juveniles under seventeen imprisoned.
1854. First Reformatory Act.
1857. Judicial Statistics first published. Penal Servitude Act II. Industrial Schools Act.
1859. Transportation to Bermuda ceased.
1862. 193 prisons in England and Wales. Coroner's inquest ordered upon prisoners dying in prison.
1863. Flogging permitted for garrotting.
1864. Penal Servitude Act III. General introduction of mark system into convict prisons. 146 prisons in England and Wales. Parkhurst closed for juvenile offenders.
1866. A fresh Industrial Schools Act passed.
1867. Transportation to Australia brought to a close. 451 sent this year. 130 prisons in England and Wales.
1868. The last public execution in front of Newgate, May 26.
1869. Habitual Criminals Act No. 1.
1870. Habitual Criminals Act No. 2.
1877. 113 prisons in England and Wales.
1878. Horsemonger Lane Gaol closed and thirty-six other prisons, leaving sixty-nine. Use of masks abolished.
1880. Sixty-seven prisons in England and Wales.
1882. Newgate closed as an ordinary prison.
1885. Sixty-two prisons in England and Wales. Coldbath Fields Prison closed.
1886. Clerkenwell Prison closed.

Even up to quite recent times there must have been a good deal of looseness in the administration of prisons, that tended to demoralize the inmates. Ned Wright, from whose story a quotation has been already taken, tells how upon being committed to prison he and the

other occupants of the prison van beguiled the journey
with a lively song. When they were within a ten
minutes' ride of the prison, the van stopped before a
public-house and the policemen asked what the
company would like before they went to " the palace."
Orders were given, driver and footman were treated,
and the happy party drove on.[1]

A MEETING ON BOARD "THE ARETHUSA," LORD SHAFTESBURY
PRESIDING.—NATIONAL REFUGES.

Neither the reformatory nor the industrial school
have realized all that was hoped from them, and we
are approaching a state of things that will be an un-
pleasant surprise in the near future for those who
have entertained the delusion that the work was
nearly done.

Miss Rosa M. Barrett, in her paper on the " Reform

[1] *Ned Wright.* Hodder & Stoughton. Report, P. S.
King & Son, 1902.

of Young Criminals," read at the third International Congress for the Welfare and Protection of Children (1902) had the following—

" I doubt if we have awakened to the terrible truth that we have not as yet checked crime in England among youths from sixteen to twenty-one years of age."

We cannot linger to argue, the present business being to record, but is it not obvious that we shall never better the old work. No institutional efforts when moral mischief has begun can ever compete for results with influences concentrated enough to be a help, brought to bear on a child living a normal life as a member of a family.

The following true anecdote, told by Dr. Barnardo, illustrates the point—

" There was a child found in a ragged school—how she got there no one could tell. Her father had been fourteen times convicted ; her mother was still worse, for she had been twenty-two times in prison. She had a brother who was then in prison ; and a sister, only fifteen years of age, who had served several short sentences and then had been sent to a Reformatory. Now this child was being cruelly beaten at home ! A clergyman heard of it and called my attention to the case, asking me to save the child. On inquiry, I found that her cries were heard day by day in the neighbour-hood, and the words caught were usually ' I can't ! I won't ! ' What was it all about ? The father was a thief and had brought up his other children to the same dishonest life ; but this one refused. ' Peggy,' he would say, ' you must steal ! ' ' I won't, father.' ' If you don't I'll thrash you.' He kept his word and cruelly beat her, and the mother beat her and sent her out to steal. When she came back bringing no stolen goods they were at her again. 'Father,' said the little one, ' YOU MAY KILL ME, BUT I WON'T STEAL ! ' I sent one of our children's beadles to inquire into the case, and if possible to get possession of her. 'Yes,' said the father, ' you may take her ; she's no good to me!' 'No good! why?' 'Because she refused to steal.' That dear child is now safe in our Home; but how came this child of nine to learn this heroism ? How was it ? She had gone occasionally to the ragged school where she had heard of Jesus, heard of the old, old story, which saved and inspired her ; purified her young life, enlarged her horizon, and gave her a new impulse of power which enabled her to say, ' Father you may kill me, but I won't steal ! ' The power of the Gospel as taught in the ragged school had truly reached that child's heart. Surely in view of such facts we must all say, ' God bless the Ragged School Union, and may it prosper abundantly.' "

Every man or woman who teaches a child as this one was taught helps to cut off the supply of crime at the main.

Such men and women are wanted by the thousand, for juvenile crime is increasing in England and throughout the world.

CHAPTER XVIII

A Check and a Halt

PERIOD 4. FROM 1870 TO 1879

" If there could be not, as I believe is the case, worse philosophy or worse statesmanship than that of giving a mere intellectual education, it behoves the people of this country to say so."—SIR THOMAS CHAMBERS, Q.C.

BY the time the late Mr. W. E. Forster succeeded in passing the Education Act of 1870, great but gradual changes had been taking place in the social aspect of England. The country had safely passed through the transition time when it changed from being mainly an agricultural to mainly a manufacturing nation. There had been employment sufficient to absorb the population as it increased, and work for children when leaving school, that is, if they were attending any before they were old enough to work. Fear of the people had ceased to be general among the upper classes, though there were still some who thought the Reform Bill and all subsequent enfranchising legislation a grave mistake.

The Rev. C. H. Spurgeon, who, through his open-air preaching experience, knew the London mob for what it .was, tells how he once had a conversation with a

nobleman upon the possibility of a revolution. The
latter said that he quite expected to see the gutters
of London streets running with human blood. The
preacher did not agree, but said, quite characteristically :
" Never you be afraid of the democracy. I always think
of the scum when I think of the top of the pot, though
no doubt there is a very nasty sediment at the bottom."

His further remarks on the same subject deserve to
be quoted, as they indicate a feeling of assurance that
was at the time of which we are writing not generally
shared :—

" There is an order and peacefulness about London
that to my mind seems miraculous. There is only
a handful of police, but still it somehow happened that
they kept the vast population in order. No other city
is like London in that respect. There is something in
the hearts of the people that keeps them from the
excesses, into which, for instance, the people of Paris
had so often fallen. It is not that they are better off,
but that there is an influence of a religious kind which,
though they scarcely know it to be so, yet operates upon
the people ; and many a man that scarce knows the
name of Jesus of Nazareth yet feels His influence, and
he is not what he would have been had he not dwelt
beneath the shadow of the Cross."

The causes of fear of the poor and pity for them
being greatly lessened, agencies that worked among
them relied more and more for their support upon the
ability to show that they were doing a needed public
work, or that they were spreading the Gospel. Of
such agencies there were now many, all dependent
upon voluntary contributions.

The Ragged School Union had for a very long time
appeared to have all its eggs, or very nearly all, in the

one basket—Education. When the Government at last took this matter up it seemed as if the bottom was knocked out of the cause. The general demeanour of some of those chiefly concerned gave colour to the view. On the part of the public there was a general disposition to hope, nay, to feel certain, that all that needed doing among poor children would now be done by the State.

" People are under the impression that Board Schools are a kind of father to poor children. That is a great mistake, as little Tom and Jim well know. The Board Schools may, perhaps, be a father-in-law to them, but they are not a father, and never will be," said the writer already quoted, and as late as 1892, after school-fees were abolished. At the time the provided schools were about to start, the feeling to which he refers was very pronounced.

The forlornness of men like Lord Shaftesbury at this time gave two bad impressions : One was that ragged school work was at an end ; and the other that the attitude of workers to the School Board was one of unpatriotic grudging towards a great public blessing, because it superseded a hobby of their own by something more efficient. But in Lord Shaftesbury's case, at least, there was nothing approaching jealousy. He verily believed that the occupation of the ragged schools was gone. He looked upon the imminent extinction of these pariah schools, with all their associated operations, as a terrible national calamity. For years he had viewed with alarm the rapid growth of a proletarian population that doggedly held aloof from all the churches. His greatest comfort lay in the hopes the ragged school held out. In that institution he saw the corrective to popular secularism. It dealt with the lowest and poorest, and at the same time influenced for good, in direct and indirect ways, the classes above. To his mind the recommendation of the cause to the public lay in the educational work alone. His estimate of probabilities was that people would not give subscriptions and pay taxes as well. An extract from one of his speeches in 1871 explains his position fairly:

" I am not going to speak in critical disparagement of the new system, for I believe that in the present divided state of opinions in England it would have been impossible to enact any law providing more minutely and definitely for the institution of children in the Christian life. Depend upon it, Mr. Forster is a good and true man. He would, no doubt, have gone much further, if he could. He did his best, and saved us from national apostasy, and *we must try and turn to account what has been done.* Ay, but then, see the wide difference between our system and this new one— cold, stiff, starched, and in buckram. Consider what must be the effect of having to act entirely under the dictates of the Privy Council."

He had, during his long career, experiences that made him distrust officialism. The tender mercies of the State, even in working out schemes devised by good men, he knew might be cruel.

" The ragged school system is the parental system," he was fond of saying.

It must never be forgotten that such men as he, had every right to speak as they did. The experience that was available at that time was in their possession. All the effort, too, had come from communities they represented, and such human material as was procurable for giving effect to the new legislation was trained by them as well. Sir Thomas Chambers very pertinently asked : " Who are they that have brought about this marvellous improvement in the amount of education given (in England in twenty-five years) and in the educational machinery employed ? Who but the members of all the Evangelical Churches throughout the country ? Who have filled the Sunday Schools ? and the Ragged Schools, and the British and Foreign Schools, and to a great extent the National Schools, with teachers ? Who but the men who have acted from religious motives, and whose conduct has been influenced by the teaching of the Gospel ? "

We owe a great debt to the first London Board, similar to that which we owe to the Poor Law Commissioners of 1833, and Sir Benjamin Hall for his efforts to unify London in 1855.

It was a gigantic and appalling task that confronted them, and in the nature of things there could not have been the needed preparation for it. But the members were patient and considerate gentlemen, who were as desirous as any could be that the moral side of the work should not suffer. What brought the Ragged School Union and London School Board into close contact was the fact that the Board Schools were meant for the poorest. The conception of " the common school " did not enter into the plan. A maximum rate of 3*d*. in the pound was the estimate for their provision. For a long time the deference of the borrower to the lender marked the behaviour of the Board to all the voluntary agencies, but all the members received in return was the repeated assurance that there was nothing against their private characters. Inquiry was their first work—then provision of teaching staff, buildings and apparatus. Only about one-third of the London children were provided for

educationally, all told. In 1872 there were still
176,000 for whom there was no school-place provided.
Upon that first historic Board, as indeed upon all
succeeding Boards, were many friends of ragged schools.
Some of them were : T. B. Smithies, Samuel Morley,
Thomas Scrutton, Lord Sandon, Sir Chas. Reed,
Alexander McArthur Lord Lawrence, Edward North
Buxton, Alderman Cotton, and John Macgregor.
But in spite of this there were too many inherent
elements of friction in the interests and duties of the
two bodies for an unruffled peace. An unguarded
expression in a press-notice of the Board, a strong
remark from the earl, would be certain to create heart-
burning on each side, respectively.

An instance of both will illustrate this point. The
first is from an officially-inspired newspaper article
dealing with the Board's work. The sting, like a
scorpion's, is in the tail :—

" These waifs and strays of the vast city received
only such instruction as they could pick up in its
streets and alleys, or in establishments which, at best,
were schools *only in name*."

The other, on the Ragged School side, is the question
Lord Shaftesbury asked in the House of Lords in the
course of a speech on the death of a child-sweep, and
which he also introduced into a letter to the *Times.*
He wanted to know what the School Boards were doing
not to prevent such employment, seeing that the boys
would necessarily be under thirteen. His letter
attracted sqme attention. The existence of chimney-
climbers in 1874 was a link with the past that was
interesting, and the death of a child stirred the public
imagination. That they were still used in the Midlands
and North Country excited indignation. Journalists

resuscitated old matter about " sweep's cancer," and the Corporation of Liverpool came in for much censure for allowing their chimneys to be swept by boys just to save a few pounds. The immediate cause of the protest was the trial of a sweep at the Cambridge Assizes. A boy in his employ had died of blood-poisoning, contracted in sweeping the chimney of Fulbourne Lunatic Asylum.

Bad blood between the two continued to be made. The Ogle Mews Ragged School had been educating children free for twenty-five years, when the London School Board, in 1876, built a school near at hand. Naturally, they wished to fill it. The Ogle Mews School stood in the way, so the conductors of the school were summoned, on the ground that the education given did not satisfy the Board's standard. It is a question to this day as to the extent to which the Board was entitled to speak with confidence about the education it was providing in 1876.

Be that as it may, the schoolmaster of Ogle Mews told the bench plainly that extermination, not efficiency, was the Board's object. ' Sir Robert Carden, Alderman of the City of London, ex-Lord Mayor, and member of the Stock Exchange, was a teacher at this school, and he being far from prepared to take such persecution lying down, was in court. The magistrate held a *viva voce* examination, and declared that the children had done very well considering that they were being questioned in public.

The counsel for the Board, however, said that the children failed to satisfy the Board's standard. Sir Robert Carden insisted that the children must be examined with other children from the Board School. How it ended does not appear, but the following papers had leaders upon it, and some of them had second and even third articles. How they were divided, whether they were divided, or which side they favoured does not transpire. They were : *The Times, Daily News, Standard, Daily Telegraph, Echo, Morning Advertiser, Globe, Church Bells,* and *Funny Folks.* The nett product of this kind of thing could only be a division of forces. Fortunately, there were peacemakers on both sides. John Macgregor and Professor Leone Levi, of the Ragged School Union, were balanced by Lord Lawrence and Lord Sandon on the London School Board.

This, at least, should be said : the Ragged School Union were continuing their educational work " by desire." A resolution was passed in 1871, by the London School Board, requesting that managers of schools be urged to maintain them in a state of efficient operation.

In addition, a letter was sent by Lord Lawrence to the *Daily Telegraph,* asking subscribers to voluntary agencies to continue their donations, on the ground that the London School Board was not really able to grapple with all its work as yet.

These two measures were hardly taken soon enough, for the managers of several schools gave away freehold buildings to the Board in the first panic of fear that they should be unable to keep their work going.

Professor Huxley was on the first London School Board, and although it was his first acquaintance with ragged schools he was very favourably impressed by what came under his notice. He wished to see them continued under the name of " Substratum Schools." Of the attainments of the masters his opinion was very favourable.

The year 1870 saw a very enthusiastic friend of the

cause called to his rest, Joseph Payne, Deputy-Assistant Judge of the Middlesex Sessions, was a figure as well known at Exeter Hall as the President himself. He was seventy-three when he died, and was a great favourite with all in the movement. He took the title of " Bard of the Poor," and his speciality was the composition of extemporaneous verses upon topics connected with the work. These " tail-pieces," as he called them, exceeded 2,400, the first of which was delivered at the first annual meeting. No meeting was

JUDGE PAYNE.

BARONESS BURDETT-COUTTS.

considered complete without them. It was natural therefore, that something should be done at his death to give expression to the universal respect that was entertained for him   In Highgate Cemetery an obelisk of white Sicilian marble, 16 ft. high, resting upon slabs of grey and red granite, and costing upwards of £100, was erected by the friends of ragged schools and temperance societies to his memory.

One of the best and oldest friends of the Ragged School Union is the Baroness Burdett-Coutts. Her connexion with Mrs. Barker Harrison has been already referred to; but during her long life there have been many other points of contact with the Ragged School Union and the ragged school movement generally. She is still President of our ladies' working parties. Though unable to do anything of an active nature now, in days gone by she did a very great deal. In 1874, she bought the " Chichester " as a training ship for £5,000. In 1867, a supper for homeless boys was held at Queen Street Ragged School, and out of this grew the training-

THE TRAINING BRIGANTINE "CHICHESTER" FOR POOR BOYS
BELONGING TO THE NATIONAL REFUGES FOR DESTITUTE CHILDREN.

ship effort. It is a distinct agency from those for which the Ragged School Union is responsible, but is, nevertheless, an outgrowth. All through these lean years, when the Society may be said to have been living upon its tissues, it can be seen what a reserve of vitality there was within the movement. All kinds of new devisings were being put into action, numbers of institutions were being formed, and the Ragged School

Union's quarterly record was usually the channel through which the first appeal was made, or the offices at Exeter Hall the place where the first meeting was held. The Destitute Children's Dinners Society and the Marylebone Home for Cripple Girls are typical of many instances where the Ragged School Union and Lord Shaftesbury were used to further a good work. The close of the period of despair and stagnancy may be said to date from the appointment of the present secretary in 1879, as well as the beginning of a period of struggle, of which the fruit did not immediately appear. Lord Shaftesbury was obliged to send round a circular letter to the schools deprecating this course of action, and pointing out that, as these schools were paid for with money from ragged school subscribers, the buildings should at least be sold in the market and the proceeds be devoted to the cause.

At the present day the legal section of the Council deal with such questions, and the group of buildings on page 394 represent salvage work of a kind that would have been useful had it been possible in the early seventies.

The position of workers can be understood who had been building up a fabric of operations demanding a considerable amount of money annually for up-keep, as well as all their spare time from business. In many instances they were sure the work could not be kept on. Moreover, they were personally liable for the expenses. In addition to these friends were the workers who had, like the majority of the English public, the idea that they might now retire as all would now be done without them.

For nearly ten years there is a constant bewailing of flown-birds and an empty nest. Outsiders came to look upon the Society as archaic in its aims, a relic of bygone days.

It is certain that the educational training given in these old schools was good, though simple and limited in its range. A chance survivor among eleven emigrant boys wrecked in the *Annie Jane* off the west of Scotland was able to write a very creditable account of the wreck, good enough to appear in the Society's magazine. The report of the Conference of Schoolmasters met to discuss the situation in 1871 can be placed side by side with the report of the meeting of the National Union of Teachers over the Educational Bill, a few months ago, and not suffer by the comparison. Several of the teachers had qualifications and attainments sufficient to warrant their being made clergymen. One, in particular, was made vicar of an East End parish. Another, upon having a living offered him by the Archbishop of Canterbury, declined it on the grounds that he could be more useful in his position as a ragged school teacher.

The works of the late Mr. Samuel Smiles were of the greatest inspiring value in these schools. "Self-help," "Thrift," and "Character" were largely drawn upon by the voluntary teachers and the schoolmasters in urging their scholars on in the path of self-improvement. These educators were able to attract the very children that under the present system it costs the London Board £150,000 a year to hunt. The cost per head annually for educating was 12s., as compared with £1 8s. in the British and National Schools. With nothing better than this equipment many a man has made his way to a position of honour and responsibility and has blessed some old ragged school for his start in life

CHAPTER XIX

Period 5.   From 1879 to 1893

" I do not believe that two-thirds of the people inside our churches and chapels know anything at all of the need for this great movement."—The late MR. BENJ. CLARKE, Sec. Sunday School Union, on the R.S.U., 1883.

THE year 1870 is the focussing point of all R.S.U. history.   All tendencies in the movement are related to it, as terminus or fresh starting-point.

It is worthy of remark that, while there has been during the past century a progress towards unities in State administration, especially in matters relating to London, in the religious social work that cleared the ground for national reforms, there has been more and more disintegration, an ever-increasing fission into fractions either mutually weakening or mutually paralyzing.

The ragged school cause has to some extent suffered in workers, money, and prestige.   Divided strength in the churches and a distracted attention on the part of the community have both had their results.   These results, combined with a too exclusive association of the ragged school with education in the transitional period, have created a position so lacking in features of direct appeal to the imagination that some amount of defensive argument seems called for. Our present period, begins with 1879, the point of lowest ebb-tide in ragged school fortunes, and a time when they seemed hopelessly beyond repair. The present secretary, upon coming into office at the Central Society, had upon the general horizon of public life no prospect of a recuperative infusion of fresh forces to bring a wasted army up to fighting strength again. The worst sign of the times was a recrudescence of the historic struggle between Church and Dissent : and this has been waged with increasing virulence up to this present moment.

The practical result, after more than two centuries of struggle in a strenuous conflict, places the oppressed party now on a level with the dominant party in this country in point of numbers. In the great English-speaking world of the Empire and the daughter republic of America it is outnumbered by three to one. Religious controversy is not a concern of this Society, but not so the deadlock.

As Lord Shaftesbury said in 1843, so are average Britons, inside and outside the churches, constrained to say in 1904, " Wherever the blame lies, it is the children who suffer." Anglo-Saxons the world over are anxious that the children of the Mother Country shall not be placed at a disadvantage ; and a theological squabble that temporarily paralyzes the effectiveness of two thousand years of Christian ideals must be brought to an end. It is not merely the establishment of an educational system that is made difficult, other good work is checked. It may come as a surprise to many, that Japan, without a conscious knowledge of a living Christ, is manufacturing criminals

at about half the rate we are. In her prisons only
21·9 per cent. of the inmates are under twenty-one,
while with us the proportion is 45 per cent.[1] After
all is said and done, a civilization must be judged by
this kind of output.

The working theory of the R.S.U. is that London
needs Evangelicalism again. With its fortunes the
Society stands or falls. The fundamental belief is
that Evangelicalism—the united force of the churches—
is not an outgrowth of Protestantism, but a super-
session that, in the world's affairs, represents a dynamic
force not met with elsewhere since Luther's days.

If denominationalism can account for the Bible
Society and the Religious Tract Society as their own
offspring, Evangelicalism must hide its head. But
history seems to show that these world-blessing
associations were the product of a religious combine.
We have misread the evidence if it be not so, and shall
be grateful for correction. The universal diffusion of
the knowledge of the Hebrew Scriptures, which ad-
mittedly, upon any theory, taking the lowest valuation,
contain the best expression that human faculty has
produced of the dealings of God with man, stands to
the credit of Great Britain.

Israel itself to whom the Human Race is indebted for
the Redeemer, cannot as a nation point to anything
that can be placed side by side with this unique instance
of active international altruism. If the Establishment
or any sect can claim it, the temptation to do so must
be strong. But Evangelicalism also produced the
Y.M.C.A.. and the Y.W.C.A., which have knit
together the Christian youth of this world. The

[1] *Report of the Int. Cong. Welfare and Protection of Children,* p. 136.

Sunday school system was one of its missionary ventures. It is true that aggressiveness, except on sectarian lines, ceased when the ideal of the Sunday school as nursery to a particular Church arose, but its concept was evangelical at the outset. Wesleyanism may say that the famous words, " I look upon the whole world as my parish," that her founder used, indicate the same thing. Moreover, she may urge that the narrowing tendencies, the specializing organization arose as defensive precautions against the extinction of her message by outside, hostile forces. Salvationism says much the same about Wesleyanism ; but both, in spite of limitations, are world-subduing agencies.

The London City Mission is another result of Evangelicalism, with a splendid record. Her usefulness has been only slightly impaired by the checks and hindrances that have operated in a more restrictive way upon the Church Army and the associations of working-men who are members of the Establishment. A grand work has been done by all of them ; but the product belongs to the actuating and sustaining Evangelical spirit.

This disquisition is necessary in the history of the R.S.U., because serious symptoms of anæmia need notice.

Our great first leader, whose name has been incorporated with the title of the Society to express its modernity, had prejudices to overcome and opposition to face when he made a stand for that union of Protestants upon which the hopes of this country and the progress of the world in reality rest.

One of the societies that sprang from eighteenth century Evangelicalism was the London Missionary

Society, that rather more than a century ago sent missionaries to the heathen to preach the Gospel. Their general instructions were not to perplex the poor Pagans with the historical controversies of these small Western Islands. In process of time missionary societies of a sectarian character arose ; so that by force of circumstances this missionary society, without altering its policy, attached itself to the independents for the pecuniary support needed for its operations.

For this society Lord Shaftesbury was asked to preside at a great meeting in 1853. He took the chair on behalf of their China missions. His diary has this entry against the date December 1 :—

" Yesterday, chair of L.M.S. in aid of Missions to China. Shall, I suppose, give great offence to my friends in the Establishment ; sorry for it, but the cause is too holy, too catholic, too deeply allied with the single name of Christ, for any consideration of Church system and Episcopal rule. What is the meaning of ' Grace be with all those who love the Lord Jesus Christ in sincerity ' ? Did not Morrison, Milne, Medhurst, Moffat, Williams love Him ? If grace, then, was with those men, shall I, vile man, presume to say that *I will not be* with them also ? "

But more than a decade before this our King's father set the earl an example by speaking at Exeter Hall at a meeting held " without practical purpose," beyond the recognition of brotherly ties among the Christians of differing communions. The early speeches of the Prince Consort cost him a great deal. The first of his Exeter Hall utterances was to help free the slave, and he was so nervous about it that he and Queen Victoria had a rehearsal beforehand. His second was at this meeting to promote Christian union. It was a grand gathering, one of the most significant in English history, having the promise of things unfulfilled to this present time. The proceedings were mainly of a devotional character, but enthusiasm and faith were high. The large hall and the lower hall were filled, and then there was an overflow of three thousand, of whom fifteen hundred adjourned to Great Queen Street Chapel.

It has been customary, and still is so in some quarters, to represent Evangelicalism as being illogical, old-fashioned, and though not dead, yet doomed to die, and carrying the marks of dissolution upon it at this present. But that view surely cannot be based upon a sound philosophy. Does not Evangelicalism, rather, seem to be an advance upon the spurious solidarity of Catholicism, while securing that freedom and opportunity for individual growth which Protestantism restored ? Is it not arguable that to have your units developed to full working value, to have also a combination which is costless, because it is the result of the spontaneous action of the units, must be superior both to Catholicism and Protestantism ? Has not Catholicism been a highly centralized system, originally constructed to save the fragments of the Roman Empire ? Is it not now wasteful of spiritual energy of leaders, and repressive of individual growth in the rank and file of Church membership ? Is it not true that a very large proportion of her strength as a Church is consumed in the maintenance of checking machinery that, where it works successfully, impairs the effectiveness of the unit as a spiritual force in the world ?

There is here no attempt to deny that Rome has had and still has much surplus missionary energy, in spite of her disastrous arrangements. The contention is that an over-centralized system in the spiritual domain is not only not the best conceivable, but that it suffers when compared with Evangelicalism. A system has recently come into existence and produced results in less than a century that eclipse all other performance. Its fortunes, at the moment, seem to wane. Is it, therefore, out-of-date, or is it merely suffering as being in advance of the age ?

Compared with Protestantism, the superiority of Evangelicalism is just as obvious. It has always been Rome's taunt to Protestantism that Protestantism has no message to the world on the subject of unity ; and we are obliged to concede that the mission of Protestantism was the protection of the individual.

But here it may be objected that there is no proof that the solidarity of Evangelicalism can be continuously secured : that in point of fact it has not been ; and that experience has shown that in drawing supplies of money and men for aggressive attack upon heathenism at home and heathenism abroad the well-wishers of Evangelicalism have had to abandon it in favour of sectarian effort.

The entire argument must be rigidly kept in this book to the concerns of the R.S.U. The points we desire to make are : (1) That Evangelicalism, upon which the ragged school movement is based, and with whose fortunes its own are inextricably bound up, is an *advance* upon the older associations of the Christian world, and within a very brief period of operation has had a better and more universal output of solid achievement.

(2) That any loss sustained by the R.S.U., and other evangelical societies, by the expediences of the

Churches, while it faithfully keeps a testimony that may not be surrendered, involves the workers in no blame.

It is greatly to be deplored that the educational work of the movement was so emphasized, to the overshadowing of all else, in the years preceding and succeeding the formation of the London School Board ; that the incradicable impression was made upon the public mind that ragged schools were things of the past. These might be allowed to continue till the School Board had grip of their work, but not after the years of depressed vitality in the R.S.U. From 1869 to 1879 were years in which sectarian influences and impulses were gaining strength in London and throughout the kingdom.

It was about 1866 that it really began, when the advances of ultra-Ritualism caused some stir among the Church laity. Lord Shaftesbury was continually urged to lead a crusade, but he considered that laymen were not sufficiently united to ensure a success. The year 1867 saw his Ornaments Rubric Bill introduced into the Lords, followed by legislation from the Bishops, and a Royal Commission ; but the effort of 1867 was made while Ritual prosecutions were as yet unknown, and no decision upon clerical vestments had been given in the courts. The succeeding years were full of Church reform proposals and prosecutions of the more advanced Ritualists. Ritualism, accordingly, became a power in the seventies.

To stimulate the Free Churches came Messrs. Moody and Sankey from across the Atlantic to conduct a revival in 1875 ; but new vigour took more or less a political tendency to combat the Church movement.

The R.S.U., as an unattached association, would

have felt the strain of these narrowing-up tendencies under any circumstances, but it had to submit to it at a time when it suffered from the prejudice that it was a dying cause. Added to these disadvantages, there was the general impression that the State services would do all that was now needed for social amelioration.

There were however, many publicists who used voices and pens to correct this error. Canon Barnett continuously attacked this fallacy, and did perhaps, as much as anyone to remove it, as an extract from one of his articles will show :—

" Far be it from anyone to say that even such radical changes as these [better police supervision of streets, improved lighting, control of tenement houses by responsible landlords] would do away with evil. When, however, such changes have been effected it will be more possible to develop character, and *one by one lead the people to face their highest. Only personal service, the care of individual by individual can be powerful to keep down evil*, and only the knowledge of God is sufficient to give the individual faith to work and see little of his work. For such men and women who will give such service there is a crying demand."

It was after a decade of eroding forces had been eating out much of the life of the ragged school movement that the present secretary of the R.S.U. came into power in 1879, though his official connexion with it began twelve years previously. For many reasons it was heartrending labour to get the attention paid to the cause that would enable it to fulfil its destiny. Yet there were not wanting men in the Establishment and in the ranks of Dissent to give a faithful testimony for a discredited cause. The Bishop of Manchester and the Rev. C. H. Spurgeon may be cited as examples of each. His lordship said :—

" It is sometimes objected that ragged schools were organized for a temporary purpose, and if they have been successful they ought to have abolished the needs which called them into existence. People have said that if ragged schools have sufficiently raised the moral and spiritual status of the destitute classes there ought to be now no ragged children. If that argument has any force it ought to be directed against all reforming institutions whatsoever, even against the Christian Church itself. The fact is, as fast as reformatory agencies are successful the infirmity and wickedness of human nature creates afresh the need which they were called into existence to abolish."

Mr. Spurgeon's witnessing was to the same effect, though briefer :—

" The ragged school is as much needed as ever it was, and I am afraid that until the millennium it will always be so."

Nevertheless, it seemed impossible to restore the work to a high position in public esteem. The process, perhaps, is not yet completed, but as far as it has gone it is mainly the work of Mr. John Kirk. Many of the most vigorous spirits had found other work ; and the aged earl, by his mournful public and private utterances, continued to do much harm. Believing, as he did, that the destruction of the system as he knew it in old days was a calamity for the country, and believing that such destruction was virtually accomplished, he proclaimed his views upon the housetops in a way that must have been most embarrassing. How black was his despair may be guessed from a few words spoken in 1880 :—

" If my life should be prolonged another year, and if during that year the ragged school system were to fall, I should not die in the course of nature, I should die of a broken heart."

The ragged school system of educational schools did not fall till the abolition of school fees in Board Schools some few years after his death; but the quotation shows how little could be expected of him in adapting the work to a need which, though permanent in its nature, is variable in its forms.

An added element of difficulty for the secretary was the state of the Society's finances. The national financial crisis of 1873 shook the fabric of ragged school interests as none of its forerunners had done. Coming at the juncture it did and lingering for six years, it was certain to affect it. The crisis was of American origin, and began on the Vienna Bourse. In the month of November of that year the Bank rate stood at nine per cent. The country, upon its recovery from this trouble, was plunged into another by the fall of the Glasgow City Bank. The collapse was due to heavy losses upon Turkish, Peruvian, American, Egyptian, and Paraguayan loans, and occurred in 1878. The ragged schools that did not abandon the struggle to keep their work going had to come to the R.S.U. for exceptional help. To such an extent was this the case between 1875 and 1878, that the grants to schools absorbed all the donations and subscriptions and over £2,000 of reserve capital. The R.S.U. had, of course, in addition, to meet its own outgoings for its work as a central society.

Yet there was no stagnancy. The evolution of boys' clubs, youths' institutes, and the Polytechnic was going on, in spite of all difficulties. Dr. Leone Levi

was deeply interested in these developments. The
rudimentary boys' club had, like so many other operations that took ambitious forms ultimately, existed
in some schools from a very early date. Mrs. Barker
Harrison had also been the first to start a working-
men's club at Westminster. This movement, during
the decade subsequent to 1879, made more and more
progress. A Mansion House Committee, under the
presidency of Sir Robert Walter Carden, had had the
matter under consideration for some time prior to
1879, but the only product had been the working lads'
institute in the Whitechapel Road. The R.S.U.
was asked to foster the institute effort, and some
important conferences were held in 1879 and 1881.
At these several broad principles of great value were
enunciated for the guidance of those interested. One
was that a paid superintendent should be employed,
where possible, to ensure absolute regularity of attendance and reliability in the management of a club
by placing it on a business footing.

Another was that no money or relief should be given.
A third was to draft lads who were earning money and
over fifteen years of age to a penny institute. In the
suggestion that the religious exercises—essential feature
—should not be unduly long, there was great wisdom.
They were not to exceed twenty minutes. At one of
the conferences (1881) Mr. Dydden, on behalf of Mr.
Quintin Hogg, reported that the work which became
the Polytechnic afterwards, but was then conducted
in Castle Street, had a membership of 400. The
tendency of games to supersede work, and the difficulty of getting lads to go in for education was brought
forward, thus anticipating by many years the discovery made by the University Settlements. In a

prize competition arranged by the Federation of
London Working Boys' Clubs and Institutes, a few
years ago, only nine essays were forthcoming from .a
united membership numbering between two and three
thousand. The whole art of inducing lads to engage in

RECREATION.

pursuits of permanent value in their leisure time was
understood in these early days to be the judicious
sandwiching of work and play, participation in any
particular game being purchased by " improving "
work done first. In 1882, the Union Général de

France failed, and a period of trade stagnation ensued in this country lasting more or less till 1888. With this period of depression came a strong socialistic influence into public life. It was independent of religious work, but it had a tendency to divide interest in efforts already being made. At the same time it brought a new constituency of helpers of the poor to the slums.

These were the years of the meetings of the un-employed, the West End riots, and the Mansion House Fund. The Franchise Act of 1885, altering the electorate, and the Local Government Act of 1888, establishing County Councils, helped to extend the spirit of the eighties into our own time. It may without unfairness be said that its distinguishing trait is to regard the individual as the product of environ-ment rather than as being a self-determining agent. It was, in a measure, a revolt from the teaching of Dr. Smiles. If it did not altogether eliminate faith, it did not make it the pivot of individual and social life. When it began to be a power, trade was very bad, and it used to be constantly urged that the State should find work for the unemployed. With those who did not entertain the socialist view, and were not of the old school either, it was a time of crusades for the general application to all social ills of special remedies. Country labourers, earning 12s. a week and supporting families, were earnestly implored to be thrifty by people who had never had to deny themselves a want. The efforts of the temperance orator are never out of season in our country : at this time he was much in evidence. State-aided emigration was another common-sense proposal, though as remedies they were not completely satisfying. The taxation of land values was suggested by Mr. Henry George. Peasant proprietary was another nostrum that found favour with many. But above all these voices rose the " Bitter Cry of Outcast London."

At the very commencement of this new era in public life the R.S.U. held a most significant demonstration. The step taken was largely due to the need of definition of relations between the School Board and itself. Political elements had somewhat altered the nature of the L.S.B. It was forgotten that the R.S.U. had been asked to continue educational work, and that the Board was not yet ready to deal with all the children in 1883.

Moreover, it was not seen that compulsory attendance, with school fees at the Board Schools, was keeping the ragged schools full because they were free. The position was most unsatisfactory. People, when asked 'to subscribe to maintain ragged day schools, were puzzled to know for what class of child Mr. Forster had asked for the threepenny rate, a rate that had not been kept to threepence. Then again, this day-school millstone, so hard to carry but worn by desire of the authorities, made the R.S.U. appear a reactionary body in the eyes of the public. All these circumstances combined to make an impressive statement of position necessary, if the association was not of opinion that it had no message for the modern age and no more work to do.

It is difficult to judge from documents only, but all the indications are in favour of assigning the merit of the great Conference of 1883 to the genius of Professor Leone Levi, aided, undoubtedly, by the business qualities of other men.

On April 11, the anniversary of the day upon which

the first beginnings were made, a rally of all friends of the ragged school movement throughout the country was called at Exeter Hall. A breakfast, at which a reception of provincial delegates by Professor Leone Levi was undertaken, preceded the general meeting at eleven in the forenoon in the Lower Exeter Hall. This gathering was distinguished by the presence of rank and fashion. The claims of the work were sufficient to secure the attendance of a large number of the aristocracy, including a duchess, as members of the audience only. Their names would mean little to the reader. A name that is remembered is that of the Right Hon. W. H. Smith, M.P., First Lord of the Admiralty. It was he who, in 1879, said, that "For his own part he confessed that he attached more importance to the work done prior to 1870—which was done as a work of love—than he did to work which was the result of orders emanating from a central authority." The Home Secretary, in opening an industrial school in Essex, in the same year, paid a high tribute to voluntary work.

The attitude of criticism was not, however, taken by the Society. The chief anxieties were to avoid overlapping, define their sphere of labour, and inform their supporters.

At the opening of the Conference letters were read from the absent. Among them one by the Rev. H. W. Webb-Peploe, M.A., contained the words: "Feeling deeply the value of the ragged schools of London and the good work done by them in the past, I earnestly hope they may be continued in full force." Another from the Bishop of Rochester had the passage: "Your ragged school work is not done yet, nor is it likely to be."

The first paper read was by Mr. H. R. Williams, chairman of the R.S.U., at the time, and a man who had pioneer experience. He was also chairman of the Hornsey School Board, and subsequently an active member of the Middlesex County Council and other bodies. His paper was a review of the history from 1844 to 1881, and a statement of what had so far been achieved. Two striking facts that were brought forward deserve mention. One was that although the population had increased between 1856 and 1881, the juvenile commitments were 13,981 in 1856, and 5,483 in 1881.

The second fact was that the School Board were still needing, in 1883, school space for 100,000 children.

The past being thus dealt with, there was next a resolution which embodied two ideas. The first was a frank and appreciative recognition of the value of the work of the educational authority ; the second that, notwithstanding the existence of that work, ragged schools were needed to deal with difficulties it could not touch.

The Duke of Westminster proposed this resolution, but not as an outsider summoned to plead for something of which he had only a slight knowledge. The use of the pronoun " we " throughout his speech is very notable.

The Earl of Aberdeen seconded it. Next came a paper by Canon Fleming, B.D., on " Religious Instruc- tion." This note of affirmation of belief at the very outset of the new work indicated to socialists how far the ragged school worker would be likely to go, and the direction in which a division would be likely to occur. Religion was the solution. The pith of the matter is contained in one passage of the Canon's address :—

"As patriots and Christians who see the evils at work and know the only cure for them, shall we not search for the precious soul, like a crown jewel in its battered casket." Next came the second resolution. This declared in effect that the day school teaching in the elementary schools being of a secular character, it became increasingly necessary to strengthen and extend Sunday schools. The late Samuel Morley was proposer, and the Rev. C. H. Kelly, of the Wesleyan Sunday School Union, seconder of this resolution.

A paper entitled "Charity and Thrift" was then read by Dr. Leone Levi. Canon Fleming's paper dealt with the religious basis, and Dr. Levi's with the superstructure of social service : these, taken together, are the principles of the movement. Nothing that has occurred since has made Dr. Levi's essay obsolete as a statement of policy, nor will anything that the future may bring forth do so. Although a political economist of equal authority to any that may be quoted whose views are of an extreme kind, it is evident that he was no doctrinaire. He seems to have belonged to a group of philosophers, of whom John Stuart Mill was one and Von Humboldt another, who were the first to break the tyranny of Turgot,[1] the French Encyclopædist, over English thought in the realm of economics. So jealous was Turgot of the power of the dead hand to affect the lives of the living, that he was equally opposed to educational foundations as to benevolent ones, and was also against State alms in any form. Even Dr. Chalmers, strict economist as he was in questions of social service

[1] *The State and Charity.* Mackay, p. 36.

and poor-law relief, had to draw the line in the matter of educational foundations.

This essay of Dr. Levi's is the best outline of R.S.U. economics that has appeared, and its principles are worth some attention.

His care to combine the idea of assistance with the idea of self-help in the title, " Charity and Thrift," indicates his position. Deprecating the notion that ragged school work was relief agency except in subordinate phases, he admitted that in bulk the charitable assistance given was considerable.

Upon the feeding of school children his views were not dissimilar to those of Mr. C. S. Loch, who, in his article upon " Charity and Charities," in the *Encyclopædia Britannica*, writes : " They [the children] should be systematically dealt with individually with the object of preserving the family life ; or if the family be so vicious that its true life is entirely lost, and there is no alternative, as privately as possible some separate provision should be made for the children."

But Dr. Levi's essay goes farther in some respects than probably this writer would do. The professor would probably have found himself in agreement with John Stuart Mill in the belief that, " When the condition of any one is so disastrous that his energies are paralyzed by discouragement, assistance is a tonic, not a sedative ; it braces instead of deadening the active faculties." His experience as a teacher would also produce agreement with another economist, Professor Marshall, in the statement that, " In every practical problem it is common sense that is the ultimate arbiter."

The encouragement and promotion of thrift was,

however, the more important branch of effort and this included assistance to the people, by suggestion, to make home brighter by the best use of resources ; in fact, a continuance of Mrs. Bayly's work of mending ragged homes by changing the slattern into an expert housekeeper and the spendthrift father into a careful provider.

But this was to be no substitute for a solution of the housing problem. Ragged school men had been the first agitators and reformers and workers, and this public action was not to be relaxed.

" Intemperance and fever are the inevitable growth of those localities (the slums). Those localities can be purified, those courts and alleys can be opened to the refreshing influences of all that is decent, comfortable, and healthy ; and until they be opened, depend upon it, your efforts will be in vain."

Such was Lord Shaftesbury's exhortation in 1852. It was annually repeated, and action agreeing with his words characterised his whole life. The legislation for which he was responsible upon the housing question is that which operates to-day. The only difference is that the powers which were then permissive are now compulsory upon public bodies.

Professor Levi wished both courses of action to be continuous. The blended charity and thrift principle included an equipment of the young for self-help in the future.

After this paper had been read, Earl Cairns, who had been for over thirty years a friend and generous subscriber, proposed that it was important to promote better dwellings, penny banks, thrift, temperance, youths' institutes, and emigration.

Other speakers were the treasurer and secretary

of the Liverpool Ragged School Union, the secretary of the Manchester Ragged School Union, and two London teachers, who were also members of the London School Board.

In 1885 the Society addressed itself in earnest to the question of country holidays for ailing children. Since 1869 a little had been done, but no important arrangements had been made for a general scheme. In this year the Council, finding that the schools were already sending children away, thought it desirable to have special homes.   Thursley and East Grinstead were the two first.   The year before this 306 had been sent to the country by headquarters, and 2,000 by the schools.

Another event of 1885 was a presentation to the Earl of Shaftesbury and to each of his children by old scholars in the ragged schools.   Carefully executed coloured replicas of Holman Hunt's "Light of the World" were presented to Lord Ashley, the Right Hon. Evelyn Ashley, the Hon. Lionel Ashley, the Hon. Cecil Ashley, Lady Templemore, and Lady Edith Ashley.

For Lord Shaftesbury there was an illuminated testimonial, handsomely framed, signed by a committee of thirteen and countersigned by Lord Aberdeen, and by the writer's father as honorary secretary of the fund.   He also had the privilege of reading the address to the earl, on behalf of all those who, like himself, had received their education and best impulses in life in the ragged schools of London.   Lord Shaftesbury expressed pleasure that he had been selected to do it.   At this interesting gathering Mr. Gladstone had intended to be present, but at the last moment was summoned to Windsor.   The presenta-

THE FIRST HOLIDAY HOMES OF THE R.S.U. BRENCHLEY,
THURSLEY, CHISLEHURST, CATERHAM, WINDSOR, FOLKESTONE, AND
EAST GRINSTEAD.

tion took place in the lower hall, Exeter Hall, and
Lord Shaftesbury's old schoolfellow, Sir Harry Verney,

and his companion in good works, the Baroness Burdett-Coutts, were present.

In 1887 the Queen became Patron of the Society.

The year 1888 saw the ragged school literary organ enlarged and re-christened under the title, " In His Name." From 1849 to 1876 the Ragged School Union magazine was a monthly, then it became the *Quarterly Record*. From 1880 it was under the editorship of Mr. R. J. Curtis.

In 1890 our genial old friend retired. For thirty years he had been in and out among the schools as guide, philosopher, and friend to the masters and mistresses of the day schools. He was adviser to the Council and examiner of the children, and a much loved man by all.

The summer of the same year saw the wedding of the model of Millais' " Love Letter," Miss Dorothy Tennant, in Westminster Abbey. She was, it will be remembered, married to Mr. H. M. Stanley (afterwards Sir H. M. Stanley), the African explorer, whose recent death is much to be deplored. As an artist she is a painter of street life, and has before now placed original sketches of urchins at play at the disposal of the editor of *In His Name*. When she was married she sent a dozen invitation cards for selected children from the ragged schools to have seats in the Abbey.

The old offices at Exeter Hall had to be given up in 1891. The dingy room and outer office at No. 13, that served all the purposes of council chamber, conference rooms, secretarial and clerical offices and warehouse, had seen the birth of some great agencies, but it was very inconvenient.

The change to 37, Norfolk Street was an advance ;

but the work was still cramped, as will be shown farther on.

Since the Earl of Shaftesbury died in 1885 the Earl of Aberdeen had acted as President. His political duties had, however, prevented any very close contact with the Society and its activities. Accordingly, when he became Governor-General of Canada in 1893, he resigned the position, and Earl Compton, now the Marquis of Northampton, became leader. 1893, therefore, for that and other reasons, represents the beginning of another period—a period marked by the emergence of the R.S.U. as a modern mission.

CHAPTER XX

Great Occasions in R.S.U. History

"I would rather be President of the Ragged School Union than President of the Royal Academy."—LORD SHAFTESBURY.

THE pageantry of ragged schools deserves a chapter to itself. Every annual festival has been a display since 1854; and although we have hearty meetings at the Queen's Hall, Langham Place, in the present day—occasions when colour, music, oratory and the enthusiasm of a great throng blend to symbolise a cause upon which God's approval has rested—yet there are vanished glories we shall never see again. There are compensations, substitutions of the modern time, uninferior but different from our recent gala days. What has gone can never be revived.

In old Exeter Hall there was less accommodation than at Langham Place, but the applications for admission were far beyond the seating power. "Thousands are inside, but thousands have been unable to gain admission," said the President, on one occasion; and that was usually the case. It was then, as now, not a cold audience of social units unrelated to each other. By the constitution the teachers and subscribers of ten shillings were members of the

R.S.U. A proportion of these friends received tickets, and of these as many as the place would hold got in. There were no queues in those days. People took chances in crowds, and even in an evangelical crowd there can be considerable pressure. A feeling that acted as a sort of *hors d'œuvre* to the banquet that was to follow was that to be there at all was a privilege and the reward of striving.

The orators found an audience all ready prepared for them to stimulate them to their finest efforts, and to be rendered incandescent by a speaker's fervour. While the hall filled, the slanting beams of a May sunset caught the dust and vapour rising in the room and filled it with a golden haze, through which teachers peered trying to distinguish their scholars on the orchestra. The school-banners were the guides to position. When friend discovered friend handkerchiefs on both sides were waved; but there were so many waving at once that the view from where the scholars sat was very entertaining.

The school-banners are never likely to be seen again in all the splendour of the early time. Painted on silk of various colours and covered with gold and blazonry, and in some instances sewn over with metal sequins, they were very effective. There was a competition for position for these on the platform and round the organ. As it grew near the time of meeting, and the twilight became more and more grey, the lights were turned on and all the moving colour of the orchestra leapt to view. Besides the banners with their devices, there were the coloured uniforms of *all* the old shoe-black brigades, and the print dresses and white caps and aprons of the domestic servants. It is safe to prophesy that no R.S.U.

meeting of the future will ever see that bit of colour again.

Solemn gentlemen, with wands they did not know what to do with, and who were expected to take up the collection, paraded the aisles, and looked for lurking-places where they would not obscure the view of members of the audience.

When the hall was packed, a good deal was done with camp-stools that a County Council Inspector would not now allow, and then the door was closed. The audience ceased bobbing up and down; ladies who had brought knitting or other work put it away; and there was a hush of expectancy as the time drew near.

On the orchestra, likewise, there was a settling down. Perpetual motion had reigned since the opening, and even as the big hand of the clock was on the stroke of the hour it seemed hopeless to expect order. We shall never look upon the like of that mob again. A country speaker addressing them once said that people who came from the country usually visited the "lions" of London; but they were the "lions" he liked to see; and there certainly was something about wild young people, uncowed by a mechanical life, that was reminiscent of lions. Henry Mayhew's description of the gallery of the "Vic." gives, as far as words can, an idea of these turbulent folk. There was an appalling boisterousness, a savage intensity that thrilled the nerves of those unaccustomed to meet with it. It has nearly all gone now—all but the factory-girls' Bank-holiday laugh.

The moment of the earl's coming being imminent, the masters and teachers skirmish around to grip the leashes of their rampant cubs, only to slip them the

next moment as those about to occupy the platform
come up the steps. Several well-known people receive
a greeting, but the roar is for the earl. From the
incense of flattery, and even the appreciation of friendship, this great man turns away, preserved from all
harm by the lonely hours of the early morning spent
with his Bible and his God; but in the enjoyment
of this music _he can indulge in all innocence and

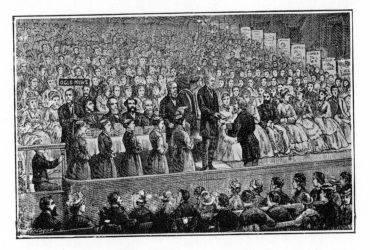

SIR ROBERT CARDEN AS A PRIZETAKER.

with thanksgiving. What those wild waves of hoarse
clamour say to him, with their 9th Thermidor under-
tone, is seen in the expression on his mobile face as
he turns to return the greeting. Something else
then occurs, never to be repeated in our time—an exhibition of the grand manner of a fine old English
gentleman. He salutes the prizetakers with the
same elaborate courtesy that he might have shown
to George IV. when walking in Hyde Park with the

Duke of Wellington, and is so preoccupied as almost to forget the audience who have been cheering all the while. He bows to them; then all are seated and all are still.

Then comes the opening prayer. It may be by a bishop, who uses a collect and concludes with the Lord's Prayer, the meeting following aloud, or just as likely a Nonconformist minister offering extempore prayer. A foreign missionary home on furough, Dr. Duff, of India, Robert Moffat, or James Chalmers, of New Guinea, may be chosen as chaplain of the meeting.

The list of names of those who have discharged this duty form a blend such as we *shall* hope to see again.

Bishop Ryan, Bishop Claughton and the Bishop of Peterborough are balanced by Dr. Newman Hall, Dr. Henry Allon, and the Rev. Donald Fraser. The negro bishop, Dr. Crowther, might be succeeded by Paxton Hood, or any of the following: Dr. Sinclair Paterson, D.D., Prebendary Cadman, the Bishop of Bedford, Canon Fleming, Rev. J. McConnell Hussey, Dr. Cæsar Milan, Dr. J. C. Miller, the Dean of Carlisle, Dean Champeneys, Rev. Wm. McCall, and others not known to this generation.

East London possessed some fine men who often acted in this capacity. One was Dr. Tyler, into whose chapel Matthew Arnold strayed and wrote verses of his experience. It illustrates the relations of Church and Dissent years ago, that this minister should, as a joke that was a tribute, be called the Bishop of East London at a public dinner by a bishop. The fun began when a Colonial bishop, who did not know him, took the matter seriously and referred to " his lordship."

Dr. James Cohen, rector of Whitechapel, worked hand in hand with Dr. Tyler for the conversion of the Jews. Jointly they were responsible for the publication of " The Jews in relation to the Church and the World," a series of powerful appeals to the Hebrew that should be translated into Yiddish as a memorial to them.

Next would come the report, of which the audience caught an occasional word and guessed the rest, taking their cue for applauding from the front rows, or the quaver, expressive of deep emotion, in the secretary's voice. After that the chairman would make one of those deeply impressive speeches which, from beginning to end, and numbers of them taken in succession through all the years he lived, are warnings to English Christian laymen to resist the secularising of the nation.

Accompanying the earl were frequently friends from the House of Peers, to whom a first visit was a surprising experience. The warmth of the greeting they themselves received, when called upon to speak, it would appear, was something novel. An instance of this surprise at the real significance of the R.S.U., decorously expressed as it naturally would be, is that contained in a speech by Lord Strafford de Redcliffe, in which he said : " In looking round him he saw that vast hall filled even to the ceiling with intelligent countenances beaming with the same sentiment of humanity, and responding so largely, and so deeply, and in so eloquent a manner, to that more formal eloquence which had proceeded from the platform. Those circumstances impressed him with the belief that that which at a distance excited his interest was *really a practical thing*." This educating of the aristocracy was not the least of the services Lord Shaftesbury rendered to his generation.

A few of these visitors were the Marquis of Westminster, Lord Drumlanrig, Lord Radstock, Lord Robert Grosvenor, and Viscount Ebrington. The Earl of Harrowby, at one time Member for Liverpool, Mr. John Holmes, the Mayor, Mr. Henry Labouchere, and Mr. R. A. Slaney M.P., were friends of Dr. Levi, some of whom signed his now famous circular to the Chambers of Commerce, recommending the formation of associations for a national and international code of commercial laws.

On such rare occasions as he was prevented from taking the chair, some good-natured friend like Lord Harrowby or the Earl of Iddesleigh would be Lord Shaftesbury's stop-gap, apologising to the audience for a disappointment the latter were at no pains to conceal. But these occasions during more than forty years were exceedingly rare. The last occasion was when Sir Robert Carden, looking preternaturally fierce from out the snow of hair and beard, took his old friend's place at the last moment at his request because he was too feeble to come.

After the speech from the chair came the resolutions, proposed, seconded, and frequently supported by some of the finest platform speakers of the day. Waves of emotion swept over the audience, and their feelings were expressed with a demonstrativeness no audience allows itself now. During the speeches the chairman thought with his eyes shut. If a fervid orator came, in the middle of a period, to the precipice-edge where pathos may drop into bathos, the heavy lids opened while he waited and feared. The danger passed, a flicker of a smile was exchanged with some platform companion whose eyes he happened to meet. Like most serious men he was a humorist as well; and some of these telepathic jokes reduced those with whom they were exchanged to convulsions behind their handkerchiefs.

His own facial expression was funereal and ex-pressed boredom. It brought many a man to the point, who forgot the time, progressing well with the audience, and looked round and saw it. If he did not look round, he heard the words, " the children," as from a sepulchre behind him.

The earl always spoke of the prizetakers, many of whom were in their late teens, as " the children." Possibly they were representatives to his fancy of all the children he had been the means of saving throughout the country.

That the speeches were a very great trial to them there can be no doubt, as scarcely a word could reach them.

Some time during the evening Judge Payne would bring in his usual tail-piece, and the relief of a little humour after so much intensity was a gain.

For many years the practice obtained of marching the lads and girls who had obtained the situation prize across the platform to shake hands with the chairman. We have not the patience of our forebears; and to sit out a matter of a thousand handshakes is probably as much beyond us now as tolerating an hour's sermon.

When the prizetakers were trained as a choir it greatly lightened the proceedings, and it disciplined the young people as a body. They were then a working entity under the conductor. Behind the chair, this friend worked wonders. Possessing a fund of spirits, much wit, and inexhaustible humour, he won fondness for himself as a wag at the rehearsals. He was a good mimic as well. On the night of the meeting a cathedral verger, could not be more solemn than he ; and in the character of a suppressed comedian he had a wonderful power over his choristers. His staidness was treated as part of the joke, and they would watch for half an hour at a time for the ghost of a sly grimace. Whoever the restlessness of the scholars offended, it never offended the chairman. Occasionally he would look round wistfully from his chair up the tiers of seats, as if to say, *our* reputations are at stake, try to bear me out in all the claims I have made for you, but that was all.

His love for sorrowing childhood was very real. " My God ! these children ! " was his exclamation in the hour of England's infamy. At the very last it was much the same. It may not be known that Lord Shaftesbury's greatest self-indulgence was an un-obtrusive visit to Hoxton or Whitechapel. It was a delight to him to be accepted as one of the family in a coster's parlour, or to go round to a few homes in Whitechapel with the schoolmaster of a ragged school. As he approached his end in May of the year he passed away he went down to George Yard. George Holland was one of the friends from whose society he derived comfort. In the dark schoolroom down a slum he pulled his coat-sleeve tightly over his arm, and said to the old schoolmaster : " Look how I have fallen away. If I should be laid aside, if I send for you, you will come to me ? " At a visit just before this he had been to see the children, and had talked with them, and the aged peer was weeping. As a privileged friend the dominie asked, " What is the matter, my

lord ? " " George, those poor children! " said he.
" Poor dear children, how will you get on with them ? "
I replied: " My God shall supply all their need."
" Yes," he said, " He will ; they must have some food
directly." He left the building, and, entering his
brougham, ordered the coachman to drive home.
A few hours afterwards two large churns of soup,
made at Grosvenor Square, were sent down—enough
for four hundred. This was continued all the winter.

His greatest trial was the poverty that prevented
him from obeying generous impulses.

In reflecting that the Lord Jesus Christ was afflicted
with such afflictions as we are subject to, he felt that
it would have been a consolation could he have included among the Redeemer's human experiences,
debt.

Yet this he struggled with, and manfully, though
misunderstood and misconstrued by those who thought
that he should give more to charity.

An entry in his diary for May 28, 1853, shows
it : " Sent to St. Giles's for two more pictures to be
sold. The house is falling and must be repaired ;
will not do it from any fund or revenue by which
money devoted to religion, charity, or cottage building would be diverted. Must therefore surrender
more heirlooms, dismantle my walls, check ancestral
feeling, and thank God it is no worse."

It is this that explains much else in Lord Shaftesbury. He was accused of being stiff to equals and
affable to inferiors (socially). It arose from the fact
that he had things in common only with those in
life who took chances.

In early life he knew what it was to be for an evening in George IV's company and enjoy it. A visit

to Crockford's in the Duke of Wellington's society may have suggested the passage in his diary : " We lose our time like guinea points at whist." His life was pure ; but he knew other men's temptations and had his own trials. That is the reason he had such a special fellow-feeling for the poor.

The poor understood him as well as he understood them. They knew nothing of his financial troubles, of difficulties for which he was not responsible. But they knew he loved them. The poor man with tattered garments, and crape on his arm, who addressed a by-stander when Lord Shaftesbury's funeral passed, represented hundreds of thousands of poor people and children when he said, " Our Earl's gone ! God A'mighty knows he loved us, and we loved him. We shan't see his likes again ! "

After a meeting, the Strand was blocked. Lads and girls from all the missions walked up to go home with the prizetakers behind the school banners and led by the school bands..

Besides the annual meetings there have been other occasions that linger in the memories of workers.

One was the presentation of a testimonial from the ragged school teachers that bore 1,700 signatures. This was presented at St. Martin's Hall, on June 28, 1857, to Lord Shaftesbury, who valued it very much.

But, perhaps, the most significant public tribute he ever received was when the Lord Mayor of London, Sir William McArthur, called a meeting under the auspices of the R.S.U. at the Guildhall, on April 28, 1881, to celebrate Lord Shaftesbury's 80th birth-day.

A portrait of himself to be retained by his family as an heirloom was to be presented. Although he was a man who could not be spoiled by praise, he was not averse to taking part in a ceremony that seemed to gather up and symbolize the ideals of his life in such a way as to assure him that he had not spent his strength for nought.

When a copy of a report of the proceedings was sent him he wrote on the fly-leaf of the copy : " Deep and lively is my gratitude to the men who conceived, organized, and executed this celebration, and much do I feel the sympathy of those who honoured it by their presence."

" If you can only go half-way in endorsing what has been said, I shall have obtained a great honour, comfort and joy," was a remark in his speech at the meeting.

It is a great pleasure to all ragged school workers to know that he did derive pleasure from the occasion. All men delighted to do him honour. " Distinguished by a long roll of philanthropic deeds," was Mr. Gladstone's testimony. " All the honour and glory belong to him," was Lord Beaconsfield's.

On this birthday festival the Poet Laureate (Mr. Alfred Tennyson) wrote : " Allow me to assure you in plain prose how cordially I join with those who honour the Earl of Shaftesbury as the friend of the poor, and who wish him many years of health and strength in which to continue his good work and to incite others to follow his example."

Probably the Guildhall never held such a company as that which foregathered on this April day. Every part of the building was crowded long before the proceedings opened. On the platform were peers and members of Parliament, bishops, clergy and other ministers of the gospel, merchants, men and women of all shades of opinion and of all stations, representing every estimable phase of political, religious and social life. Distinguished ornaments of the bench and bar, the army and the navy were there, while literature and journalism were well represented.

The Earl of Aberdeen, Mr. W. E. Forster, and Mr. H. R. Williams were the principal speakers, but Mr. Forster's was the speech that pleased the earl most. " If anything is told of my life after I am gone, let those words of Forster's be recorded. I don't think in the whole course of my life any words ever gratified me more," was his wish and his opinion respecting a certain portion of Mr. Forster's speech. The words were : " The good conduct on the part of the population [in the factory districts] was in a great measure due to the moderating influences which were brought to bear on them by Lord Ashley. How I do wish that all agitators, when they are advocating the removal of great and real grievances, would take an example from the way in which Lord Ashley conducted that agitation, and remember with what care they should consider both the immediate and the ultimate effect of what they say upon those who are suffering."

But brilliant as was the throng that surrounded him, his greatest happiness would be derived from the presence of old and valued friends, and the members of his family. The Baroness Burdett-Coutts, his upholder in many a good work was there, so were Sir Harry Verney, Lord Kinnaird, Sir Robert Carden, R. C. L. Bevan, Samuel Morley, and C. H. Spurgeon. Seated near him, too, were the three authors, Miss Catherine Marsh, Miss Hesba Stretton, and Miss Frances P. Cobbe.

Of Miss Marsh he had written at one time : " Catherine Marsh is ill. Let every one who cares for Christ's kingdom over the hearts of the human race pray that she may be restored " ; and again : " Ran down to Feltwell Rectory for the day to see Miss Marsh and the O'Rorkes. A pleasant time : had, what I ever desire but seldom get, some sympathetic talk—some talk of this world and some of the next."

Miss Marsh was a pioneer worker among the navvies at the Crystal Palace. She also wrote *English Hearts and English Hands*, and was the biographer of her father, Dr. Marsh, and of Captain Hedley Vicars.

Miss Hesba Stretton, the author of *Jessica's First Prayer*, is well known to all.

Miss Cobbe, who has just passed away, was also a ragged school worker. She had sent the hero of the day a poem for the occasion by that morning's post.

The most significant part of the entire demonstration were the wooden barriers erected in Guildhall Yard to keep the people back. Their share of the function was not inappropriately in the street, where they made an even more impressive display. Ragged school children and costers with decorated donkeys and barrows were there, while flower-girls strewed flowers for him to walk upon, and all poured upon him " the blessing of the poor and of Him that was ready to perish."

> Oh, tarry long amongst us. Live, we pray ;
> Hasten not yet to hear thy Lord's " Well done ! "
> Let this world still seem better, while it may
> Contain one soul like thine amid its throng,

wrote Miss Cobbe, on this occasion ; and for four years

longer he was spared. When at last it pleased the Lord to summon him home there was mourning throughout the land. At the memorial service in Westminster Abbey over 150 religious societies with which he was connected sent deputations. Royalty was represented, the Church, both Houses of Parliament, diplomacy. municipal power, and society also.

As the coffin rested under the lantern, Charles Wesley's beautiful hymn, " Let all the saints terrestrial sing," was sung ; and perhaps never before in an English church had representatives of so many sections of Protestantism met together for worship, nor so near an approach to the aspiration of that first line been realised.

The coffin was buried beneath masses of the loveliest flowers from the offering of the Crown Princess of Germany to " The loving tribute from the Flower Girls of London." He had, indeed, " clothed a people with spontaneous mourning, and was going down to the grave amid the benedictions of the poor." As at the Guildhall, so now—the respect of the poor was displayed in the open-air. There was a poetic fitness in it that the street-folks' tribute should be quite their own. Right down the east side of Parliament Street deputations of working-men, with the banners of clubs draped with crape, deputations from the homes, refuges and training ships, and from various missions and charities, stood to keep the way. Bands of music stationed at intervals played " The Dead March ; " and as the procession, consisting of a plain hearse and five coaches, and a few carriages and cabs passed by, these bands headed the deputations and fell in behind. They then accompanied the cortège as far as the Abbey door. But it must not be supposed that rank and privilege appropriated the national treasure-house of greatness, and that the poor were excluded. They were well represented.

At the western door the coffin was met and carried through the nave and choir by eight pall-bearers, representing the chief societies of which Lord Shaftesbury was President. Six of these were, or had been, ragged school men : John Macgregor, H. R. Williams, W. J. Orsman, Joseph G. Gent, William Williams and George Holland. The other two were George (now Sir George) Williams, Y.M.C.A., and J. M. Weylland, of the London City Mission ; John Kirk acting as honorary secretary of the Funeral Committee.

After the service the costermongers' band preceded the hearse, playing " Safe in the arms of Jesus." The poorest of the poor had secured black from somewhere, and sorrow was universal. This was the saddest and the darkest day in R.S.U. history, but there was a deep joy as well in the knowledge that a good but much enduring man had entered into everlasting rest.

CHAPTER XXI

Literary Friends of the Cause

TINKERS and tailors, soldiers and sailors and men of many other stations and callings have worked in the ranks or for the cause of the Ragged School Union. Few, however, have been able to do so much for it as its journalistic and literary friends. Conspicuous in a distinguished group are the two great novelists who have made their art an instrument for promoting social service. Charles Dickens and Sir Walter Besant did more to rehumanise British middle-class opinion than any other writers of the Victorian Age. Charles Dickens interpreted the generalizations of Carlyle into terms understood by ordinary people. He reached the judgment, conscience and feelings through the family affections which nearly every one possesses, and tried to help forward the reforms the country needed. From 1838 onwards there was a serious purpose underlying nearly all his writings, and his effort ran parallel with the practical work of philanthropy. For that work he created a sympathizing and supporting public irrespective of religious people. In 1838, *Oliver Twist* appeared to arouse sympathy and interest in workhouse children. *Nicholas Nickleby* came next in 1839, exposing certain scandals connected with child life and education. The purpose is never obtruded, but it is always attained.

There is no gain in attempting to delineate so familiar a figure except so far as his friendship with the ragged school movement is shown to fit in with his life-work—

CHARLES DICKENS AS A BOY AT THE BLACKING FACTORY.
THE HARDSHIPS OF HIS CHILD LIFE MADE HIM THE
FRIEND OF POOR CHILDREN.

a natural part of it, and not a special hobby. The serious business of every book he wrote was to make certain of securing the sympathy of every reader for some typical ill-used creature, or produce a feeling of aversion for some corrupt individual, also a type.

But the great advocate seemed to have chiefly child clients, though adults such as the poor debtor and the chancery victim also came in for help.   Charley Bates, the Dodger, Little Nell, the Marchioness, Smike, David Copperfield, Oliver Twist—how well we know them all ! So did the fathers and grandfathers of some of us. With them there was this gain : that when the magician had woven his fireside spells a prejudice was killed, an injustice seen and a wrong hated.   So numerous were the people to whom this happened that reforms did not linger long.   It need not. therefore, surprise us that Charles Dickens was in close friendship and association with Lord Shaftesbury.   They were drawn together because they were both reformers.   Probably Lord Shaftesbury never felt more complimented by any one than when Dickens told him his Act for the registration of lodging-houses was the best measure put upon the English statute book.

Be that as it may, the great writer was a friend of the Society throughout his life.   His paragraphs and editorials about the work were very helpful.   It was through an article in *Household Words* that the late C. H. Spurgeon was drawn into the Ragged School Union.   When he lived in Doughty Street and the Marylebone Road he was actually in touch with the work at one of the schools, as the following letters will show :—

> " BROADSTAIRS, KENT,
> " *September* 24, 1843.

" DEAR SIR,—

" Allow me to ask you a few questions in reference to that most able undertaking in which you are engaged with a view, I need hardly say, to its advancement and extended usefulness. For the present, I could wish it, if you please, to be considered as put in confidence, but not to the exclusion of the gentlemen associated with you in the management of the Ragged School on Saffron Hill.

CHARLES DICKENS AS A YOUNG MAN.

" It occurred to me, when I was there, as being of the utmost importance that, if practicable, the boys should have an opportunity of washing themselves before beginning their tasks.

" Do you agree with me ? If so, will you ascertain at about what cost a washing-place—a large trough or sink, for instance, with a good supply of running water, soap and towels—could be put up ? In case you consider it necessary that some person should be engaged to mind it, and to see that the boys availed themselves of it in an orderly manner, please to add the payment of such a person to the expense.

" Have you seen any place, or do you know of any place, in that neighbourhood—any one or two good spacious lofts or rooms—which you would like to engage (if you could afford it), as being well suited for the School ? If so, at what charge could it be hired, and how soon ?

" In the event of my being able to procure you the funds for making these great improvements, would you see any objection to expressly limiting visitors (I mean visiting teachers—volunteers, whoever they may be), to confining their questions and instructions, as a point of honour, to the broad truths taught in the School by yourself and the gentlemen associated with you ? I set great store by this question, because it seems to me of vital importance that no persons, however well intentioned, should perplex the minds of these unfortunate creatures with religious mysteries that young people with the best advantages can but imperfectly understand. I heard a lady visitor the night I was among you propounding questions in reference to the ' Lamb of God ' which I most unquestionably would not suffer any one to put to my children ; recollecting the immense absurdities that were suggested to my childhood by the like injudicious catechising.

" I return to town on Monday, the 2nd of next month ; if you write to me before then, please to address your letter here. If after that date, to my house in town.

"With a cordial sympathy in your Great and Christian Labour,

"I am, dear Sir,

"Faithfully yours,

"CHARLES DICKENS."

"Mr. S. R. Starey."

CHARLES DICKENS' HOUSE IN DOUGHTY STREET.

"DEVONSHIRE TERRACE,
"*February* 1, 1844.

"DEAR SIR,—

"Will you have the goodness to turn over in your mind, and to note down for me, as briefly as you please, any little facts or details connected with the Ragged

School which you think it would benefit the design to have publicly known ? If you· could make it convenient to favour me with a call any evening next week or on Sunday week, and will let me hear from you to that effect, I shall be glad to make an appointment with you. But pray do not hesitate to let me know what time suits you best, as I can easily accommodate myself to your engagements.

" The kind of thing I wish to know is—your average number of scholars—whether it increases or falls off— whether any boys are pretty constant in their attendance—whether after absenting themselves they return again—whether the ignorance of their parents is one of your rocks ahead—and the like. In short, I think I can turn any result of your experience and observation of these unfortunate creatures to the account you would desire.

" Pray, mention to me the discouraging as well as the encouraging circumstances, for they are equally a part of the sad case, and without a knowledge of them it is impossible to state it forcibly.

" You are at perfect liberty to mention this to the masters of the School. But beyond this, or such other limits as you may consider necessary I could wish our correspondence to be confidential.

" Faithfully yours,

" CHARLES DICKENS."

" Mr. S. R. Starey."

His later interest was mainly concerned with work in Westminster, with which the Baroness Burdett-Coutts was connected. But he was often found interesting himself in particular cases. For instance, John Macgregor tells us that he paid for a poor boy's admis-

SIR WALTER BESANT.

sion to a refuge, then for an outfit upon his entry into
the shoe-black brigade, and "Smike," as the boys

called him, was a great favourite and did very well.

Sir Walter Besant was in some respects the successor of Charles Dickens, though his special line was the history of manners in the eighteenth and nineteenth centuries. But to him it is we owe the short-lived interest in slumming that for a time was quite a craze among the upper classes, and which indirectly did more than a little good. It is common knowledge that the People's Palace in the Mile End Road is the visible, tangible result of the novel, *All Sorts and Conditions of Men.* His expert knowledge of the forces that have made English Society during the past two centuries would naturally put the hall-mark of value, from a certain standpoint, upon the efforts of an old Society if the criticism were unfavourable. At the jubilee of the Ragged School Union, in 1894, in the *Contemporary Review*, he bestowed upon it unstinted praise, ascribing to its originators the re-birth of social service in England, which he maintained had practically died out with the Franciscans. A passage from the article may well be quoted here, as indicating how powerful his support was :—

" These children of the gutter were sent out by their mothers as soon as they could walk to pick up their living somehow in the streets. They sang ballads : they sold matches : they picked up coals on the river bank, they pilfered from the open shops and stalls ; whatever else they did, or pretended to do, they always pilfered. Why, out of 260 children who were collected for one of the first Ragged Schools, 27 had been in prison, 36 had run away from home, 19 slept in common lodging-houses, 41 lived by begging, 29 never slept in beds, 17 were barefoot, 37 were bareheaded, 12 had no body-linen. What prospect was there for such children ? . . . In Cold Bath Fields Prison there were 2,690 prisoners under twenty-one. Of these, 259 were under fourteen. One prisoner in every ten was a child under fourteen. These unfortunate children were without religion, without knowledge, without a trade. They entered upon manhood with nothing but a pair of hands, and in their heads nothing but the continual desire to steal—steal—steal, in order to enjoy the simple pleasures they desired—especially warmth, food, drink and idleness. What has become of that army of 100,000 ? Some few, one supposes, have been dragged out by the efforts of the new agencies ; those who are living must now be from sixty to seventy years of age. How many survive to tell the tale ? And how many of them who still breathe these upper airs venture to look back and to remember ?

" A few more figures may bring home to us the condition of things. An army of 100,000 children reckoned from the age of seven to twelve, means allowing five children to each family, 25,000 parents. On the same estimate it would give to these children a following generation of 300,000, and to a third generation of 900,000, without allowing for early deaths. Making every allowance, we understand that these were the children of a great army of parents ignorant, dissolute, or criminal ; that unless preventives of some kind were found they would themselves follow the example of their parents ; and that they would most certainly, of this there was no manner of doubt, bring into the world a greatly increased army of those who, without preventives, would naturally, perforce follow in the same course. But these figures assume only 25,000 as the parents. In 1847 it was reckoned that there were in London 150,000 men and women, boys and girls, who were criminals and prostitutes.

" Consider the cost, the mere money loss, to the nation of such an army.

" First, it is fair to suppose that 10 per cent. would always be in prison.

" Next, the 90 per cent. left would have to maintain themselves by stealing.

" Thirdly, the country would lose the wealth that those hands and brains should have created.

" Fourthly, the country had to pay for an efficient police force, not to speak of magistrates, courts, etc.

" As to the first proposition, the convict charges at £120 a head, including the whole cost of prisons £1,200,000

" As to the second, the lost wealth reckoned at £100 a year (if a working man could make £1 a week for wages, what he has made was certainly worth double) £9,000,000

" As to the third, we must reckon that they would want at least 25s. a week, for the criminal class lives well. In order to get this they must steal property worth at least three times as much, say £3 15s. a week, in all over £16,000,000

" As to the fourth, the police force, etc., that may be left for a more exhaustive estimate.

" We find, therefore, that in 1847 London actually lost, by its army of ignorance and crime, the sum of £26,000,000 every year. That, remember, was when the population was less than half its present number. Had the proportion been maintained the criminal class at the present day would number 300,000 ; the loss to the city every year would be £52,000,000. Had there been no preventives, the proportion would not have been maintained ; the number of criminals would have increased with greater and still greater acceleration.

BELIEVERS IN THE F.A.F.

One knows not, indeed, what in the long run, would have been the end of a city whose convict class was left unheeded and unchecked, save by the lash and the prison, to work out its own damnation."

Among our own workers have been several who handled the pen to some purpose in the cause.

The late Miss Cobbe, nicknamed " Cobweb " by the Bristol urchins, was one of them. Upon the staff of the *Echo*, she was able to give helpful notices. Mrs. Sewell, Hesba Stretton and Mrs. Bayly were other lady writers. A.L.O.E. secured a cottage in Berkshire as a place of rest for our jaded workers. By the bankside near old Cherry Garden pier is a ragged school called Stephen the Yeoman School. It is so named after the principal character in *Ministering Children*, and was built out of the profits of that book by Miss Charlesworth. John Macgregor was no mean writer, nor was Dr. Leone Levi. Lord Shaftesbury, as has been stated, wrote about ragged schools for the quarterlies. When he went slumming to get the copy for his articles, he used to take a humbler friend, and to him he afterwards gave the honorarium the articles earned. Dr. Guthrie was of the group perhaps the most influential advocate of all.

Journalist friends the cause has always had, but at a time when newspapers, magazines and reviews were relatively few in number, when life was slower and people were not surfeited with printed matter, advocacy of ragged schools told. At Queen Victoria's accession there were but 479 British newspapers ; at her Diamond Jubilee, 2,396. The work stood alone also. There were not numerous other charities of a similar nature to distract attention. *The Times* gave preeminently splendid help. As for the *Illustrated London News* half pages of ragged school interiors and ragged school excursions were always appearing.

The money paid to artists and wood-engravers for pictures illustrating ragged school work must have been considerable. The *Graphic* at a later date was just as liberal. Mr. *Punch* occasionally stopped joking, to give serious praise to the new effort. *Chambers' Journal* gave the widest opportunities for full descriptive articles upon the work in all its aspects, as did also the *Quarterly Review*. Among illustrators who have given aid, George Cruikshank, John Leech, and Thomas Sulman were conspicuous, and the succession has been maintained by such artists as Lady Stanley and William Rainey to the present day.

It is not very clear what caused the late Henry Mayhew to attack ragged schools as he did. The explanation may perhaps be found in a preference he had for reforms and self-help agencies arising from the efforts of the people themselves. That he was not intentionally unfair is shown by his appreciation of Lord Kinnaird's lodging-house, but his criticism of the liability of the lodgers to the intrusion of the curious, gives us a clue to the thoughts that made him such a bitter enemy. He never knew the work or its spirit. The view from inside was never vouchsafed to him. His distrust of philanthropic effort that seemed to have inseparably associated with it patronage on the one side and servility on the other, does him infinite honour. He was a man to whose opinions upon poor life great weight was attached by his contemporaries, and rightly so. If we had not had a Henry Mayhew we might possibly never have had a Charles Booth. His great work on London Labour and London Poor, is a human book that will live without need of revision, while the great statistician's work needs correcting every few years.

It is an indication of the hold the workers had gained upon public opinion that his merciless onslaught in the *Morning Chronicle* in the year 1850 affected the work so little. At the annual meeting of that year the late Earl of Harrowby read out a series of testimonies from prison chaplains, traversing the statements of the *Morning Chronicle*. Mayhew had gone so far as to suggest that the ragged schools instead of lessening crime, actually produced it. It is just possible that in isolated instances boys and girls may have met others at the ragged schools worse than themselves, who initiated them in criminal ways, but such a fact was too slender a basis upon which to found a sweeping generalization. Judge Payne turned the discussion to account for his " tailpiece." Addressing the scholars, he said—

> May you be taught, may you be fed,
> May you in wisdom's ways be led ;
> May you be happy night and day
> In spite of all Mayhew can say.
> May you from filthy homes be free ;
> May you improving parents see ;
> May you grow wise, and good, and strong,
> Till Mayhew owns that he was wrong. :

But in spite of his misinterpretation of the ragged school movement Mayhew was a good man, intensely sympathetic with the poor, and desirous of helping them. He formed benefit societies among the costers and patterers and also gave and lent money to them himself.

The same may be said of his brother Horace, who survived him many years. The *Daily News*, during the editorship of Charles Dickens, secured some invaluable workers, and since then has many times furthered ragged school interests.

From 1856, when it was first started, the *Daily Telegraph* has also been a friend. The most marked instance of interest was in the autumn of 1895, when an appeal for money to give Christmas hampers to cripple children, brought so remarkable a public response as almost to embarrass the staff in dealing with it by its unexpectedness. Thanks to the organizing ability of Mr. J. Hall Richardson and the voluntary labours of R.S.U. friends, a great scheme was carried through without a hitch.

James Greenwood, brother of the first editor of the *Pall Mall Gazette*, Mr. Frederick Greenwood, was the writer of the articles that stirred the hearts of the people of England. At the offices of the National Refuges is a framed picture drawn originally by James Greenwood, representing the Lambeth casual ward about 1865. Anything more terrible and loathsome than the scene depicted, it is scarcely possible to imagine.

The late Thomas Archer, like the late Mr. Clement Scott, used his gifts frequently for the benefit of poor children.

Apart from the very generous treatment the R.S.U. received at the hands of the daily Press at all times, there is an exceptional indebtedness in connexion with raising the funds for the annual children's banquet at the Guildhall and for the New Year's Gifts for London cripples. Sir William Treloar from the very commencement of these enterprises has been greatly assisted by the London and provincial papers.

Among the earliest of the alliances between the

R.S.U. and the Press for carrying out philanthropic schemes was that whereby the scholars of ragged schools shared in the benefits of the Robin Dinner Fund, subscribed by the readers of *Home Words* and other publications founded by the Rev. Charles Bullock.

Mr. F. A. Atkins, editor of the *Young Man*, *Young Woman* and *Home Messenger*, helps forward the good work through the Guild of the Good Samaritan, the members of which supply garments to meet the needs of the Poor Children's Aid department of the R.S.U. In point of time this was earlier than the Barefoot Mission of Mr. Hartley Aspden's publications, but very soon after its formation the latter was seen to be a very powerful auxiliary to the same department. A few months after it started in 1895 it had as many as 40,000 members.

An enormous body of sympathisers with ragged school work have consequently been recruited from among the readers of *Sunday Stories*, *Golden Stories*, and the *Sunday Circle*.

In 1892 Pearson's Fresh Air Fund commenced work in London, subsequently extending operations to the provinces. The R.S.U. has been the advisory agency on account of the expert knowledge of London the staff possess in judging the merits of the applications from schoolmasters, clergy, city missionaries and other workers in slum-land. In the provinces also, it has used the old ragged school link with the towns to introduce the promoters of " the cheapest charity " at once to the right people for dealing with the right children.

In addition to this, the R.S.U. does all the work connected with the London excursions, of which the chief centre is the Retreat on the borders of Epping Forest at Loughton, able to accommodate with ease a thousand children.

The Crutch and Kindness League, though mentioned last, is perhaps the most valuable of all the R.S.U. Press alliances. It is the product of the advocacy of the Rev. J. Reid Howatt. Its first home was the *New Age*. From thence it was shifted to the columns of the *Temple Magazine*, and now has found a permanent resting-place in the *Sunday at Home*. Starting in a very simple way it has grown until there is a probability that before long every cripple child in London will have a friend to correspond with. The members not only write to the cripples, but in many instances give substantial help as well. The most interesting feature of this association is the way in which the members of it are scattered all over the world, which makes the matter in the letters extremely interesting to the children.

The position that the R.S.U. takes in placing its machinery and influence at the disposal of those who wish to help the poor is, that it is, the Society's duty to assist in giving expression to the best impulses of every section of the community.

CHAPTER XXII

The Ragged School Movement as a Modern Mission

We are still asked, as our fathers were asked, "What is the work of the Ragged School?" The answer is the same as in the old time: "To improve the child-life of our great cities. To improve the most neglected, the most abandoned, the poorest child-life on the face of the earth, to better their condition and prospects in this life, and to give them the glorious hope of the perfect life of the hereafter."

LORD NORTHAMPTON.

BY 1893 there had been so many changes that such dramatic features as the work originally had, were greatly reduced. From the abolition of the soap duty to the abolition of school fees all public action had tended to tone down the picturesqueness of squalor or to break down the barriers between the regularly employed and the street-folk. Among these, while on the one hand reforming missions, amendment of prison treatment, and improved chances of employment made great inroads among the criminals and semi-criminals, Economic forces greatly changed the law-abiding. The continuous application of machinery to every kind of manufacture, the growth of the railway system, and the working of Cobdenism had gradually made London into a labour market capable of absorbing the casual workers, displaced from their old pursuits.

The result of these influences has been the production of an enormous mass of workers, not sharply divided in their characteristics from skilled labourers, but less self-reliant than the units of the old mob. The mob itself though not wiped out, had shrunk in numbers, and had been leavened with the surrounding spirit of subordination. Moreover so long a period had elapsed since their turbulence was provoked, that pugnacity was a tradition rather than an active force. But poverty, vice, weakness and misfortune were at work as of old, destroying human bodies and souls.

The first industrial census of London was taken in 1851. Thirty years from that date, undefined factory labour had increased 309 per cent., and of those employed in the lower branches of the printing trade, 124½ per cent. The London building trade had also shown enormous increase. Other new industries sprang up, or old ones expanded, such as the making of electrical fittings, pottery, india-rubber articles, the working up of tobacco, and manufacturing of matches, jams and pickles. The first street-folk to find other means of livelihood during the sixty years were those who had picked up odds and ends of maintenance through the coaching trade Sixty-eight thousand passengers left London inns daily in the year of the Queen's accession, and it was many years before the train services drove coaches from the roads. The police and parochial authorities as soon as they were working together in a fairly unified London, secured obedience to regulations that had long been on the statute-book. This also pressed not a few into other callings, and quite destroyed those more than doubtful occupations that could only be carried on in an ill-lighted city, the supervision of which had been in a chaotic state. The abolition of the newspaper tax in 1855 and the paper duty in 1861, made havoc of the trade in broadsheets of public events, by cheapening newspapers. When public executions

ARTHUR'S HOLIDAY HOME, BOGNOR.

ceased, "last dying speeches and confessions" went out also, and as soon as there was ability to read the papers as well as to buy them, among the poor, the patterers and the chaunters found their occupation gone.

When the great markets of London became more and more the centres of wholesale trade in provisions, and the old retail ones were swept away, or decayed, many more of those who had lived by their wits in the open air had to seek situations. The mere enumeration of the vanished markets suggests a considerable amount of industrial displacement. They were— Hungerford, Farringdon, Finsbury, Clare, Portman, Carnaby, Oxford Street, and Cumberland.

The mere distribution of population in the great growing city, taken together with increasing facilities and ever cheapening rates for transport of goods and conveyance of passengers, interfered seriously with costermongering, as did also the universal use of carts or barrows by tradesmen in the suburbs as they undertook delivery. Never a provident race, the costers felt increasingly a disadvantage in purchasing, in competition with the settled traders, in spite of their simpler home expenses. Then from time to time came scarifying epidemics that kept people from buying at stalls or from barrows for long periods. Accordingly, while there was no incentive, but many a deterrent, to taking up the trade in normal times, in times of plague like the year 1849 or 1862, they were forced in large numbers, to live by some other means. The indigent Irish and Jewish aliens may have augmented their numbers, but the ranks of the genuine coster tribe were much thinned. Mudlarks, in consequence of alterations in the methods and character of the trade of the Port of London and the formation of the embankments could not after a time pick up enough on the Thames shores to make it worth their while to delve in the mud, and as common sense and public spirit gradually caused the vestries to attend to their duties, there was less need of crossing-sweepers.

At the same time that these changes were taking

place, changes that entirely altered the habits and character of our London poor, there was the wholesale destruction of rookeries that has been already noticed.

But from this it should not be inferred that there are not still large areas composed entirely of the homes

PRINCESS CHRISTIAN'S HOLIDAY HOME, ENGLEFIELD GREEN.

of the old class of poor, districts that have been scarcely altered.

The sum total of changes in the populace were first, the conversion of a vast number of individualist workers with initiative and power of self-adaptation, although they might be living erratic lives, into a body of tamed wage-earners just above, just on, or just below the poverty line. These people were dependent for the maintenance of themselves and their families upon machines and the operations of financiers. The second result was an intermingling of these people with the artisan and labouring population, among many of whom there is a normal family life, but a large proportion exhibit recklessness and wastefulness.

The changes within the missionary movement which had hitherto dealt successfully with them were fourfold : A weakening of the personnel of local groups of workers by denominational absorption and removals to the far-suburbs ; a general discrediting of evangelicalism in favour of other schemes ; a support not increased proportionally to the size of the work to be overtaken, through the apathy that the removal of the grossest social injustices, and the application of palliatives to the most appealing needs had produced ; and a distraction of attention and dissipation of resources due to the number of charitable funds and other remedial efforts now claiming a share.

But the bed-rock truth was there all the while, that the only social workers whose work tells, are the individuals who can reach the motives of others and affect them for good, and that the only workers who stand this test are those who use the religious life that sustains them in their labours, as the chief implement in their work. The expedients that human nature and common sense suggest for the amelioration of condition, and the removal of disability to live a natural family life being of course a common meeting ground for all workers.

At this time, many schools were depleted of numbers of capable workers, and were overstaffed with home-reared ones, lacking often in grasp, outlook and opportunity. Some schools were shut up, so that in old districts there was deficient provision. In the rapidly growing new districts there was scarcely any provision for the child of the pariah at all.

The steps taken by the R. S. U., the central society, to meet the situation were in strict accordance with

CRIPPLES' HOLIDAY HOME, SOUTHEND.

its original intention. Its abstinence from direct work in the slums at ordinary times has been a marked feature, but at junctures it has undertaken such special work, or work supplementary to that of local independent centres as the maintenance of a London scheme might involve. Such efforts have always been conducted on lines and within limits as would leave the local schools uninjured and unembarrassed.

At the period of expansion, the R.S.U. came into the field with industrial schools, refuges, and an emigration scheme.

In a time of depression it now came in with a clothing agency and a drift movement. The first was dependent on the co-operation of the masters and mistresses of the elementary schools. The second was the Society's own. The two together, on the benevolent and evangelical sides of the work among the poorest children, though not covering the entire ground, witnessed for the old tradition and also kept alive the ever-new hope of an unhampered and perfectly adequate citizen-service for the poor children of the whole metropolis.

The Society still maintained its grants to affiliated schools, still supported that solid unvarying work that is the backbone of the movement, but it supplied sufficient of what was yet lacking, to re-furbish the ideal. At no period of its history can the ragged school cause claim that it has been more than an object lesson to the community. Its successes within its opportunities do certainly imply increased successes with a more general application, but it has never yet had the chance to do all it might.

The agency for supplying loaned clothing grew with the assistance of the press and has now reached a point at which the year's outgoings are no less than 27,536 new garments, 42,360 worn garments, and 7,572 pairs of boots.

Increased opportunities for storage at the offices in Norfolk Street made the work possible; the ladies' working parties of which the Baroness Burdett Coutts has been so long President, supplied the chief material at the outset, supplemented as time advanced from other sources.

It is now an amalgamated concern, embracing The Poor Children's Aid Society, The Guild of the Good Samaritan, Hearts and Hands League, and the Bare-Foot Mission, and the whole is under the Ladies' Auxiliary.

It was a bold and ambitious undertaking, for practically this clothing store is at the mercy of the head

PASSMORE EDWARDS' VICTORIA HOLIDAY HOME, BOURNEMOUTH.

teachers of all the elementary schools in London. Very few, if any, applications have been refused where the proper guarantees were forthcoming.

In effect the R.S.U. by this action ranged itself beside the School Board, that had now taken up one part of the R.S.U.'s work, to assist the masters and mistresses wherever possible.

A general scheme of feeding was not attempted—

an expedient of that kind bristles with difficulties and dangers. A very close association between such agencies as exist for feeding children and the R.S.U. has been maintained. All the help that could be rendered to keep such efforts within wise and useful bounds has been available. Schools, utensils, and honorary labour for preparation of meals or supervision of children, have been at disposal, but the plan that has chiefly commended itself to the Council has been the nurturing of penny dinner schemes and half-penny dinner schemes at the poorest local centres. With clothing, however, they feel on safer ground. Abuse can be guarded against better.

The applications from elementary school teachers supply matter for reflection on the part of those who think that ragged school work is at an end as the following cases will show :—

A girl of eleven, one of five, father a stableman earning 18s., rent, 9s. 6d. The child seems underfed ; needs pretty well everything. Another girl of eleven, in a family of seven, living in one room, toward supporting whom the father earns 18s. a week, appears to be in a like case. A girl of seven, daughter of a widow with seven other children to keep, which she does by taking in washing, needs a new rig-out. A foot-note says that the children have to stay in bed while their clothes are washed. In the case of a boy of twelve, recommended for clothing, it appears that the father earns 25s. a week in the summer and nothing in the winter, and nothing of course during the temporary fits of insanity to which he is subject. Mother keeps the home together. Another boy of fourteen has no mother, and his father, an elderly bent man, can only

get a job as a watcher on Saturday and Sunday. For
this he gets 5s. 3d. a week.

The letters accompanying the forms are very
illuminating.

One is a plea for clothes and boots " for some of
my poorest ones." They are going into the country in
July and *must* have a rig-out before they go. Then
here is the reply, after the request has been granted :
" The parents are very grateful, the boots will be a

CLOTHING DEPARTMENT, R.S.U. HEADQUARTERS.

boon to us. Our children are worse than barefoot
half the time. After the holidays I want some boots
on the payment system."

Another teacher, in asking for boots, says she always
has them properly repaired before giving them to the
children. It should be mentioned that the second-
hand ones are given, and the new ones sold cheaply.

The poverty of all London is felt in the storeroom
of the Ladies' Auxiliary—the poverty of north, south,
and west, as well as east, and there *is* acute poverty in

the west. Take, for example, the state of things a worker found existing one winter in a little West End street, with 100 families in it ; 115 adults, the majority of them men, were out of employment : " A number of families, even in the bitterest times of the long frost, lived for days without fire and light, and often with no food but a chance morsel of bread or tea ; the children's boots even were pawned for food."

Occasionally letters that accompany gifts of clothing are as heart-moving in another way as the requests for help. One received in 1902 is of this kind—

" We have sent you," says a mother, " a few clothes belonging to our youngest boy, who died in 1896. We never intended to part with them, but feel it would be very selfish to keep them when so many poor little things are naked. It has cost a great wrench to give them up, and we hope they will prove a blessing to one or two of Christ's poor little neglected children."

The Drift movement is a missionary agency for gathering into any buildings that can be borrowed for the purpose, the roughest and the poorest children, who presumably get little religious instruction, and so far as circumstances permit, imparting some. It is not a substitute for schools, being inferior in every respect. In the old districts, it supplements what the schools do, and in the suburban districts it is regarded as being pioneer work for schools that are to be.

The new President, when Earl Compton, threw himself heartily into this effort and wrote an article in the magazine entitled " Brooms wanted." It was indeed a renaissance, a return to the practices of the City missionaries who swept in the waifs to the early schools.

From it originated the Cripple Mission, that will receive notice after another important department of labour, that came into prominence in 1893, has received attention.

The Fortnightly Holiday for ailing children and run-down adults was no novelty in the movement in 1893, but it was in that year that the first specially built Holiday Home of the Society was opened at Bognor. The previous history of the holiday branch can be briefly told.

Very soon after the R.S.U. began, the Day in the

CRIPPLE DEPARTMENT.

Country became a feature in the summer programme, and a great novelty was the massed gatherings from the schools in Richmond and Bushey Parks, and other suburban spots. The R.S.U. excursion was a demonstration that the *Illustrated London News* thought it worth while to depict. The Day in the Country has never been relinquished, though in recent years the Fresh Air Scheme of the Pearson publications and the *Daily Express* takes its place, which the Society administers. Not only in London, but the provinces also, is the fund at work, and the R.S.U. is responsible for the arrangements.

From the Day in the Country to the extended stay was but a step, and it was taken early. In a desultory fashion, ailing scholars were sent away by teachers to friends of their own in the country, and paid for. An article in one of the early volumes of the magazine entitled, " The Ragged School Convalescent," proves this. In 1869, however, the well-known authoress, " A.L.O.E.," whose books, such as *Idols in the Heart*, were widely read a generation ago, came forward to help the R.S.U. to do this work in a more definite way. Those who went to the cottage at Sutton first, then Holmwood, and finally Bracknell, where the arrangements were made, came back blessed in soul as well as recruited in body. The next steps were taken with the aid of Mr. George Courtauld, M.P., and his daughter, Miss Courtauld, by sending a number of the poorest children to be entertained in cottages at Halstead and Witham ; Chobham, Thatcham, Apsley Guise, Barnet following soon afterwards ; and the results in benefit to the children were most satisfactory, although a difficulty was felt in securing proper supervision. A further advance was made when the Holiday Home on Thursley Common was taken, capable of accommodating twenty children at a time. Though relinquished at a subsequent stage of progress, it is endeared to the hearts of not a few who found it, as the Bracknell cottage had been, a Bethel and very gate of heaven.

After Thursley came East Grinstead, Folkestone, Windsor, Brenchley,Chislehurst, Caterham, and Bushey, and the plan of working having been found, a thoroughly satisfactory system was soon in operation, and the Council, in 1892, were able to speak of some 5,000 children and run-down adults having had a fortnight's change during the year.

Arthur's Home, Bognor, was the gift of a friend who wished to remain anonymous, and was erected as a memorial to a beloved child, " To make some children happy." The Brenchley Home in Kent was soon afterwards secured for senior scholars, then within a few years the cripple homes at Windsor, Southend, Margate, and Bournemouth. The last is the gift of

COUNCIL ROOM, R.S.U. HEADQUARTERS.

Mr. Passmore Edwards. A home at Addiscombe, consisting of three cottages, has recently been bequeathed by Lady Ashburton to the Society. These institutions afford accommodation for such of the children and young people as it is desirable to have under the care of the Society's own agents while on their holidays, but the system is very considerably supplemented by the use of cottage homes, in various

country and seaside towns by resident associates of
the R.S.U.

Some six thousand children annually for many
years past have had a holiday fortnight through this
means.

In 1892 Pearson's Fresh Air Fund started, and by
1893 was being well used for reaching " Drift " children.
Reference has been already made to the growth of the
Fresh Air Scheme under the heading " Literary Friends
of the R.S.U." House-to-house visitation in connexion
with Drift work brought the cripples that were then
found, under special consideration, although from the
very outset of the work, cripples had been dealt with
and helped, and institutions for them had arisen from
the general cause.

But now an entirely new work dealing with between
six and seven thousand cripples, came into existence.
It has grown into a vast surgical aid and holiday
providing agency, in addition to being a religious
mission.

It was thought by not a few when " Drift " work
began, that in this there was danger of retrogression
concealed. Assuming that the tendencies towards
local decay and headquarters aggressiveness to increase, there might conceivably come a time when the
" established principle " against which Lord Shaftesbury warned the workers, might supersede the " voluntary principle " to a mischievous degree. Such possible over-centralization was completely outweighed
when during 1894-5-6-7 upwards of a thousand
volunteer workers were recruited for the visitation of
cripples in their own homes. This influx more than
redressed the balance.

Another grand result is the sub-division of London

and the suburbs among the honorary workers of the Society of the entire London and suburban area, an achievement which alone brings work within the region of possibility that could never have been attempted in past times. Some 6,000 children, more or less handicapped, are by a most economical arrangement watched over and their needs made known.

The organization, though very complete is extremely simple. The system is territorial. A large block of houses, situated between main roads, contains within it a certain number of cripple children. These are given into the care of visitors by a friend who has charge of the block, and is called a Local Superintendent. A number of these blocks combined is called a division, and the friend who is the link between the Local Superintendents in a division is called a Divisional Superintendent. The visitors undertake the trying, and often discouraging, duty of bringing religious influences into the homes where cripples are found. The Local Superintendents strengthen the visitors' hands in various ways, and have charge of most of the local business arrangements of the Society.

With the Divisional Superintendents rests the discretion upon all the larger questions of policy that affect the mission as a work for London.

The Society is fortunate in the possession of officials taken from the ranks of the honorary workers. It has always been so ; Mr. J. G. Gent, Mr. Kirk's predecessor, was a volunteer before he became secretary, and Mr. Kirk is honorary secretary of one of the affiliated schools Most of the staff are engaged in honorary work in the cause, apart from their official connexion. But were it not so, if officialism of the worst type were entrenched at headquarters, this powerful body of workers would give a tone and character to the work that officialism could not possibly affect for evil.

So distinct a change in the extent and nature of headquarters' undertakings has been introduced in this period, that some recognition of it in the description of the Society's objects was called for.

It is not surprising, therefore, that a modification of its title should be made in 1893. It was still the old Union, but it was more. To have dropped the word "ragged" would be to lose much in sentiment and tradition that it was desirable should be kept. Something to denote a new attitude and amplified responsibility must be added. With much the same difficulty to encounter that a firm in business has, when choosing a word that shall be a telegraphic address, and at the same time descriptive, a second title was sought. The Shaftesbury Society was the name chosen, and it is probably better than any other that could have been found.

Lord Shaftesbury in his own person stood for so many things that this movement represents. He was a man of many hobbies, giving countenance to every plan making for social righteousness. At the same time he regarded religion as being the chief concern. While firm. and even rigid, in his own views, he was an advocate of liberty of opinion, and has shown us perhaps as well as any man ever has done, how to work with others with whom we may not on all points be agreed. A moderate man, as firm a believer in a reasonable medium in economic questions as in other things, he was neither in favour of lavish and thoughtless almsgiving on the one hand, or of crushing people who were in need of encouragement on the other.

The clothing and holiday movements were after his

LAMB AND FLAG.   DODDINGTON GROVE.   CAMBERWELL.

HAMOND SQUARE.   ASHLEY MISSION. KIMPTON ROAD.
LOCKSFIELDS. SNOWSFIELDS. BRENTFORD.
SCHOOLS DIRECTLY UNDER THE CONTROL OF THE COUNCIL.

time, though he annually appealed for the day in the country.

But the greatest modern adjunct, the Cripple Mission, can claim him as a pioneer worker for the cripples of England. One loathsome evil at least he quite stamped out. "Sweep's cancer" is off the list of chilhood's diseases for ever, through his efforts.

But by his factory legislation he has probably done more than any man that ever lived to save children from becoming cripples, and these not only in our own land but throughout the Empire.

Pleading for the factory women and children of India in the House of Lords in 1879, in a speech that occupied an hour, he said—

"Creed and colour, latitude and longitude, make no difference in the essential nature of man. No climate can enable infants to do the work of adults, or turn suffering women into mere steam-engines. What say you, then, of children—children of the tenderest years? Why, they become stunted, crippled, deformed, useless. I speak what I know; I state what I have seen."

Then came a reminiscence of 1838 at Bradford—

"I asked for a collection of cripples and deformities. In a short time more than eighty were gathered in a large courtyard. They were mere samples of the entire mass. I assert without exaggeration that no power of language could describe the varieties, and I may say the cruelties, in all these degradations of the human form. They stood or squatted before me in the shapes of the letters of the alphabet. This was the effect of prolonged toil on the tender frames of children at early ages. When I visited Bradford under the limitation of hours some years afterwards, I called for a similar exhibition of cripples; but God be praised there was not one to be found in that vast city."

Lord Shaftesbury won his case, and a Factory Act for India was passed.

If the second title, Shaftesbury Society, represents the new work, it has not superseded Ragged School Union, although the word ragged was offensive to many, both inside and outside the movement. It has been retained because of the splendid service it has rendered to the cause. No device could keep an agency such as this, absolutely true to its purpose. The perpetual transference of improved scholars to other agencies that it involves, and the necessity for seeking new material to replace the gaps from among the lowest and most disgusting children are against it. But the word " ragged " has within certain limits been an automatic rectifying influence through the entire period.

But even as a means of keeping the work approximately near to the class for which it was and is intended, it has only had a qualified success, and for one important reason. You cannot take scholars in their teens and do as you will with them. If they leave those who have an influence over them, they probably at that age leave religious influences and interests behind them altogether. So the idea of handing them on to other friends in the hope that they may fuse them with communities recruited from other social levels, though fascinating, is impracticable. The more successful the school, the sooner is it likely to lose its characteristics as a ragged school. To keep its character it must be continually parting with enough of its scholars to allow of a continuous flow of the outside barbarism into it and through it. The only way to " stick to the gutter " has ever been to continuously use a ragged school building and never allow it to be empty *at night*.

By that means, varying grades of children occupy it at different times, and at night the very lowest are not ashamed to come.

In so far as the word " ragged " predisposes the public to expect every child under ragged school care to be in a state of semi-nudity, it is as imperfect a definition as it has always been, but it is hard to better it.

Professor Huxley suggested " substratum " as a substitute. He saw the all-round difficulty, for as a member of the first London School Board he came in close contact with the work. As between " substratum school " and " ragged school," the associations and history of achievement of thirty years weighed down the balance in favour of " ragged " in the early seventies. It was much the same in the early nineties, when the Free Education Act had created new conditions. The new conditions were, however, only superficial, sufficient to mask the old permanent difficulties.

Never has there been a time when the majority of the children in any school had not enough clothing to place them above the line of destitution in that respect, though a very close scrutiny would reveal insufficiency, uncleanness, and want of repair in the apparel of most.

In the second report of the R.S.U., where an evening ragged school of 260 children is described, the external appearance of most of the scholars was not bad enough to have supplied startling copy for a sensational journalist. Only seventeen had no shoes or stockings. Only thirty-seven had no hats, caps, or bonnets, and there were but twelve who had no body linen. The tragedy of their lives was only apparent to the patient seeker who looked beneath the surface.

Thus there- were—42 who had no parents.

          21 had stepmothers.

           7 were children of convicts.

          27 had been in prison.

          36 were runaways.

          19 slept in lodging-houses.

          41 lived by begging.

          29 never slept on beds.

Around the word " ragged " the efforts of Lord Shaftesbury, John Macgregor, and Mr. S. R. Starey have centred in their anxious endeavours to keep the work true to purpose. To remove it, would be as sacrilegious as to take St. Edward's staff from the English regalia. Sentiment might be in either case the only thing sacrificed, but surely a noble sentiment is too valuable in these materialistic days to be lightly parted from.

The word " ragged " has served to bring out most prominently the uncalculating passion for veracity that has possessed our best men.

At the most inopportune moments from a worldly point of view, our prophets have broken in with warning and reproof. It was not an unusual thing for Lord Shaftesbury at an Annual Meeting to rebuke some of the schools for rising above their work and threaten the formation of new schools and a new Union with himself as President. Although he did it in a half-bantering way he meant what he said : " I feel that my business lies in the gutter, and I have not the least intention to get out of it."

John Macgregor in the very heart of an appeal for

ragged schools frankly admitted to the reader that
" There is one great and prevailing error which we are
prone to fall into —we are apt to escape the difficulties
of our work by rising above it."

Mr. Starey, the founder, at the important conference
of 1883, which was intended to impress the public
favourably, got up and complained that in some of the
schools the right children were not to be found.

These are three instances out of many that show
how jealously the standard has been kept, and the
word " ragged " has made it easier for those who have
done it.

The chief events of the last eleven years are the
Jubilee of the Society in 1894, the expansion of the
cripple movement in 1895 and 1896, Queen Victoria's
Diamond Jubilee celebrations in 1897, the receipt of
a letter from her late Majesty during her Irish visit
in 1900, and the Empire treats to poor children in
1903–4, when for the first time, and in a small way,
sympathisers from four different colonies provided
Christmas cheer for London waifs.

The two great changes of the period are the removal
from Exeter Hall to Queen's Hall in 1894 for the
Annual Festivals, and the taking of the present offices
in John Street, with the greatly enlarged facilities for
work that they offer.

A broad generalization of the operations of all the
constituents of the entire movement has to be made
if its present-day meaning is to be understood.

First come the local centres, independent as to their
management, responsible for the raising and expenditure
of their own funds.

" I love the independence of each local school," said
Lord Shaftesbury in 1856. " We avoid centralization,

which I know is distasteful to many, and endeavour to increase local and personal responsibility." That position has always been maintained. While there is independence of the R.S.U. there is neither absence of financial obligation nor absence of loyalty on the part of the 151 schools. The statistics of their united efforts for the past year are as follows—

Sunday Schools. Morning .. 6,397
      ,,   ,,   Afternoon.. 23,535
      ,,   ,,   Evening .. 20,044
Sunday Average   43,579
Bible Classes   5,010
72 Christian Bands and C.E.'s, 2,677
180 Prayer Meetings, 9,532 in attendance
Adult Services   17,281
254 Young People became communicants.
3,904 Teachers.
36 Educational Night Schools. 2,456 pupils.
62 Industrial classes, 2,458 in attendance.
22 Boys' Brigades, 837 lads.
242 Recreation Classes. 7,989 in attendance.
146 Bands of Hope. 12,759 members.
67 Libraries, 17,726 volumes.
60 Penny Banks. Deposits £7,561 17s. 1¾d.
48 Clothing Clubs. Deposits £1,629 16s. 4d.
121 Mothers' Meetings, 8,768 in attendance.
7 Crêches.

That record of work is the output of one section of the movement.

There is a slight falling back as compared with ten years ago, but it is still well ahead of the year of crisis, 1870.

The supplement to this on the part of the R.S.U. is first of all a salvage work by means of its legal sub-committee, and its funds to keep buildings and other property from passing out of the movement into other hands. For such rescued schools it assumes responsibility, working them on the same economical principles as the other centres. They are—

> The Latymer Road Mission, Notting Hill.
> Ashley Mission, Bethnal Green.
> Doddington Grove Mission, Battersea.
> Cabul Road Mission, Battersea.
> Lamb and Flag Mission, Clerkenwell.
> Camberwell Mission.
> Locksfields Mission, Walworth.
> Brentford Ragged School.
> Snowsfields Mission, Bermondsey.
> Vincent Street Mission, St. Luke's.
> Kimpton Road Mission, Camberwell.
> Hamond Square Mission, Hoxton.
> Neal's Yard, St. Giles'.

Intermediate between the work of the schools and the headquarters' agencies are the " Holiday Homes Fund " and the prizes for steadiness in situations. In these local and central effort are combined.

An emigration agency has been revived during the past year. Then apart from the school interests, its second branch of operations are the schemes that aim at fulfilling the first intentions of the pioneers, to cover ultimately the whole ground of need among the poorest children.

First, there is a religious agency for ordinary children, not stationary in its methods, and intending to deal with all London.

Secondly, a religious and benevolent agency among cripple children that does deal with all London.

Thirdly, a correspondence system between charitably disposed adults in all parts of the world, and the cripples of London, promoted and sustained.

Fourthly, a clothing agency working through the Elementary schools for the destitute children of all London.

Fifthly, a treat agency working in the summer in conjunction with Pearson's Fresh-Air Fund, and in the winter through the Robin Dinner Fund, Sir William Treloar's Fund, the Australian Sunbeam and other funds, supplied by municipal and local generosity. The aim here is to give, as nearly as may be, all the little ones who otherwise would not get a treat, some of the enjoyment they ought to have. All such trusts are discharged in a public-spirited way, not for ragged school children only, but for all who should receive benefit.

Lord Northampton has succeeded as president where his predecessor, Lord Shaftesbury, might have failed in annealing five new general agencies with the old work, though now that the task is accomplished doubtless the result would receive his approval. By means of them the old unrelinquished ideal of an extension of the school system to the entire city may yet be realized.

The peroration of one of Lord Shaftesbury's speeches will fittingly close this chapter as that of his successor commences it.

" If the work is to be done it must be done collectively and individually. Some may aid the cause in one way, some in another ; but all must do something for the mighty end in view. Done, I say, it must be, in order that you may act up to the dictates of your conscience ; done it must be by those who profess obedience to the Word of God, and believe in the truths of Christianity."

CHAPTER XXIII

A Worker's Opportunities

" We have been aware in the past, and as we are still better aware in the present, that thousands—I suppose I should not exaggerate if I said hundreds of thousands—of the little ones in our very midst are growing up without the knowledge of God, in spite of the great religious efforts, the magnificent work done by our clergymen, and by our ministers, then I say it behoves our Union, above all societies, to go down again to the depths and to carry out the wishes and intentions of the first founders of our Society."—LORD NORTHAMPTON.

THE present chapter gives a near view of some of the newer agencies of the Ragged School Union, through the medium of a worker's reminiscences and experience. The Society is not committed thereby to an endorsement of every opinion expressed upon unsettled controversies, but in the main there is little to take objection to in the manuscript. The movement has always been one in which the absolute liberty of the individual had to be allowed, and not unfrequently it has been found that the heretics of one decade have been the orthodox of the next. The general unanimity of the entire body, considering the absence of artificial restraint, is not the least remarkable thing in the history of the work.

Although in a sense a personal document, it is only so as far as was necessary in giving testimony, and all that is local in the work described has been excluded.

This friend writes—

" Believing, as I always have done, that the present secularism, ritualism, and sectarianism, will pass away, and believing that we shall again see in our midst great leaders like Gordon, Leone Levi, Macgregor and Quintin Hogg among men, and Mary Carpenter, Mrs. Barker Harrison and Mrs. Bayly, among women, only in larger numbers, the chief duty of the present day worker has seemed to be to keep the work broad and elastic enough to receive them.

" The promise of their coming lies in an incident that happened years ago in Exeter Hall at an Annual meeting. An orator paused in the middle of a fervid speech, and, inviting the vast assembly to rise, led them in the following prayer—

" ' Lord Jesus ! take us for Thy servants, use us for Thy service, and make us followers of them who now through faith and patience inherit the promises.' And all the people said ' Amen.'

" Turning to the chairman as if nothing unusual had been done, the speaker said, resuming his speech—

" ' And now, my lord, for work.'

" To such men and women as have been named, of spiritual power, capacity, means, and leisure, the movement looks for a repairing of the waste places, and an extension to the unoccupied fields.

" Knowing the great Drift, Cripple, Clothing, and Treat Agencies in their present form from their commencement, I believed that it would be through participation in them that such leaders would come.

" Knowing the need of the schools by years of work in the older branches of the cause, I rejoiced to see these introductory and training services started, and owing everything in life to the pioneer efforts of such worthies in a preceding generation, I longed with a longing unspeakable to see the work revived and extended beyond all past achievement. The new agencies had within them the promise of the future, if they could be kept pliant enough for those who, as they came, would require space for the full stroke of their giant blows against evil.

"Against paid agency it has seemed to me there is nothing to be said on abstract grounds, but in a great voluntary mission the limits wherein it can be usefully introduced are well defined. Its sphere would seem to be that of expert direction of technical matters that volunteers would be wasting strength upon.

"Elsewhere, however faithful it may be, it becomes mischievous by the rigidity that inevitably results, from numbers of paid men, through a series of years, having to be supervised, checked, and watched, on account of the money sunk in the concern. If an equal spontaneity be preserved to that in an honorary work, a few years after establishment, it is almost miraculous.

"When unpaid workers put effort of the best kind and to an exhausting degree into a cause, they have rights in the cause, or they think so. Rules, wholesome enough and quite necessary in the public interest for controlling an established society disbursing large funds for salaries, are intolerable and without meaning for honorary workers. It becomes impossible to retain them. They either leave, or the salaried staff become hewers of wood and drawers of water to the volunteers, otherwise they rise to the position of advisers and leaders through superior knowledge and experience. There is no intermediate position for them.

" At one time, the bulk of the ragged schools were in the hands of City missionaries, but they could not hold them, because they had to work by rule, and the volunteers who came in to help them were not so controlled. A more instructive instance could not be given, for in most cases the volunteers were per-

THE JOYS OF FREEDOM.

sonal friends of the missionaries, introduced by them, and entertaining the profoundest respect for them. Besides the check upon freedom, there were the other dangers and difficulties attending the established principle applied to a work among the lowest. Chief amongst these is the possible moral deterioration of the men employed who should be able from a business point of view to show results, but would not be able to do so. A hint at the cost of a mechanical treatment of spiritual problems to a sensitive man is given by the well-known police-court missionary, Mr. Thomas Holmes.[1]

" ' I wonder how many times in the small hours of the morning my wife has said to me, " Now, you are not asleep. You are bothering your head again." Why, they were looking at me, mowing and gibing at me, mocking at me, with outstretched hands appealing to me—the people whom *I was paid to save and didn't !* '

" Another objection that weighs, is the increasing difficulty that any one seeming to derive profit or mere maintenance even, experiences in getting really close to the life of the people to influence it for good. These reasons seemed sufficient to make me wish to see voluntaryism applied to ' Drift work, ' when I became acquainted with it in 1892. Paid agency for rank and file effort, as a temporary expedient, did not matter, if once it could be shown that ' Drift ' work was an opening for new workers and gave all the scope that the most earnest, capable, and leisured could desire. It was a great enfranchisement, this access to a pioneer's career in the closing decade of the nineteenth century without possible hindrance from anybody.

" I found sufficient to justify the belief that, arduous as the work is, it is possible for a man of even limited leisure to engage in it on a considerable scale. Moreover, I found that the personal gains in knowledge of life, reverence for human nature, sympathy for one's fellows, and an intensified belief in the power of an

[1] *Pictures and Problems from London Police Courts, p.* 21.

uplifted Christ to save to the uttermost, far outweighed all the trouble taken. The indebtedness,

PROBLEM, 'HOW TO BEGIN AND WHERE AND WHEN TO FINISH.''

the humbled feeling, the ever-abiding joy of recollection, can never be described, and I feel, as others have

done who have been privileged to come very near to
the poorest people, that nobody can have that experience without surprise at the amount they learn as to
their own limited power to confer benefit, and
despair of communicating much of the teaching received. If a faint impression of the richness of the
deepest mines to be worked in this city can be given,
the writer will be satisfied. There are no successes
to record, except surface ones, not worth time to go
into. One dying man pointed to the Saviour, and
finding peace in believing, is perhaps all that would
really come under the head of definite achievement.
All the rest was uncertain influence upon fluctuating
crowds during seven years of severe labour. Some
companions who joined as the work progressed, can
claim more. But even they would admit that personal gain to themselves was the chief feature in their
experience.

" Having taken a few lessons from the workers in
the East End, to which area the work was then confined, I proceeded to apply the knowledge to a very
poor, rough district, without friends or helpers, but
with abundance of material. The conditions could
not perhaps all be exactly reproduced now—it is not
necessary for success that they should be—but they
assisted greatly a first experiment. Editors of various
magazines and journals had begun to develop that
cult for social service among their readers that has
proved so useful. Schemes of various kinds have
since been launched of permanent utility, but at this
particular time they all took the form of large treat
demonstrations. Folks had not grown accustomed
to using them as they have now, and there was not the
same competition for the tickets then,

" Thousands of children within a certain area were taken to public parks. Anything that gave the chance to go round to every house in all the streets of the district and schedule the families was sought after, and in a short time we had four thousand names. Up to this point several lessons were learned.

" The first was, that to keep to the lowest, even in a new effort, is always extremely difficult. Self-distrust, constant examination of the work of colleagues, a perpetual weeding out, and an unceasing

WAITING FOR " A FRIEND."

search for the poorest and shyest, are conditions that imperiously govern 'Drift' missions, as they should govern the entire work.

" All influences and circumstances seem to conspire from the earliest moment to compel a settling down on the part of the workers.

" A Board school master or mistress who tried to help by distributing tickets for one in their schools, would invariably supply children whom one could see at a glance were for the most part above the type.

A school in the worst districts always has a large element from artisan families attending. These are 'the best children' by all standards of school measurement, and must come first when the teacher has anything to give away.

" The Sunday schools, and even an old-established ragged school, were worse. They scarcely touched the poorest at all. How it may be in other localities, or even here at the present time, I cannot say. In dealing with a Board school, if *all* the children were taken out, a certain percentage of the right kind could be relied upon, but it meant a loss of material on the whole transaction. The ne'er-do-wells even from the Board schools were the last to receive invitations, and that when all other wants were supplied. Even 'Drift' workers get fond of special children. One needs to dig and delve and dive without pausing and keep at it for years, trusting nobody, oneself included, as being untainted by favouritism.

" The second lesson learned was, that directly work of this kind is started, helpers come. The first helper was in our case an old lady, now gone to her rest, whose boots had to be soled and heeled before she could accompany a party to the Forest. Then came others, working men and tradesmen, who made time, at their own pecuniary loss, to give a helping hand. The staff grew as the work grew, until in four years there were sixty adult workers. The most instructive deduction from watching that growth is, that while a vigorous work is being done in a devotional spirit, there is an assimilative power in such a staff. It is easy to understand, after such an experience, how those groups of teachers, that were made up of tinkers, cobblers, and other slum residents, moved by pity, in the early forties, should, long before 1850 was reached, have absorbed men of mark in politics, commerce, and the professions. The absorption took place without injustice to, or displacement of, the early workers. It is this parallelism that marks the ' Drift ' work, as the new wood of the old tree. For the numerous men of leisure and means that London possesses who keep aloof from social work because nothing they have met with satisfies them, there is the joy of definite usefulness here, and deep draughts of life's cordial elixir such as they have never known, and within easy reach. Leadership in such work demands no brilliancy ; the qualities it asks for are all negative except a very firm belief in a universe planned upon righteous lines, and a power of recuperation accessible to the human soul, that desires to take its proper place in harmony with it. This much of affirmation there must be ; the other qualities are, suspension of judgment, distrust of fads and dogmas, absence of personal aims except to find truth and obey it, avoidance of all that curtails the liberty of others, a tardiness to make alliances with organized schemes.

" Men with time and money to devote to the cause of the poor can find helpers and advisers for their first steps, after which, if they have average thinking power, they are best employed at the work itself, which will instruct them.

" Returning to my story, there is another experience to record. I did not find that ' Drift ' work could ever take the place of schools. When the very best was done in the way of hunting after, coaxing, and attaching the poorest waifs, and then by registration, sifting, and continuous visitation of homes, the right children were secured and kept under influence at

meetings, personal influence over these masses of
children was a very feeble affair. They needed sub-
dividing into little groups, among whom earnest souls
could bring home the truth with real hope of success.
Tempted and needy children can hardly get the help
they require when taught in crowds.

" Our first operations were conducted from the
base of a ragged school, on such nights as were not
utilized for its own agencies. Afterwards there were
several centres. There were two floors in the building, each accommodating two hundred and fifty
children. One vacant night was Monday for the top
floor, and another, Friday, for both floors.

" The place was filled, always by personal invitation
at the houses in the neighbourhood, on both nights.
Not only were the numbers large, but the district
being large as well, there were long intervals between
the attendances. The Sunday school accommodation
as compared with that of the day schools was absurdly
inadequate, on Sunday nights especially. : On both
nights lantern services were held. The school was
lent, the lanterns came from the R.S.U., the slides
were borrowed from Mr. Stead's National Society of
Lanternists, and all the labour was unpaid. Seven
hundred weekly were gathered in, two hundred of
them being lads who had left school. These youths
we used to intercept on their way to a cheap music
hall. The old gaff was a penny for admission. The
modern two-houses-nightly music hall is twopence.

" We found, as our fathers found, that competitive
entertainment was out of reach. But we coaxed the
lads, and reasoned with them about their future, in
the streets. When they elected to join us at the
little tumbledown stuffy school, in preference to

yielding to the attractions of the hall, the very choice was a heart-gladdening moral victory for us. For a time a night school was held, at which some seventy lads attended, but although it gave us hints as to the usefulness of such work and its hopefulness under proper conditions, circumstances were against its continuance. Failure taught us more than success would have done.

A PRISONER OF PAIN.

" One result of the effort expended was to produce a Sunday morning class of urchins, absolutely barefooted all of them, fourteen in number. Such a thing the school had not known for many a long year.

" Nevertheless, it was found possible to impart a good deal of real telling influence into the work, in an indirect way. When eight hundred children were lined up two deep and in companies on the asphalted

portion of an open space, ready to go to Loughton,
it was a moving scene. The mothers present on the
ground to see them off were in the right mood for a
few earnest words to affect them, and a dear old
friend, now departed, used often to address them.
Though in the general way careless and defiant, they
could not but join in the prayer, commending the
children to the care of Almighty God.

" A close bond with the people was created. They
were taken into confidence in everything we did. If
tickets were being distributed in a street at the rate of
two in the family, it was put to the people that if
children who had had or were about to have treats
went, others, and those very often the children of
widows, would be deprived of an outing. This plan
worked better than any scheme of treating them as
all conspiring to defraud.

" When the children were taken out for a day, or to
a treat, we always had a thanksgiving service first,
and the duty of making others happy throughout
the day was enjoined. Not without their value, we
are persuaded, were those meetings before return, on
the hillside overlooking the forest, when as the sun
was setting the children sang, ' Praise God from
whom all blessings flow.'

" In one season nearly five thousand, being representatives of nearly three thousand households, took
part in the Fresh Air Scheme. Plans were specially
made to foster the sense of partnership on the part of
the people. They helped us find all the orphans for
a treat at one time, and all the old people over seventy
at another. When we began to find cripples they
helped us there also.

" The headquarters agents had some three hundred

when we had fourteen, and a friend on the south side of the river, a worker who had been a ragged school boy, had forty. The people, combining with the R.S.U. in half the cost, sent not only our fourteen, but others they found, bringing the total to thirty-five, to Folkestone. Full of teaching was the sight at the send-off. A livery-stableman lent a large brake and a pair of greys to take them to the station ; women stood at their doors waving farewells ; a publican—an ex-pugilist—who contributed to the fund, and put all the fines for broken glasses into the treasury, was active in lifting the children into the

A CRIPPLE EXCURSION.

brake ; a greengrocer of his own accord brought fruit ; and then, as we passed a gasworks, on the top of a huge gasometer the forms of numbers of burly men were seen silhouetted against the sky. They waved their caps to the cripples as they passed.

"These and other experiences taught me that, as indicated at the outset, the incompleteness of the experiment made all boasting impossible, even if the disposition for it were present to indulge in it. Its great value was its teaching to the worker.

"All the lessons were given in the Valley of Humiliation.

"Never counting myself to have attained to the height and depths of the truth to be grasped, reading proceeded side by side with work. With judgment fixed for the moment by reading *The Purse and the Conscience*,[1] I went down in the slums upon one occasion, but I learnt more from watching an old woman for half an hour than I ever learnt in books or by the exercise of my own mind. She was sitting behind her counter in her chandler's shop with blanched face, reading through thick-rimmed spectacles not unlike Chinese goggles, from a large print Bible. All the life-problems of justice and mercy demanded solution from her just then. Bread-winners by the hundred were out of work all around. She had to think of the travellers of firms that would call for the settlement of accounts before long, and to look into the pleading eyes of helpless children, who asked for family credit every few minutes. Alike when she yielded and when she was obdurate, the godly old soul asked herself if she did right. As mother and grandmother her impulses seemed to drag her into criminal courses, and yet how could the withholding of bread be in harmony with the Will of God ? She looked to me for help, but there was none forthcoming except the evasion of supplying the simple needs of those who came when I was there, and we bade each other a tearful farewell. As the shop bell tinkled at my shamefaced retreat, she applied herself to the Word of God, and I realized that all the red books of the Fabians had failed me.

" On another occasion I attended one of those committees where representatives of differing interests, supposèd to balance each other, meet for the discussion of the affairs of such of the poor as, driven by necessity

[1] By Herbert Thompson, B.A. Swan Sonnenschein & Co. (1891).

allow them to be discussed. They do so in the fond
hope, often deceived, of receiving assistance. We
sat around a table in judgment. A wicked sense of
humour that will obtrude on serious occasions suggested that we were not unlike those lifeless ' happy
family ' collections in menageries, whose distinguishing virtue is, that the members do not bite each other,
though they might be expected to do so. The case
of a child needing help came before us. She was one
of nine, and her father earned thirty-five shillings a
week. Upon festive occasions this man had been known
to imbibe intoxicants beyond the limit that is lawful,
but whether at his own expense or that of friends who
wished to make him happy in spite of being so much
married, did not transpire.

" All sat silent. A comfortable-looking bachelor of
means and leisure seemed to be balancing the pros and
cons. Well-drilled in theories as to what ought to be the
condition of the ' economic man,' he seemed unable to
fit them to nine children and 35s. a week. But a young
lady from a University Settlement had no misgivings.
If London were ever to be saved, such men must
feel the screw of pressure applied to them. A genial
old surgeon was in the chair. His hand covered his
mouth as he leant upon his elbow, that his expression
might influence no votes. Matrons who knew housekeeping, and spinsters who knew the poor, shrugged
their shoulders, wavering clerics joined them, and
' the economic motive ' was sacrificed. But the
University Settlement girl was no harsh virgin. Her
means could provide her with a Riviera holiday and
she needed it. Her whole time was given to the
poor. Her dress showed that she made sacrifices for
them. An occasional facial twitch or a jerk of the

arm were signs of hard work and presaged breakdown.
Everybody there was in earnest and working from
the most lovable of motives, but who could escape
the conviction that our method wasted energy.

"With this and other exciting thoughts uppermost,
a walk across a West End park near at hand suggested
itself as a means of getting rid of surplus energy.
Who is sufficient for these things ? was the ever
recurring question. Not the individual of narrow
means and leisure, certainly, thought I, and there
before me in the Row I saw scores of well educated,
physically fit people who probably were bored by the
kind of lives they had to lead. If one could, if one
dared, speak to them of real genuine social service—
but it was of course impossible. A messenger of any
sort was almost inconceivable, unless it were a Carlyle
redivivus. He, wandering from Chelsea, might accost
a lounger without offence, and, repeating his message
of 1843, say to him—

" ' My brother, the brave man has to give his life
away—give it, I advise thee.'

" From others, such a hint would be an impertinence.
Yet, in the midst of a ' Democracy akin to Atheism,
which means despair of any heroes to govern you and
contented putting up with the want of them,' how
much we need the people with capacity and advantage
to work for the common weal.

" In revolt against limitations, and an extreme
' individualist,' for the moment, I went down the
same night into the slums, to be confronted with
conspiracy to exploit charity in one case and an
instance of the working of that ' previous and better
mechanism of society ' in which Dr. Chalmers had such
faith, in another. In the first case one of those

fibreless but plausible and cunning men the worker
often meets, had attempted to trade upon supposed
weaknesses. In the second an orphan upon whose
behalf efforts were made to secure admission to Dr.

FLOWERS SENT TO THE RAGGED SCHOOL UNION BY
H.R.H. THE PRINCESS OF WALES.

Müller's Home had been taken to live with an aunt.
Securing copies of the birth certificate of the child
and marriage certificate of the parents, and consent
of relatives to his admission had brought this about.

So I had to admit against my will that Wisdom was justified of her C.O.S. children.

"Lord Shaftesbury left us an example in this by presiding at their meetings, and defending the costliness of their checking machinery. But while he did this, he claimed liberty for his own action, and liberty to criticise as well. Ever-increasing uncertainty, but an ever-growing teachableness, resulted from this intercourse with families. An extensive reading was necessary to hold one's own. From an aged widow, for example, I heard a more searching and just examination of the deadening effects of sacerdotalism upon a poor population than I have ever met with elsewhere. She was a lady in reduced circumstances. As a young woman she saw the rise of the Oxford movement, and had ever since watched it with misgiving. She had living with her a deaf and dumb son, at the time aged seventeen. During a hard winter just before I knew them, this mother and son, having purchased bread with their last penny, shut themselves in their rooms to wait for death, but neighbourly benevolence intervened.

"Clear hard thinking upon social questions one constantly meets with among working men, and it is folly for any man to expect to do much among them, or, as in my own case, even find favourable conditions present, if in such matters he has been content to

> Sail on, away, afar,
> Without a course, without a star.

Extravagant socialism and extreme individualism I only encountered in two men, one a very young and the other a very old one. The latter was a survival of Chartist times. But they were neither of them easily disposed of in those arguments we had, and that could not be avoided. To shirk discussion invariably, when you are accustomed to make calls upon men in their own homes, is to give the impression either that Christianity is out of date, or you are unable to champion it. If not these, then that you despise your hosts as controversialists. You can afford to allow none of these ideas to remain, yet at the same time argument seldom does much good, and its chief value in these cases was that it gave the opportunity of showing a love for truth, and the expectation of being a receiver as well as a giver. The point towards which I always tried to make the argument tend was, that communism and individualism both required comparative perfection in the social unit for successful working.

" But the general position of the thoughtful working man I met, was not an extreme view of any sort. It seemed to be that as there are some forty millions or more of people in the United Kingdom and thirty-six millions have no money to fall back upon, some better way of distributing wealth needs finding. They were not for confiscation or mechanical sharing, but were far from contented with things as they are. They judge Christian men by the extent to which they apply the Christian ethic to the housing and other working class problems, and distrust philanthropy that hinders reform.

" Without having read Mallock's *Aristocracy and Evolution*, they have a very shrewd notion that crowds, to make progress, need leading, that the time limit within which capable men could be coerced to lead, would be one generation, and that leaders of men need rewarding unless altruism takes the place of self-interest in these captains of the human race.

They know that a species of bargaining between men able to lead an advance, and the community that needs leading is always taking place, and that were it not for the rewards, the discovery of individual power would never be made. They see the crudities of socialism, but they do not see equity in a social system that uses them during their best years and then flings them aside when they begin to grow grey. In the late nineties, the tendency to amalgamate small concerns into large ones, with effects that regarded the workman and small business man last of all, were keenly felt. Middle aged men were feeling the difference between working for ' the old governor ' and for a manager changed every few years, of a concern that had to grind out dividends. The very washerwomen were being superseded by large laundries. Twenty years before, every milkman was a master man, but they had nearly all of them been absorbed by this date, into huge centralized systems making 60,000 calls daily. Smithfield companies had taken to buying butcher's shops all over the kingdom. The grocers were beginning to feel acutely the competition of stores. Brewers bought up public-houses. Enormous amalgamations were everywhere made. These did business on such a scale, with one set of working expenses, instead of the multiplied cost of many establishments, that profits could be cut low. The owners of other businesses of the old-fashioned sort either failed, were content to just turn over their capital, or to work at a very low profit. By 1897 a huge combine for the manufacture of gunpowder in Germany made the eighteen firms in this kingdom work in some departments of their trade for hardly as much as the capital sunk would have yielded had it been invested in Consols.

"It was in this year that the London General Omnibus Company had to make terms with the London Road Car Company. In agriculture it was the same. Large farms, worked with sufficient capital and the best machinery and under competent management, paid ; small farmers were very generally retiring from the contest, more or less broken and beaten.

"Just as when Henry VIII tampered with the coinage, and when modern financiers have gambled in stocks, it has been the poor who have ultimately suffered most, so it is in the case of these inevitable changes. Wages are cut, and unskilled labourers and old men are discharged. Those in employment are full of anxiety for their own positions, and while doing what they can for those who are out of work, feel themselves to be helplessly in the grasp of a pitiless law.

"You cannot go to such folks and invade their homes if all you have to offer is some nostrum or other that has a certain amount of feasibility in a time of prosperity, but is arrant nonsense when applied to their serious troubles.

"Evangelicalism of the right sort wears well at these times, and scarcely anything else does.

"There is, however, another type of working man I have met, far too common—the man with good wages, who is self-indulgent to such an extent that home, wife, and children suffer. The worst and most difficult problem lies here. If he keeps well within the law and if his family never seeks pecuniary help, what can regulative processes do for them ? Here again the old influence that springs from an unimpertinent sympathy is the only possible assistance. ' Drift ' work, I have found, gives access everywhere.

"If space permitted, a most pathetic series

of instances of the value of the R.S.U. clothing department in such work could be given. Widows especially need assistance in their struggle. Memories of these come crowding up so, it is difficult to select them. I remember one especially to whom it was a great boon to have some of her children clothed. She had seven to support, and had just been laid aside by an explosion of the mixture with which she was making crackers at home. Another, with five to keep, two of whom were cripples, was a doll stuffer. She worked in a mound of sawdust filling the linen bodies. The pay for this could not have been lavish. A third example may suffice for these. A family of nine, six of whom helped the mother at match-box making, were found dwelling in two wretched rooms in a house down a court. Four of the children were in most deplorable rags, but through this agency we were able to rig them out and take them for an excursion—the first in their lives. As ailing and sickly children have been found, the Holiday Homes have taken them and sent them back hearty and strong One case of many just comes to mind that made a dramatic impression upon the inhabitants of an entire street. They had watched a girl with a broken leg depart for the seaside, the injured limb swathed with bindings around a supporting splint. When she came back, able to skip and jump, and play at ' higher and higher ' with the best, plumper and rosier than she had ever been, the gossips of the neighbourhood were much impressed. If instances were multiplied—and scores and hundreds there were—no strengthening of the story would result. Mutually helpful were all the headquarters and local agencies, used under a sense of responsibility.

"The cripple work that grew out of this 'Drift' work had its own peculiarities and special features, as had all other work of the same kind that soon came into being throughout London. But they belong to local history, consisting of memories that are dear to those concerned and stimulating to fellow workers. They in exchange can give experiences that are just as inspiring and suggestive for fresh effort because different in kind. Its special glory is that it was a growth, though one of the larger divisions of the Ragged School Cripple Mission. All others were confederacies of independent groups. That it was so was due solely to the help of the people. That it did not fulfil all that was designed is due to the absence of those elements without which all democratic efforts are faulty. Yet the very fact that within five years a work extending over miles of surface could be held in hand by the people among whom the first workers went as strangers, should be full of encouragement to intending workers. The value of the time and money of the gifted are in no danger at any time of being overlooked, but there is a danger that the fact that the *people* must have a share in any mission that is to live, may be forgotten. To gain their sympathy there is no new recipe. It is the same as the correspondence of Lord Shaftesbury suggests. It is the same as the book *Ragged Homes and How to Mend Them*, by Mrs. Bayly, throughout enjoins. If a notion of leavening ' a stodgy mass ' [1] has led some workers astray, they have to hark back to that earlier conception of individual interest.

"Lord Shaftesbury wrote to Mr. W. J. Orsman, hon. superintendent of that Coster's Benevolent

[1] *Heart of the Empire.*

Club to which he belonged, ' Do not forget the woman who made the braces,' and of a poor cabinet maker, ' Let him have what he wants in his necessity.'

" These are but two of many such references.   Mrs. Bayly has this passage in her book, characteristic of the whole of it and containing the secret of her success—

" ' When a poor mother tells us how much misery the bad behaviour of her children is causing her, we must not say . . . but it must be, " Ah ! I can feel for you, for my children trouble me a good deal sometimes, and occasion me much anxiety." '

" Friendships of this kind are not, however, without their amusing embarrassments at times, as the following will show.

" A box of flowers had been given me for distribution.   Flower distributing in a low street is not an unmixed pleasure.   The gladness of the old country-bred people, with nothing on their consciences, is more than counterbalanced by the sadness of those whom the sight of fresh blooms causes conscience to torment.   The sighs they produce are not all caused by the scent.

" An old Scotchman had witnessed the incident, and knowing me beforehand, and being very full of whisky, became affectionate.   He linked his arm in mine and insisted upon accompanying me.   We had had some talk upon previous occasions, and on this afternoon he was determined to uproot heresy in my soul on the subject of evolution and the verbal inspiration of the Scriptures.   He would not go back, he had taken ' a real liking,' so there was no help for it.   Down a long street we made our devious way. His straight thinking and crooked walking were full

of surprises. What the neighbours thought I
can pretty well guess, for he was heavy to hold up.
At the corner of this long lane I thought to break away.
But he pressed his hospitality upon me. Lord
Shaftesbury enjoined upon us ' to drink a glass of
wine with a fellow man,' and ' never give up the
convivial system.' Now, if I should ever depart from
teetotal principles, it would be in the company of this
genial old fellow, but I had to decline. The refusal
seemed to hurt him, so, as there was a milkshop at
the opposite corner, we went in and had a large bottle
of sodawater between us. He would not go back
home without me, and I did not want him to come
further, so I got him to a lamp-post. Clinging to
this, he called after me, ' Hold fast that thou hast.'

" By 1897 the cripple mission of the R.S.U.
for all London was a federation of visitors caring
for some six thousand cripples, and it has continued its work since on the lines which the past
history of the entire movement seemed to determine
(1) That it should be a religious mission ; (2) That it
should, in the benevolence connected with it, seek to
help those for whom least was done. Other societies,
were at work, and with them co-operation was established ; but the R.S.U. had its own special sphere to
occupy. One important subject to which a good
deal of attention has been already paid and still
more is likely to be given in the future, is the supply
of surgical appliances for curing or remedying the
physical defects of the cripples.

" Although other Surgical Aid Societies and
Funds are at work, the means employed for protecting
the treasuries of these charities make them inaccessible
to most of the poorest. By supplementary funds and

the work of the visitors, who study the charities and show the parents how to comply with their conditions, a much larger number of cripples than formerly now get the appliances that the surgeons of the hospitals order them to have.

" My experience of a share in this work has been that, like the Drift Work, it offers the finest opportunities for usefulness. As in that agency and in the work in the schools there are many vacancies, especially in the higher posts. With additional leaders a larger number of rank and file visitors could be set to work, and would doubtless be forthcoming. That many more may respond is the sincere desire and earnest prayer of all at present engaged."

CHAPTER XXIV

The Waiting Fields

" So long as their strength (voluntary religious agencies) is not' united so long will the fruit of their labours be scanty, unattractive, and scarcely worth the gathering."—*Heart of the Empire.*

WE are assured by a distinguished writer " That the progress of the century has seen the breaking down, at least in the great cities, of a consciousness of individual responsibility and consecration of individual energies ; until now in the broken populations of the congested districts all religious agencies find themselves baffled amidst masses heedless of their message."

Is it to that that we have come ?   Have we indeed sunk so low ?   Is all the pessimism we find in the books on social topics just now quite justified ?   Times were bad enough in all conscience in 1847, but for the healthy thinker there was hope and encouragement. How black the prospect was has been described ; yet here is a cheery, breezy speech from a man of that period when addressing the members of the Y.M.C.A. It has in it the ring of British Valour and Faith towards God combined ; and as that happens to be the combination London needs at present, the mere perusal of it may give us heart :—

" The Churchman takes his view of the age from the

top of a steeple ; a Dissenter from the roof of a chapel.
A Tory takes his view from the steps of the throne, or

MORE IN NEED OF LOVE THAN BREAD

the town-house of a rotten borough ; a Whig stands
on the shoulders of the multitude, and looks through

spectacles made of the parchment of the Reform Bill.
A Radical looks at the age, and examines it from the
window of a Great Western Express carriage, proceeding at the rate of seventy miles an hour. A Chartist
takes a peep at the age from a seat upon the orifice of
a volcano. One man sees in it the thickening gloom,
another brightness and sunshine ; one picks up nothing
but withered leaves, another nothing but beautiful
flowers. One is the ancient philosopher who laughed
at everything ; another is the rival philosopher who
cried at everything. You see, therefore, how difficult
it is to hit on the *juste milieu.*

"Our age has smiles, but it has tears also; it has tombs,
but it has also temples ; it has a warp of sorrow, but
there runs through it a woof of gladness ; and the years,
as they rush, are the flying shuttles that work up the
web of our existence. It is not an age of scepticism,
nor yet of Christianity ; it is not an age of tyrant despot-
ism, nor yet of democratic crow-bars. Our gaols and
hospitals, our palaces and arsenals, are all more or less
huddled together. There is not a spot upon the earth
that may be called a Paradise, if I except a happy
home, and there is scarcely one that can be called a
Pandemonium, except it may be, a long-hour warehouse
in the City of London. The age we live in is coloured
more by our own country, that is, Old England, (and
it is very fair in a Scotsman to say so,) than any other.
Its religion, its liberty, freedom, power, are stamping
the impress of Old England upon the currency of years,
and the age we live in receives an English hue. I
do not think that the sun, after all, shines on, or the
age sweeps over a finer country, with all its faults,
than this same old country of ours."

If a ragged school man could say as much as that

in 1847, it ought to be much easier·for us to be hopeful in 1904.

After all, of what is this pessimism in social literature a symptom ? Surely it is nothing more than re-action after a check to an unjustified assurance, the effects of a stunning blow received from Nature, whom the smartest cannot bluff.

Examined in a spirit of candour it will be seen that the hopelessness of the " stodgy mass " of the London proletariat has only come to light since some of the schemes of superior persons have not worked out as planned. Like the Educational Commissioners of 1862, who could not find the schools, yet patronised the ragged school workers as " intending well," they felt certain they could put London right, and pitied the men and women they found already at work. Now that it is clearly seen that the position cannot be taken by storm, that intellectualism carried the worker but a short distance, they are discouraged, and the city has in their view no future. But the sober fact is, that human nature can always be reached when tact, sincerity and love go hand in hand. It is quite as certain, too, that there is no other way to get there, and that it is just as gloriously worth the doing as at any past time in history.

The only mistake was in supposing there would be royal roads for cleverness other than the rough ones of patience, self-forgetfulness and labour.

Now that many attempts have been made to reach the people, and the insolent audacity that marks a new touch brought to an old difficulty has been somewhat tempered, we may ask for a fair examination of the R.S.U. in its relation to the work of the future. If the R.S.U. were a home of lost causes and obsolete faiths, then it would be vain and inconsiderate to thrust its interests upon the attention of the busy makers of the England of to-morrow. If our faith in it were not firm, importunity on its behalf would be in the worst of taste. But, grounding a claim to a hearing

EDMONTON CHILDREN. A SURPRISE PHOTO TAKEN
ON A WINTER'S DAY

upon the right to it that has always been conceded to the absolutely convinced, we submit that there is a case. It can be established that an extension and a deepening of the ragged school movement is one of the chief wants of London to-day.

Abhorring all dogmatism and arbitrary uncharitableness, may we not examine why it is that " People have become tired of the poor," why " The Condition of the People " problem, once so insistent, ceases to trouble the public mind ?

Since the R.S.U. started, the entire period of successive, unpersistent experiments in social amelioration has been covered. It began with the group of prophets who denounced middle-class indifference, and may be said to have opened with the publication of *Past and Present*. Carlyle, Ruskin, Dickens and Kingsley were the men referred to. Of these, neither Dickens nor Ruskin had gone far as yet in 1844, and Kingsley was only just taking home his bride to Eversley Rectory. Then arose a generation, outside the " Clapham set," outside the evangelicals, who took a tepid interest in the poor and gave financial support. From among these, when *How the Poor Live*, or *The Bitter Cry of Outcast London*, or the novels of Sir Walter Besant appeared, there were numbers who determined to go down into the abyss themselves and see what they could do. Most of them expected too much; many of them, on the other hand, went with too little in the way of tools for the work. The wedge of faith and the hammer of doggedness were cast aside as old-fashioned, and a set of keen chisels preferred. But the " stodgy mass " turned the edges, and the travellers returned dispirited. Reforming the poor by supervising and drilling them has also proved a hopeless cause. So has living next door to them, but under different conditions. Next came a set of workers with a special object of their own to secure, collaterally with and by means of service to the poor. The motive was high because in the worker's mind the two things were identical. These were the recruits whom the High Church party enlisted. But two things have happened : the people have not responded to any

MARQUIS OF NORTHAMPTON.

extent ; and a mischievous counter-demonstration by the dissenting sects in the slums has been provoked. Such are the chief ameliorating social influences of the last half of the nineteenth century, if we except the brief " Age of Slumming, when, stimulated by the cloying pathos of the popular novelist, the wealthy and good of the West descended, halo-crowned, into hovel and cellar, to demonstrate by songs and smiles and sympathy the affection of the rich for the poor." [1] as we are told somewhat spitefully. Meanwhile, the R.S.U., representing opinions that it cannot abandon, whatever the passing fashion in philanthropy may be, has been marking time. In the fancy of some, she should have been a dismantled hulk, beached high and dry years ago; but they never sailed in the ship, and know nothing of her sea-going qualities.

The point to which the superior person has brought social service in London is the substitution of competing proselytisers for co-operating citizens.

Will any man who knows the poor dare to predict an ultimate success for the axe-grinder of any school ?

A clerk in holy orders, intimate to a rare degree with the life and spirit of the slums, has been bold enough to put the poor man's protest against pettiness into these lines :—

> Oh, I'm sick, sick to death o' their rantin',
>   And there's many another like me ;
> Fer we're sweatin' an' pinin' an' pantin'
>   In this England the 'ome of the free.
> Let 'em chuck all their rantin' an' cantin',
> It's Hope with a big H I'm wantin'
>   Fer the boy at my knee. [2]

Not only is this a reliable expression of what the people feel, but it contains a hint of where the point of access to their hearts can alone be found. That is just

[1] *Heart of the Empire.*
[2] *A Cry from the Darkness.* Richard Free.

what has been said with almost wearisome reiteration by our workers from the first. " Seek the child." They did seek the child ; and it is due to them that there is now enough law on the statute books of the nations throughout the world to secure protection for children wherever there is an executive strong enough to enforce the law.

But in what way can we give hope for the child ? If we were a syndicate of millionaires, would the problem be much easier for us now than at the outset ? The chances are, we might do more harm than good by seeking one of those tempting short cuts to moral progress that money offers but which so seldom leads to the goal. We should have to be human first, come face to face with essentials in life, and then apply the money. There is room for money, on a lavish scale, when the groundwork is ready.

Now granted that there is much in the child's environment to work at—the housing question, economic questions, and so on—it will be conceded that the springs of his own character have more to do with Hope for him, than all his surroundings, whether good or evil, can ever amount to. Moreover, it has been so ordained that when the springs of character are vitiated in an individual, the position of society is much the same towards him as that of all the king's horses and all the king's men towards the unfortunate humpty-dumpty.

Then here we come to issue. Is the Gospel the power of God unto the full salvation of the entire personality of the individual, and does it secure the healthy Evolution of Society ? We believe that, and we start with it, " and stick to it." Dr. Barnardo—himself an old ragged school teacher—said upon one occasion : "There is one reason why we should support generously, heartily, and in no grudging spirit, with a full purse and an open hand, this Ragged School Union. Because it has ever been

FAITHFUL TO GOSPEL TRUTH,

MR. JOHN KIRK, PRESENT SECRETARY OF
THE RAGGED SCHOOL UNION.

which it is now so much the fashion to decry. The masses, the people are sick at heart, and do not know what ails them ; they are crying, struggling in pain and weariness and bondage, yet cannot utter their need. There is a deep insatiable longing in the hearts of men which bursts forth sometimes clamorously, and in ways and expressions at which society stands aghast ! Many nostrums have been tried to palliate and in vain ; but only one remedy gives satisfaction and rest, and that is the Gospel of our Lord Jesus Christ. Ragged School teachers understand that, and bring to the people the true remedy. Hence—must I say it—our churches have been empty and our Ragged School Missions thronged. What has been the secret of this strange phenomenon ? Apart from all questions of methods, men, and organizations, the secret is the matchless power of the Gospel of Christ to attract, win, bow down, conquer and civilize. The Ragged Schools have been, I believe, loyal to the Gospel. Alas ! the churches have not always been ; and there is one secret of the success just mentioned. Because the Gospel is declared and taught, I love the Ragged School, and ask you to support it. And observe how the Divine Remedy has been applied. On the face of our dead children—morally dead—Ragged School workers have not been content to lay the dead, dry staff of ecclesiasticism or formalism, but they have brought into contact with the little ones living men, living women, face to face and heart to heart, hand to hand and eye to eye, and this personal contact, this human touch of those who themselves know and have felt the Gospel in its power, this has, through the blessing of God, in thousands of instances, caused the dead to live."

What form does the application of this general principle take ? In the first place there are the schools. In some of them the difficulty acknowledged by John Macgregor in the first decade of their existence is ever present, the difficulty of keeping them down to

the lowest class after the schools have been some time at work. Still, they attract a class that would keep aloof from Sunday schools of a middle-class standard, a class that is poor and tempted and need an all-round support and stimulus. Some of the schools on the other hand, do deal with the very lowest. Then as a supplementary work we have the " Drift " work, which is the scouting work of the City Missionaries of old days revived. In either of these, a citizen to whom the principles exhibited in the history of this work appeal, can find a sphere. He can obtain the privilege that Gordon valued, the pleasure of a downright, persevering interest in a few children. There may be a hearty welcome for him among his fellow teachers: there may not. They are not always demonstrative to new-comers.

A sufficient number of offers of service from the right people ready to show some initiative would mean covering the ground : and when that is done there is no agency in existence or that can be conceived that would be so effective, so simple, or so economical in working

In the suburbs where no ragged schools may exist
" Drift " work must be the form of effort, but conducted with a view to a future school. An organiser
in such a work would see the advantage of " thrusting
the obligation " to do something in the matter upon
every religious community within reach. His experiences would be mixed. There would be encourage-
ments, but there would be difficulties. " I pray thee,
have me excused," is what he must expect from clergy,
ministers and laity. It should not embitter him ;
many of the excuses are real grounds for exemption.
Perhaps, if he sticks to it, a godly coalheaver, a cobbler
or a navvy will join him. Then may be seen, perhaps,
the spelling of hope with a big " H " for one boy. A
boy in the Midlands who worked at the Potteries sixty
years ago was the victim of shocking brutalities.
Thrashed with a rope's end, his blood glued his shirt
into the wound-dints, and his mother had to get it off
by bathing his back. This boy attended a Sunday
school, and was under the teaching of a labouring man.
Last year the old potter wrote a book, in which he paid
this tribute to his teacher :—

" I remember, as I sat among the other scholars,
Ralph Lawton's face shone as if transfigured as he sat
in his pew under the gallery. He little thought that
sixty years after, the vision of his ecstasy would be
like a ' bright cloud ' hanging over an old scholar's
life, at once an inspiration and a joy."

But whether the man be a sweep or a Prime Minister,
it is only along such lines that a child's nature can be
reached and the character buttressed, the will directed
and the aspirations quickened.

In that simple story there is the work in germ. Its
unlimited multiplication is what London needs. The

man who wants Hope for his boy can be reached after-wards. Magistrates, police-court missionaries, jail chaplains, schoolmasters, all assert that a mission to parents as parents is a crying need. But who will go? or shall we not say, Who can go? The man who has gained the love of the boy is the only man with a chance.

Such is the work! You begin with the child. For, as the Talmud says, " The World stands on the Breath of the School Children."

Quintin Hogg under the Adelphi arch with a candle, a Bible, and two crossing sweepers is the *beginning* ; a Polytechnic is the *finish*, of an ideal school.

And this is where the millionaire should come in. Men are found who can give with imagination. Libraries, baths, and other institutions are given to towns and boroughs by wealthy men; why not inex-pensive schools that would be self-supporting from the moment they are opened?

But though the movement would welcome million-aires it has never yet waited for them. " Do what you can with what you have " has been its motto, and God has not forsaken it.

But as to methods? it may be asked. The R.S.U. never dogmatises. It has sought in all its enterprises to give an embodiment to unchanging truth, at the time of need, in such form as then seemed possible and best. No man need fear to enter the work lest he be strangled by mummy swathings. The reply of the Founder, when asked upon what lines he started work, holds good to-day and will for the future as well : " Expediency and love."

Experience is accessible, but liberty is the law of R.S.U. life. There is no red tape. A happy thought, a successful experiment by the humblest individual is made public property by the monthly magazine, *In His Name*, and is in the pulsing blood of the entire movement in a very little while.

Need it be said that hope is not fixed on the millionaire. The subscriber of any sort deserves the gratitude of his colleague at work. God has been mindful of His own : but when we look upon the waiting fields, the longing for more labourers, barns and tools must be forgiven.

Those vast stretches of squalid suburb where we might muster friends, but where we have no representation in bricks and mortar, and where no buildings can be borrowed or hired, cause many a heartache to those who know that there, and very rapidly, the troubles of the future are arising. As a writer has so well expressed it, "Come to think, it is all the Child. The Future is the Child. The Future. What are we—any of us—but servants or traitors to that ? " But our confidence is in Him. Remembering how many a difficulty has vanished from the path in past times, we rely on Him, whose work it is, to send more labourers into His vineyard.

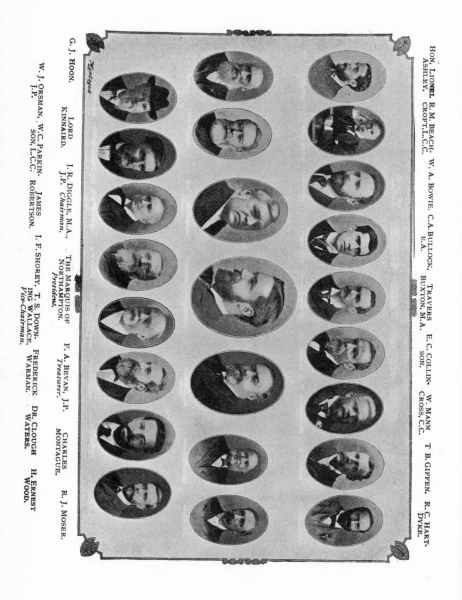

HON. LIONEL R. M. BEACH. W. A. BOWIE. C. A. BULLOCK. TRAVERS E. C. COLLIN- W. MANN T. B. GIFFEN. R. C. HART.
ASHLEY. CROFT, L.C.C. B.A. BUXTON, M.A. SON. CROSS, C.C. DYKE.

Montague

G. J. HOON.

LORD I. R. DIGGLE, M.A., THE MARQUIS OF F. A. BEVAN, J.P. CHARLES R. J. MOSER.
KINNAIRD. J.P. *Chairman.* NORTHAMPTON. *Treasurer.* MONTAGUE.
President.

W. J. ORSMAN. W. C. PARKIN- JAMES I. F. SHOREY. T. S. DOWN- FREDERICK DR. CLOUGH H. ERNEST
J.P. SON, L.C.C. ROBERTSON. ING WALLACE, WARMAN. WATERS. WOOD.
Vice-Chairman.

Ragged School Union

SHAFTESBURY SOCIETY

THE COUNCIL

A S a supplement to the volume, a group of thumb-nail portraits of the members of the governing body of the Society are given, in the belief that a completing touch is thereby added.

For executive purposes, the detail work of the Society, apart from general questions of policy and matters involving a large expenditure, has been divided into ten sections. Each section is placed in the charge of a group of the Council from year to year, the positions held being frequently changed ; an enlarged experience to the members of the work as a whole is the result. The sections are : 1. Finance and General Purposes ; 2. Legal (Trusts and Properties); 3. Oversight of Spiritual Work ; 4. Drift Mission ; 5. Cripples ; 6. Holiday Homes ; 7. Benevolent, Social, and Temperance ; 8. Clothing and Boots ; 9. R.S.U. Mission Centres ; 10. Literature.

THE PRESIDENT.—Lord Northampton has succeeded to the position held in former days by the Earl of Shaftesbury in the hearts of the teachers and workers. His May-meeting speeches for thirteen years past, giving all-round views of the work, have formed a strong personal tie between them. His public work on the Technical Education Board, and in the House of Commons, and on the L.C.C. in connexion with the great housing problem, is well known. The Bible Society, of which he is President, the Y.M.C.A., and many an other good work, has his warm and active interest.

THE CHAIRMAN.—Mr. J. R. Diggle, M.A., J.P., who is Chairman for the year, is a close rival to the President as a useful public man.   His vigorous and experienced work on the London School Board of which he was Chairman, is well known to most.   He was also Chairman of the first Technical Education Board of the L.C.C.   Into the chinks of well-filled time in a busy life, he fits such trifles as the management, with others, of the People's Palace, Christ's Hospital, and the Regent Street Polytechnic.

THE VICE-CHAIRMAN.—Mr. T. S. Downing Wallace has local interests in the Hoxton Market Ragged School, of which he is the beloved President.   He is also known as an active Church worker around his country residence at Potter's Bar, which is always available for dispensing generous hospitality.   Both Mr. and Mrs. Wallace are never more happy than when surrounded by a number of guests, whether it be factory girls, crippled or ragged school children, or Christian workers. Although a comparatively new member of the R.S.U. Council he has won the fullest confidence of his colleagues by his business-like aptitude, and his whole-hearted interest in the extension of Christ's Kingdom.   Hence his unanimous election to the vice-chairmanship.

THE TREASURER.—Mr. Frank Bevan, upon the death of his father, Mr. R. C. L. Bevan, in 1890, succeeded to the office the former had held.   The Church Missionary Society, the London City Mission, Thames Church Mission, Church Pastoral Aid, Bible Society, Evangelisation Society, Open-air Mission, our own Society, and many others, have found father and son to be their staunch friends.   Mr. and (now, alas ! the late) Mrs. Bevan were both at one time teachers at Gray's Yard Ragged School.

THE HON. LIONEL ASHLEY.—In Mr. Ashley the R.S.U. has an official link with the family of the first president.   We rejoice, however, in the possession of the full sympathy of all the other members.   The name of Shaftesbury is not only imperishably enshrined in the past history of the movement, but forms an integral part of its present title, because nothing better can be found to express its policy and objects.   Mr. Ashley is on the section of the Council dealing with Mission Centres.

R. M. BEACHCROFT, L.C.C., who is on the Legal Section, has represented Paddington and Clerkenwell on the L.C.C. He is at the present time Chairman of the Metropolitan Water

Board. His position in the Clothworkers' Company, with which members of his family have been associated for six generations past, as well as his duties as solicitor to Christ's Hospital, identify him with the City. In addition to serving upon the Council of the R.S.U., he has a local ragged school interest in Holborn.

W. A. BOWIE.—Mr. Bowie was actively engaged in work among poor children for many years in Glasgow before coming to London. He has brought with him much valuable experience in connection with the working of the Poor Children's Fresh Air Fortnight scheme of that city. His local London ragged school interest is in the Borough. Upon the Council he is Chairman of the Drift Section and a member of four others, viz., Holiday Homes, Cripples, Supervision of Spiritual Work, and General Purposes.

C. ASHTON BULLOCK, B.A.—Mr. Bullock is a publisher and editor of magazine and other literature having a wide circulation among Church of England families in this country. He is the Hon. Secretary, in conjunction with Mr. Kirk, of the now famous " Robin Dinner " Fund. " Robin " has earned the gratitude of all R.S.U. workers, for their children have, with others, come in for a plentiful share of the good cheer he annually provides.

TRAVERS BUXTON, M.A.—The name of Buxton will always be associated with the cause of liberty in the minds of Englishmen. Mr. Buxton is Secretary of the British and Foreign Anti-Slavery Society. His local ragged school interest is in Camberwell, (where his honoured father was Hon. Secretary for many years,) as well as a member of the R.S.U. Council. Upon the Council he serves on the Legal and General Purposes Sections.

E. C. COLLINSON.—Bristol and London have both been the scenes of Mr. Collinson's unpaid evangelical labours. At the present time he is co-pastor with his brother-in-law, Mr. Orsman, at his mission in Hoxton. He is Chairman of the " Mission Centres," and a member of the " Holiday Homes " Sections of the Council.

W. MANN CROSS, C.C.—As a member of the Common Council since 1891, Guardian of the City poor for a large number of years, and holder of several important honorary positions entailing unceasing labour and great experience, Mr. Cross is a man with both hands full. All his life he has been identified with ragged school work, and his special sections on the Council are " Holiday Homes " and " General Purposes."

T. B. GIFFEN.—Mr. Giffen, like Mr. Bowie, was connected

with Christian social work in Scotland before he came South, and still retains some connection with it. He has been engaged in the " Children's Day Refuges " and the " Poor Children's Sabbath Dinner " schemes of the Glasgow United Evangelistic Association, and was the founder of that Society's Cripple work. Although a recent member of the Council, he is on the " Mission Centres," Holiday Homes, Cripples, Drift, Supervision of Spiritual Work, and General Purposes Sections.

R. C. HART-DYKE.—Like many another man who has gone before him, Mr. Dyke has not found that intercourse with the well-to-do unfits a man for taking a direct personal interest in poor children. His ragged school work is in Westminster, and he is on the Legal Section of the Council. He is one of the members who have already occupied the position Mr. Diggle holds this year. As solicitor to the Duchy of Lancaster, he has been, and will be again, a useful friend in Court.

G. J. HOON.—Mr. Hoon is the oldest member of the Council. Of the local work in Kingsland that he is connected with he has been fifty years Superintendent. As a Guardian of the Poor of Hackney Union he has done good work. Notwithstanding his long career of useful service, Mr. Hoon was quite active until overtaken by enfeebled health.

LORD KINNAIRD.—Lord Kinnaird is a member of long standing, and was Chairman in 1891. Like the President and the Chairman for the year, his lordship has very wide interests. The Y.M.C.A., the Y.W.C.A., that he and his family have done much to found, the Blind, the Lock Hospital, the Zenana Bible and Medical Mission, the Open-Air Mission, and many other grand enterprises, own him for a friend.

CHARLES MONTAGUE. Mr. Montague, another old member of the Council, has an experience of philanthropic and religious work in East London extending over a period of nearly half a century. He was connected in his earlier years with Mr. H. R. Williams, the Rev. William Tyler, and other worthies who have passed to their rest. His own work is in Spitalfields. The Benevolent, Social, and Temperance, and the Holiday Homes are the sections upon which he serves this year.

R. J. MOSER.—Mr. Moser, on the Literature and General Purposes Sections, has been Chairman of the General Council. He is a deacon of Dr. Horton's Church, Lyndhurst Road, Hampstead. For many years he was actively engaged in ragged school work in St. Luke's.

W. J. ORSMAN, J.P.—Mr. Orsman has been Chairman of the R.S.U. Council upon two occasions. A unique training in the Government service, in honorary work connected with

Mr. Spurgeon's Tabernacle, in the founding and building-up of a large Mission, in service on the L.C.C. and the Magisterial Bench, as well as numerous committees, combined to fit him for the distinction. He is this year on the Literature, Benevolent, Social and Temperance, Cripples, Drift, Supervision of Spiritual Interests, and General Purposes Sections.

W. C. PARKINSON, L.C.C.—Mr. Parkinson, another member who has passed the chair, has a record which, in catalogue form, will fill the paragraph our space allows. He is Chairman of the Finance Committee of the Baptist Missionary Society, Vice-President of the Orphan Working School and Alexandra Orphanage, has a good deal to do with the Chest Hospital and Sick Man's Friend Society, as well as the various Committees of the L.C.C. On our Council Sections he is Chairman for the Holiday Homes, and a member for Cripples, Drift, Spiritual, and General Purposes.

JAMES ROBERTSON.—Mr. Robertson, who was introduced to ragged school work by the late Professor Leone Levi, joined the Council in 1885, and has been three times Chairman. Like many of his colleagues, he is associated with other good work in the metropolis, notably, the London City Mission. His local ragged school work has been done mainly in St. Pancras. Of the Literature and General Purposes Sections he is a member, and Chairman of that supervising the spiritual work.

J. F. SHOREY.—Mr. Shorey has laboured in connection with Gospel Temperance work in New York, London, and the north of England. For his interest in cripple children he is known in districts so far apart as Mile End and Westminster. His sections for this year are " Cripples " and " Drift."

F. WARMAN.—Mr. Warman, to whom both the parent Society and many of the affiliated schools are deeply indebted for his professional advice and help as an architect, is another of the members who have passed the chair. His local work in Islington extends over a period of some thirty-eight years. For this year, upon the Council's sectional committees, he is Chairman of two : the Legal and the Benevolent, Social, and Temperance, and is a member of three others : Holiday Homes, Cripples, and General Purposes.

DR. CLOUGH WATERS.—Dr. Waters is one of our honorary physicians. He has been for many years Medical Adviser to the Cripples' Home at Southend. His election to the Council is not only a recognition of indebtedness to all the medical men who place their services gratuitously at the Society's disposal, but it also, in this instance, creates a direct link with the important group of workers living in Southend.

H. ERNEST WOOD.—Mr. Wood is the son of the late Mr.
Henry Wood, J.P., at one time Chairman of the Council. His
father was well known as a generous supporter of the Baptist
Missionary Society, the London City Mission, and other good
work. He was also deeply interested in the work among
cripples. His son follows in his footsteps. Mr. Wood's local
interest is in Camberwell, and his sections of the Council are
R.S.U. Mission Centres and Supervision of Spiritual Work.

The Gordon Memorial Fund,

FOR THE

BENEFIT OF POOR CHILDREN.

THE above Memorial Fund was formed on April 8, 1885, and its management confided to a Board of Managers selected at a united meeting of members of " The Ragged School Union " and "The Reformatory Refuge Union," which formerly included the name of the late Sir Henry W. Gordon, K.C.B., brother of the late General Gordon, who was one of the trustees, together with the late Mr. H. R. Williams and Mr. W. E. Hubbard. Messrs. John Kirk and A. J. S. Maddison are the Honorary Secretaries.

The object of the Gordon Memorial Fund is to retain the Fund in Trust, and to apply the income only, not in the erection of buildings or the founding of new institutions, but for the benefit of poor children more directly in the following among other ways :—

1. Paying for the maintenance of poor children in existing Homes and Institutions under conditions to be agreed upon by the Committee.
2. Providing funds, wholly or in part, for the conveyance of weakly and convalescent children, and for their maintenance, for such periods as may be deemed necessary, in the country or at the sea-side.
3. Aiding and encouraging young emigrants, and providing them with necessary outfits for a start in life in the Colonies ; and generally to strive to extend a helping hand to promote the present good and the future welfare of the children of the poor on the benevolent lines so dear to the heart of the hero of Khartoum.

A " Boys' and Girls' Gordon Memorial " forms part of the general plan, all subscriptions for that branch being kept apart from the fund, and applied, if desired, to a specific purpose.

Contributions to " The Gordon Memorial Fund for the Benefit of Poor Children " are invited, and may be sent to the Honorary Secretaries, Messrs. John Kirk and Arthur J. S. Maddison, at 32, John Street, Theobald's Road, W.C. ; or to the London and Westminster Bank, Lothbury, E.C., and its branches.

INDEX